A HISTORY OF
TORTURE

CHINESE TORTURE OF THE RACK

From *The Punishments of China*, 1808, by courtesy of the Department of Oriental Antiquities, British Museum.

A HISTORY OF
TORTURE

GEORGE RYLEY SCOTT

SENATE

A History of Torture

First published in 1940 by T. Werner Laurie, London

This edition published in 1995 by Senate, an imprint of
Random House UK Ltd, 20 Vauxhall Bridge Road,
London SW1V 2SA

Copyright © this edition Random House UK Ltd 1995

Reprinted 1997

ISBN 1 85958 174 9

Printed and bound in Guernsey by
The Guernsey Press Co. Ltd

PREFACE

" It Can't Happen Now "

THE sophistry and superficiality which are such outstanding characteristics of the product of twentieth-century civilization; the elaborate and rococo environment in which the human animal of to-day works and plays; suffice to suggest an atmosphere of weakness and appeasement. The rapid extension of State control and coincident interference with the freedom of the individual suggest the development of an improved social organization.

The collective result is merely a veneer on the surface of a human nature that, in its elementals, changes little. Such apparent surface changes as do occur, are largely impermanent, being environmental in character, and due to those moral, ethical and social reactions which are mutable and sporadic rather than stable and eternal.

The larger humanity displayed by the individual and by the State, while praiseworthy enough in its way, is deceptive. Its illusory expression is due to the growing factitious character of modern life, which more and more results in man being out of tune with nature. The increasing intricacy of the machine, and the ever-increasing production of rubber-stamped mentality, are bringing man and machine nearer together. If twentieth-century man were to formulate a deity, he would not create an anthropomorphic godhead but a glorified robot—a robot god who would be conceived to possess even greater power than the old-time fire-and-brimstone Yahveh.

The machine may be excellent so long as it serves man in a truly utilitarian sense: it may be catastrophic the moment it concerns itself solely with the work of destruction —a comparison of the aeroplane in peace and war presents a pertinent example.

In examining mankind to-day one cannot altogether ignore these somewhat alarming repercussions. The decrease in brutality which has been so marked a feature of the past half century must not blind one to the potentialities for evil which are ever present and which may conceivably exhibit, should the occasion arise, a new ruthlessness in keeping with the competent mechanistic age in which we live. This, in itself, would appear to present possibly the most sinister aspect of modern civilization.

Something of the remorselessness and something of the lack of emotion, so intimately associated with the machine, are featured in the human product which has evolved contemporaneously with the development of the modern Juggernaut. The surrealists, in their artistic manœuvres, have, I think, managed to convey this automatistic remorselessness into the expressions of the humans they have depicted. The realistic American novelist similarly has succeeded in depicting the modern reactions and thought-motivations, which, when they become unmoral, are perhaps more cold-bloodedly inhumanistic than anything which we have ever been able to envisage from the literature of the past. The cruelty of the criminal of to-day seems all the more pitiless and correspondingly capable because of the mechanistic forces behind him and the mechanized soul within.

These points seem to me of vast significance. They seem to indicate that whenever and wherever a wave of cruelty or persecution does occur, it is likely to be all the more terrifying, not alone because of the capacities for cruelty inherent in this soulless mechanistic group-mind but because an outburst of persecution is always more frightful when it occurs in a State where cruelty, in its grosser or more sensational aspects, has for long been inexistent.

Recent happenings in other countries have suggested that the outbreak of mass cruelty is never an *impossibility*; that, on the contrary, as the Very Rev. W. R. Inge pointed out recently, " torture has been reintroduced into Europe."[1] The history of the past decade has smashed the contention that the horrible cruelties of the past are of no interest or significance to the present generation because " they can't happen here " or " they can't happen now."

---

[1] In an article in the *Evening Standard*, January 19, 1939.

A Dangerous Viewpoint

At a recently held meeting in the Queen's Hall, Lady Astor, because she supported the abolition of flogging, was booed and jeered at by 2,500 women. Here we have an example of women, in the mass, acclaiming themselves to be supporters of torture. That such support may be restricted, in its application, to certain crimes, does not affect the basic significance of the demand for the continuance of torture in the guise of punishment. The moment an attempt is made to justify any form of torture, whatever the circumstances may be, there arises the possibility of creating a dangerous precedent.

Justification on the ground of its efficiency, which was so often attempted in relation to torture as a means of securing confessions of guilt from those charged with heresy and sorcery, is actually conditioned by the need for finding a victim upon which to wreck the vengeance of society, and, vicariously, the vengeance of God. Such justification acts also as a means of suppressing or obviating any sense of injustice in society as a whole, and in those individuals immediately and specifically concerned with the infliction of the torture or persecution, either as executioner or onlookers. On these lines it is easy to justify any form of barbarity, and it is in this way that, through the ages, the most monstrous inquisitions and persecutions have been vindicated. Thus the justification, in our own time, of negro lynchings, of Bolshevist atrocities, of " Black-and-Tan " outrages, of brutal floggings, of " third degree " methods.

If there is one lesson that history teaches it is that any possibility of abolishing torture is endangered by the *existence of cruelty in any form and for any purpose*. In all circumstances and at all times *cruelty may easily develop into torture*, and the toleration or sanction of one form of torture may easily lead to the introduction of other forms. For this reason alone, any openly expressed approval of cruelty is as dangerous as it is alarming. The spectacle of 2,500 women crying aloud for the retention of torture is disturbing, and presents a significant footnote to any examination of modern sociological trends.

The Ostrich Attitude

There are people who persistently refuse to discuss or to witness anything that is unpalatable. They contend that it is much better to look upon the bright, the pleasant, the agreeable and the soporific things of life than to concern oneself with the sordid, the revolting and the unpleasant aspects. The world is full of people who persistently subscribe to this doctrine.

Now I am unaware whether or not these persons think that in adopting such an attitude they are exhibiting some form or other of mental superiority. But what I do know is that in this way they *encourage* the evils that are all too prevalent in modern society. Smugly and complacently, they shut their eyes to anything that is disturbing, repellent or offensive, affecting to believe it does not exist. They hold the view, or at any rate they act upon the concept, that ignorance of cruelty excuses the support of cruelty. Thus the well-to-do woman displays her astrakhan coat in ignorance of the fact that she is contributing towards a detestable and revolting form of animal torture; the masses cheer the antics of performing animals and thus encourage the continuance of a form of cruelty that is a disgrace to civilization.

This attitude of the public is one of the greatest enemies to reform. It may be that the majority of people view with disfavour cruelty to animals, to individuals, and to races; but this reaction is conditioned by individual desire and ambition. Wherever the result of prevention of cruelty is in opposition to personal interests I find there is no real enthusiasm for abolition. And so it goes on: the cruelty connected with the fur trade; the butchery trade; the perfumery trade; the cruelty associated with sport; with amusements; *et al*.

I make no apology for the presentation, in the following pages, of a gruesome picture of man's inhumanity. The record, stark and terrible though it be, should drive home to all thinking persons the need for every effort being made to eliminate cruelty in all its forms: the grim account of torture in our own time should make clear to every reader the danger, as well as the possibility, of an outbreak at any time and in any place.

It has been essential to my project that nothing should be shirked, evaded or suppressed. In any full consideration of the subject with which this book elects to deal, a thorough knowledge of the historical background is necessary. If the problems connected with this particular branch of sociology, in so far as they affect and apply to civilization to-day, are to be grasped properly, and the means of dealing with them, in any adequate sense, are to be comprehended, one must lay bare the root causes of torture, and examine its march through the thousands of years which have separated the appearance of the first crude specimen of *homo sapiens* and the elaboration of the 1939 model.

Acknowledgments

In the bibliography are included particulars of the many historical, criminological, anthropological, legal, and other works, which have been consulted. To the authors of these publications I am indebted for much information and help in the study of a sociological problem which, admittedly, bristles with difficulties. Incidentally, I may say that I have made every effort to provide as complete and comprehensive a bibliography as possible (even to the extent of including certain works from which I have drawn no data) with the view and hope that it may prove of value to future researchers and historians. There seems to be a strange lack of bibliographical matter relative to this particular subject.

For much information respecting present-day aspects of cruelty to animals and children, I would express my thanks to the Secretary of the Royal Society for the Prevention of Cruelty to Animals; to the President of the Massachusetts Society for the Prevention of Cruelty to Animals; and the Director of the National Society for the Prevention of Cruelty to Children.

The illustrations are the result of a diligent search through the artistic productions of many centuries and several nationalities. I am indebted to the Syndics of the University Library, Cambridge, for permission to reproduce a number of these pictures from their collections.

GEORGE RYLEY SCOTT.

CAMBRIDGE.

CONTENTS

PAGE

PREFACE V

"It can't happen now"—A dangerous viewpoint—
The ostrich attitude—Acknowledgments.

PART I

PSYCHOLOGICAL ASPECTS OF TORTURE

CHAP.

I. THE MEANING AND LIMITATIONS OF TORTURE . 1

A question of terminology—The reality of psychological torture—Illegitimate, surreptitious and camouflaged torture.

II. THE FUNDAMENTAL PRINCIPLES OF TORTURE . 6

A primary means of exacting vengeance—An expression of power—The physiology of hate—The toleration of
torture by society—Mob psychology in relation to the
development of torture.

III. SADISM AS A BASIC CAUSE OF TORTURE BY THE
INDIVIDUAL 14

The sadistic concept of torture—Sadism developed by
public exhibitions of torture—The indulgence of private
sadism.

IV. THE PLEASURE PRINCIPLE IN MASOCHISM . . 21

The submission to torture—Martyrdom and masochism.

V. THE CAUSES OF WHOLESALE OR MASS TORTURE . 24

Sacrifice in relation to torture—The weak and the despised—State domination and power.

VI. THE EFFECTS OF TORTURE 29

Paralysing influence upon the individual—Futility of
torture in the securing of confession or evidence—Psychological effects on society.

xi

PART II

THE HISTORY OF TORTURE

CHAP.   PAGE

VII. TORTURE AMONG SAVAGE AND PRIMITIVE RACES   .   35

The transition from torture as a religious rite to penal
torture—The place of torture in initiatory rites—Punishment by torture.

VIII. TORTURE IN ANCIENT GREECE AND ROME   .   .   44

Torture of free citizens—The torture of slaves—The
Roman gladiators.

IX. THE PROGRESS OF TORTURE   52

The attitude of the Church—The Christian approach
—The persecutions suffered by the Waldenses—The
persecutions suffered by the Quakers—The growth of
judicial and penal torture in Europe.

X. THE HOLY INQUISITION   64

The birth and development of the Holy Office—The
examination of the accused—Inside the torture chamber—
The *auto da fé*—Influence of the Inquisition—Victims of
the Inquisition.

XI. TORTURE IN GREAT BRITAIN AND IRELAND .   .   86

The rise of judicial torture in England—Judicial torture
in Scotland and Ireland—Torture in the guise of punishment.

XII. THE PERSECUTION OF THE WITCHES   .   .   95

The war upon demonology—The mark of Satan—
Witch-hunting in Britain.

XIII. TORTURE IN CHINA, JAPAN AND INDIA   .   .   102

Judicial torture in China—Methods of punishment—
Capital punishment in China—Torture in Japan—A
terrible campaign of religious persecution—Japanese
methods of punishment—Torture in India—The terrible
kittee and other Indian tortures—Torture of school children—Some bizarre forms of torment.

XIV. THE TORTURE OF SLAVES IN THE WEST INDIES,
MAURITIUS AND THE UNITED STATES OF AMERICA   119

The traffic in human beings—Methods of torture employed—Torture will who torture can—The horrors of
Mauritius—Torture of American slaves.

CHAP.   PAGE

XV. THE WAR UPON TORTURE 134

    The growth of opposition—The decline of torture—
The war upon animal torture.

XVI. SOME NOTORIOUS TORTURERS . . . 141

    The ancient tyrants—Torturers of the Middle Ages—
Some eighteenth and nineteenth century torturers.

PART III

THE TECHNIQUE OF TORTURE

XVII. IMPALING METHODS 153

    Crucifixion—The " Dice "—*Peine forte et dure* or
pressing to death.

XVIII. BURNING AT THE STAKE, BRANDING, BOILING TO
    DEATH, THE FIRE-PAN AND THE BRAZEN BULL 157

    Burning alive—Branding—Boiling and frying—The
brazen bull.

XIX. SQUASSATION, THE RACK, THE WHEEL, THE BOOT
    AND THE SCAVENGER'S DAUGHTER . . 168

    Squassation or the torture of the pulley—Torture of the
rack or wooden horse—The torture of water—Torture of
the wheel—Stoning to death—Torture of the boot—The
Scavenger's Daughter—Hurling from a tower or height.

XX. WHIPPING AND BEATING 188

    Flogging implements and methods of the Middle Ages
—The Jamaica cart-whip—The technique in Mauritius—
England's cat-o'-nine-tails—Cart's tail and other penal
floggings—Private and sadistic floggings.

XXI. MUTILATION, DRAWING AND QUARTERING, DECAPI-
    TATION, ETC. 208

    Mutilation—Scalping—Drawing and quartering—De-
capitation—Flaying alive.

XXII. BURYING ALIVE, HANGING ALIVE IN CHAINS,
    STARVATION, THE " VIRGIN MARY," ETC. . 217

    Burying alive—Hanging alive in chains—The Black
Hole of Calcutta—Torture by starvation—Drowning—
Torture of the boats—The kiss of the " Virgin Mary."

XXIII. TORTURE BY ORDEAL 227

    The red-hot iron ordeal—Ordeal of boiling water—The
cold-water ordeal.

CHAP.		PAGE

XXIV. MISCELLANEOUS FORMS OF TORTURE . . . 234

The pillory and the stocks—The thumbscrews—Torture of the "iron gauntlets"—Torture of the glove—The ducking-stool—The scold's bridle—Torture of the pendulum—Torture of the bath—Military tortures—Some bizarre tortures—"Little ease" and "torture of the rats"—Various prison tortures.

XXV. METHODS OF SELF-INFLICTED TORTURE . . 256

The Flagellants—Self-tortures of saints and penitents—The Indian *suttee*.

XXVI. MODERN METHODS OF TORTURE . . . 264

Torture in Russia in the nineteenth and twentieth centuries—The Bolshevist atrocities—Torture in Abyssinia—Torture in South-West Africa—The Chinese communist atrocities—Torture in modern warfare—Terrorism in Ireland—The American lynchings—The "third degree."

XXVII. FORMS OF TORTURE OF ANIMALS . . . 278

The criminal prosecution of animals — Bull-baiting and bear-baiting—The Spanish bull-fight—Miscellaneous forms of modern animal cruelty.

PART IV

THE CASE AGAINST TORTURE

XXVIII. THE FUTILITY OF TORTURE IN THE FIGHT AGAINST CRIMINALITY 287

The aims of punishment—The limitations of fear as a deterrent—The nullity of punishment in a reformatory sense—Experience confounds the arguments of the floggers.

XXIX. THE EVILS OF TORTURE AS A FORM OF PUNISHMENT 298

Dangers incidental to excessive pain—The brutalizing effect of punishment—The suppression of humanity.

XXX. THE PSYCHOPATHOLOGICAL ELEMENT IN TORTURE, AND ITS TREATMENT 302

The limitations of punishment—Treatment of sadism and masochism.

XXXI. THE ABOLITION OF TORTURE . . . 306

Preventing the torture of children and animals—Difficulties in the way of abolition—The real solution.

BIBLIOGRAPHY 315

INDEX 321

LIST OF PLATES

CHINESE TORTURE OF THE RACK . . . *Frontispiece*

Facing page

VARIOUS ANCIENT TORTURES 8

TORTURE AND SACRIFICE OF PRISONERS BY THE AZTECS . . 36

" SLICING TO DEATH " 36

CLUBBING A CRIMINAL TO DEATH IN THE SANDWICH ISLANDS . 38

INITIATORY TORTURE RITES OF THE MANDANS . . . 38

TORTURE OF ROASTING ALIVE 42

TORTURES OF THE PROTESTANTS IN THE PIEDMONT VALLEY DURING
THE SEVENTEENTH CENTURY 58

THE TORTURE CHAMBER OF THE INQUISITION SHOWING THE METHODS
USED 66

TORTURE OF A NATIVE GIRL IN TRINIDAD 70

AN AUTO DA FÉ 70

ROCHUS BURNT AT THE STAKE BY ORDER OF THE INQUISITION . 80

TORTURES INFLICTED ON THE PROTESTANTS, BY THE IRISH PAPISTS,
IN 1642 94

TORTURE OF THE CHAIN 104

CHINESE PUNISHMENT OF THE TCHA . . . 104

TORTURE OF DEATH BY THE THOUSAND CUTS . . . 106

PEINE FORTE ET DURE OR PRESSING TO DEATH . . . 106

CHINESE TORTURE : TEARING THE LIMBS . . . 118

CHINESE TORTURE : SAWING A WOMAN IN TWO . . 118

DRAGGING AT THE HORSE'S TAIL AND CRUCIFIXION . . . 144

VARIOUS FORMS OF CRUCIFIXION 154

VARIOUS FORMS OF TORTURE : BRANDING, FLAYING, AMPUTATION AND
BREAKING THE LIMBS 154

TORTURES OF THE MACCABEES 164

TORTURE OF THE BRAZEN BULL, THE FRYING-PAN AND THE GRIDIRON 166

TORTURE OF THE WHEEL 166

CUTHBERT SIMSON RACKED IN THE TOWER OF LONDON, 1557 . 170

THE TORTURING OF JOHN COUSTOS BY THE INQUISITION OF LISBON . 170

WILLIAM LITHGOW TORTURED ON THE RACK . . . 174

WHIPPING AT THE CART'S TAIL AND OTHER TORTURES . . 174

TORTURE BY FLAGELLATION 200

TORTURE OF THE ENGLISH PRISONERS AT AMBOYNA, IN 1622 . . 200

TORTURE BY CASTRATION 208

Facing page

BURYING ALIVE, DISEMBOWELLING, ETC. 208

BREAKING ON THE "WHEEL" OR CROSS 218

IRON CAGE USED IN JAMAICA FOR HANGING CRIMINALS ALIVE . 218

THE "VIRGIN MARY" 226

VIEW OF THE CUTTING APPARATUS IN THE CHAMBER BENEATH THE
   "VIRGIN" 226

EGAN AND SALMON ON THE SMITHFIELD PILLORY . . . 236

TORTURE OF THE TREES AND OF DRIVING SPIKES UNDER THE FINGER
   AND TOE NAILS 236

THE SCOLD'S BRIDLE 240

TORTURE OF THE ROPE 240

TORTURE OF THE RATS 250

THE TREADMILL AT BRIXTON PRISON . . . 250

PROCESSION OF THE FLAGELLANTS 256

THE PENANCE OF KING HENRY II 260

PENITENCE OF THE GERMAN JEWS IN THEIR SYNAGOGUE . . 260

A REMARKABLE PHOTOGRAPH TAKEN DURING THE CHINESE COMMUNIST
   ATROCITIES OF 1927-28 268

EXECUTED COMMUNISTS, CANTON, DECEMBER 1927 . . . 270

VICTIM OF THE CHINESE COMMUNIST ATROCITIES IN CANTON,
   DECEMBER 1927 270

CLEARING UP AFTER THE COMMUNIST INSURRECTION IN CANTON,
   DECEMBER 1927 278

A SCENE AT A SPANISH BULL-FIGHT 278

BULL-FIGHTING IN THE PLAZA DE TOROS, MADRID . . . 280

LIST OF ILLUSTRATIONS IN TEXT

page

ROMAN FLAGELLUM 48

TORTURES OF THE MIDDLE AGES 54

ANN WILLIAMS BURNT AT THE STAKE . . . 161

RICHARD TURPIN TORTURING A WOMAN BY FIRE . . 162

JANE BUTTERSWORTH BEATEN TO DEATH . . . 206

TORTURE OF RUTH OSBORNE AND HER HUSBAND BY THE "COLD
   WATER" ORDEAL 233

JOHN WALLER PELTED TO DEATH WHILE ON THE PILLORY . 235

For kindly permitting the reproduction of illustrations, acknowledgments are gratefully given by the author and publisher to the Department of Oriental Antiquities, British Museum (frontispiece); to the Wellcome Historical Medical Museum (Torture of Death by the Thousand Cuts); and to the University Library, Cambridge (illustrations facing pages 8, 36, 38, 70, 104, 118, 154, 164, 166, 170, 174, 200, 208, 218, 226, 236, 240, 250, 256, 260, 280, and, in the text, on pages 48 and 54).

PART ONE

PSYCHOLOGICAL ASPECTS
OF TORTURE

CHAPTER I

THE MEANING AND LIMITATIONS OF TORTURE

A Question of Terminology

It must be admitted that the meaning of torture is not easy to define. Invariably is one likely to formulate a definition which is either too wide or too narrow in its scope. Realizing to the full that a serious error in either direction is bound to detract from the value of any study of torture, I feel it to be essential that I should, at the outset, define with some exactitude what, so far as this book is concerned, the word torture implies. It is important, for instance, to realize clearly that there is no rigid line of demarcation between torture and punishment. Any distinction is dependent largely upon the reaction of the *individual victim* to physical and mental suffering. It is necessary to consider in what circumstances the one implies the other. It has always been customary for society and the State, from the beginning of civilization to the present day, to attempt the justification of torture by placing it within the category of punishments, and, further, in this way to deny that any form of torture is used at all. Largely because of this almost universal practice, in which the term punishment is employed as a euphemism for torture, it has never been thoroughly and adequately realized to what extent torture has been employed in past ages, and, additionally, to what extent it is employed to-day.

Much of this lack of knowledge concerning its extent and

universality has arisen through the wide acceptance of the legal definition in contradistinction to any comprehensive elucidation of torture; which acceptance has in large part been due to the fact that no other more exponential and truer definition has been presented. According to the legal definition, torture was a form of cruelty or method of tormenting sanctioned by the State, and executed by duly accredited or appointed officials, through its judicial authorities. It was held to be justifiable, and was authorized and executed for the purpose of inducing a person accused of a crime to confess his guilt or a witness to present evidence. In those countries, of which England was the most notable, which *at no time* allowed accused persons or witnesses to be subjected to the *quæstion* in order to secure a confession or to extract information, it was contended that torture was inexistent. By observing a sharp line of demarcation between those forms of cruelty authorized and practised for a specific purpose, as in the case of judicial torture, and cruelty imposed as punishment, it was easy to deny an allegation of torture even where criminals, under the name of retribution or prison discipline, were subjected to the most fiendish, barbarous and terrible forms of persecution.

At the same time, the error must not be made, as it so often is made by those whose humanitarianism has run to seed, of classifying every form of punishment and every form of cruelty, *in all circumstances*, as torture. It is true that, under certain conditions, as we shall see when we come to consider psychological torture, a form of punishment considered by one individual to be relatively mild, might, to another, constitute a most horrible form of torture; but, generally speaking, the majority of the punishments inflicted to-day in civilized countries and under the ægis of the law, cannot be placed within the category of *physical* torture.

Torture is not a mere matter of terminology, however. Death, in itself, deliberately induced, in many cases, does not rank as a form of physical torture. But torture exists where death is preceded and caused by acts which involve unjustifiable suffering or pain. Where any procedure involving cruelty, suffering and pain is inflicted upon an individual, in any circumstances, and for any purpose, whether the punishment ends with such persecution or is followed by the extinction of life, it does most assuredly constitute torture. The objects of persecution, whatever their nature and however serious their import, neither justify the torturing of the individual nor the description of the torture by another name.

The acceptance of the legal definition means the acceptance of the view that torture is applied only by the State, for the express objects defined. The act of cruelty used by the State as a form of torture, if committed by an individual or by a number of citizens, without the authority of the State, would not be legitimate and would not constitute torture: it would rank as an assault. Obviously such an interpretation is most unsatisfactory and logically indefensible.

From the viewpoint of the unfortunate person who is being subjected to any act which entails suffering and pain analogous to that experienced by the victim of torture, it is a matter of indifference by what precise term this persecution is described, and whether it is being executed by a private individual or by a State official.

Clearly the sufferer, provided the degree of persecution or cruelty is sufficiently severe, is being subjected to what can be described as nothing less than torture. And equally clearly the sufferer is the one person who is in a position to provide the most fitting evidence as to the reality or otherwise of such torture. The judge responsible for the sentence, and the executioner responsible for the infliction of the punishment, apart from the fact that they are prejudiced witnesses, cannot be so reliable in their decision as to whether or not the specific sentence ranks as torture, as is the actual victim.

The Reality of Psychological Torture

Here we come up against the fact, all too imperfectly and all too rarely realized, that there is in existence a form of torture distinct from physical injury or torment: a form of torture which is psychological in its trend. It may exist in addition to physical torture. It may exist where there is no physical torture at all.

The substitution of psychological methods of dealing with crime in the place of many antiquated physical methods does not necessarily mean, as is generally thought, that torture has been removed *in toto* from the prison system. It merely means that physical torture, in the shape of corporal punishment, the treadmill, the crank, *et al.*, has been to a big extent ·replaced by other and more subtle methods.

The reformation in prison methods has been coincident with the evolution of a new type of prisoner. Man to-day is, *generally speaking*, and in *normal circumstances*, more humane and less brutal than was his prototype of fifty and a hundred years ago. He is, to use another form of terminology, " softer." This applies to the criminal element in society exactly as it does to the respectable element. The popular notion that the criminals of the world are " tougher " specimens than are the law-abiding members of the public is a fallacy. It arises through the error of accepting those exceptional cases of " toughness " which figure in sensational newspaper accounts and in crime fiction as representative of the criminal world. The majority of criminals, as Dr. Amos Squire, one-time chief physician of Sing Sing, has pointed out, are indistinguishable in physical or mental attainments from the average respectable golf-playing, cinema-going, radio-listening citizen.

The mental torture induced by imprisonment, with its destructive effects upon initiative, will-power, originality and ambition, can be incalculable. Upon some natures the segregation of mind is even more paralysing and cumulative in its effects than is any form of physical segregation. The contention that the modern prison is a convalescent home or a rest-camp, and errs on the side of leniency or beneficence, is as erroneous in its implications as are the ideas secured by visitors who are conveyed around a " model " prison upon a tour of inspection. *A prison is a prison* whatever amenities form part of the curriculum. Moreover it is possible for a governor or a warder, even in a modern " humane " prison, to render the life of the prisoner a veritable hell. Ninety years ago, in Birmingham borough prison, the governor subjected the prisoners to various illegal tortures unknown to the visiting justices. It is not impossible, in relation to psychological torture at any rate, for an analogous state of affairs to exist to-day.

Illegitimate, Surreptitious and Camouflaged Torture

The prohibition of torture and persecution during criminal investigations and in prison management, by the State, is no guarantee of their non-existence in the community. Any such prohibition does not even mean that the State itself *never* employs such methods. For instance, although torture, either by the State or by private individuals, is prohibited in Great Britain, flogging is still included among the punishments prescribed in the penal code. The use of corporal punishment is justified as a legitimate means of correction; it does not rank as (what it actually is) a form of torture. In the United States of America, for many decades, torture has been prohibited both in the penal code and in private life, yet flogging has been employed in several States and on many occasions since 1868; and the " third degree," which incorporates many forms of torture, is surreptitiously but widely resorted to by the police in the securing of confessions. The American public, the American judges, and the American Government *know* that this " third degree " is in constant employment: they make no real or sincere attempt to suppress a practice which is as much a crime as are any of the offences of the individuals upon whom it is used.

To what extent torture is employed privately it is quite impossible to do more than guess at. Although it is true that the individual has the right of appeal to the law in any case of assault, there are lots of instances where no such appeal is made. There are wives and there are children who suffer severe physical punishment and take no action against those who have inflicted such punishment. There are hundreds of cases where terrible mental suffering is borne in silence, often, too, in circumstances where it would be difficult, if not impossible, to prove anything which would secure a conviction in a court of law. There are other cases where, for many reasons, the suffering and persecuted party cannot face the publicity and exposure which a court action ensures. There are prostitutes in the power of bullies and pimps, and there are criminals tied up with gangs, who cannot seek the protection of the law.

CHAPTER II

THE FUNDAMENTAL PRINCIPLES OF TORTURE

A Primary Means of Exacting Vengeance

ONCE it is conceded and accepted that there are forms of
torture in addition to the type acknowledged and defined
by law, we have gone a long way towards realizing that
torture is something which has existed from the beginning
of time. In relation to its true and wide significance it is as
erroneous to assert that torture was inexistent before the
time of the Romans as it is to assert that it disappeared from
most European countries in the eighteenth century. Both
these assertions have been made. Each assertion represents
a perversion of the truth.

It is no exaggeration to say that every man and woman
is a potential torturer. The scope of this potentiality, and
likewise its expression, are extended by the fact that what,
by the persecuted party, is recognized as torture, may not, and
probably in many circumstances will not, be so recognized or
admitted by the individual responsible for putting the torture
into operation. This non-recognition or non-acceptance of
torture by the individual, by the mob, and, in certain circumstances, by the State, is responsible for the wide extension
of persecution in any one period of history, for its continuance through the ages, and for its existence to-day. It is
further the cause of the abolition of torture being a much
more difficult affair than the average person realizes, involving matters which are outside the scope of ordinary vision
and which have implications that are seldom fully recognized.

In its simplest and most ecumenic form torture represents
a ready, an efficacious, a satisfactory, and a crude means of
exacting vengeance; especially of exacting that type of vengeance which is more concerned with the individual than
with the State. That is to say, torture in any ordinary
circumstances, appeals more to the sense of retribution

developed in the injured individual for a crime or an offence concerning himself or his immediate family, than it appeals to the State as a means of securing satisfaction for a crime committed against the community, or an offence concerned with abstract principles. It is this attitude which is responsible for the view expressed so often by those individuals intimately concerned with a horrible crime that the penalty of death, in itself, is not enough to satisfy the call for justice. The personal cry for vengeance demands that before death the criminal must suffer long and severely; in other words, that torture must precede death. This primitive cry for vengeance is as common and as urgent in the civilized countries of to-day as it was among the North American savages careering around the captives whom they were burning at the stake. It is merely that society, in virtue of laws passed by citizens, who, *at the time of making those laws*, were not imbued with this passion for private vengeance, has diverted or submerged the urge. It is not that, fundamentally and individually speaking, the urge does not exist.

An Expression of Power

In this vengeance inherent in all forms of torture lies the key to its use as an expression, by the individual, of the will to power, and, by the State, of authority and autocratic domination. The expression or satisfaction of this demand for vengeance on the part of a group of individuals or of society as a whole, which is an extension of the individual's private urge for revenge, has formed a part of the policy adopted by every leader of mankind, starting with the chief, the king, or the emperor, and descending, through various stages, to the mob leader, whether he be the incendiary calling to arms a rabble of political rebels, or the gangster chief directing the criminal activities of a mob of social outlaws. Nothing was, and nothing is, better calculated to enhance the prestige and authority of the leader than the handing over to his followers, for punishment, of their enemy.[1] It was due to a realization of this primeval fact

[1] A modern example of this appeal to the mob's desire for vengeance was the promise made, either directly or by implication, during the war of 1914-18, by some of England's leading statesmen, that the Kaiser would be tried and executed at the termination of hostilities.

that torture was first adopted and authorized as part of the penal code of a race, a government, or a branch of society. The more the leader showed himself as an advocate and a devotee of vengeance against the avowed and suspected enemies of the branch of society he headed, the more did he find himself respected by his immediate followers. Coincidentally the tyrant fed, in true anthropophagous style, upon his own tyranny. The more tyrannous he became the more powerful. Torture proved itself to be a footstool to greater power just as it was a means of developing personal vanity in one's own power.

As society developed out of savagery into civilization, and as codes of laws and regulations were enacted, the torture which was inflicted by primitive man to satisfy his vengeance against enemies without and within his race, crystallized itself into a definite method of torture justified as a system of punishment; as a means, adopted by the ruler in an autocratic country and by the State in an oligarchy, of compelling subservience to authority; and, in the case of smaller mobs or gangs, as a method of maintaining discipline.

Torture, more perhaps than any other factor known, justified itself, in the opinion of those in positions of authority, irrespective of the nature, degree and circumstances of such authority, as the best available means of limiting the freedom of the individual to think or to act for himself. Torture justified itself as the most satisfying method of compelling acceptance of dictatorial jurisdiction, by repressing and preventing all attempts to rebel against that authority or the tenets of its creed. In the State, as in the Church, in waging war upon treason on the one hand and heresy on the other, torture was admitted to be the most powerful instrument available. It is, although any practical expressions are hidden and camouflaged in a thousand ways, the most powerful instrument available to-day. Because of this basic fact, torture has always been existent in some form or other, and, in the course of the world's history, has made spectacular and sporadic emergencies, which, in themselves, have been partly instrumental in distracting attention from those forms of persecution which have been continually present since the beginning of man's urge to power, and which are existent in our own time.

From Clark's *Martyrologia*, 1677.

VARIOUS ANCIENT TORTURES

The Physiology of Hate

Interlinked with all this is the virtue of cruelty, which represents a physical expression of hate, in the fight for self-preservation. The rival or the competitor, even within one's own race, is a potential enemy. The primeval law of self-preservation demands that everyone should think and act on the supposition and in accordance with the selfish realization that, in the ultimate struggle for existence, it is, in popular parlance, every man for himself. In mass formation this transcends itself into the assumption that every powerful neighbouring tribe or nation is similarly a potential if not an actual enemy.

Whether the question is one concerning the individual or the family, or the tribe, or the nation, the possibility of hatred towards someone implied or expressed is always existent. Everything or everybody that possesses dangerous possibilities is a potential subject for hate.

Now just as cruelty or tyranny is an expression of power over the inferior or the despised; so, too, is it an expression of hatred for the powerful rival or competitor. The more that rival or competitor is feared the greater will be the degree of hate, and when the opportunity for overt activity arises, the greater the expression of cruelty.

It is the existence of this fundamental potentiality for hate, which may be, and probably is, in many cases, functioning unconsciously or semi-consciously, that, in the interests of self-preservation, leads to the formation of gangs, societies, associations, groups; and, in relation to nations, pacts, alliances or treaties. These organizations may be open or they may be secret.

In modern civilization this tendency is apparently a growing one. It is not a tendency which can be viewed without disquiet, though one may perhaps secure some degree of consolation from the fact that the multiplicity of such groups has a weakening effect upon any individual organization.

The Toleration of Torture by Society

It is an ironical commentary upon society that the masses have always contributed towards their own enslavement by encouraging the lust for power in their leaders, whether those leaders have been chiefs of gangs and mobs functioning locally; or kings, dictators and oligarchies functioning nationally. If it is too much to say that society itself actually initiated the putting into operation of torture in any organized and universal sense, it is certainly not too much to say that sections of society, by their actions, first suggested to ruling individuals or governing bodies the virtues of torture as an indication of power and a means of compelling obedience. " It is," says Sumner, " of the first importance to notice that it was the masses which first applied death by burning to heretics. The mob lynched heretics long before the Church began to prosecute."[1]

The root cause of this reaction of society, as we have already seen, is in the primeval thirst for revenge which is inherent in the individual, and which has existed all through the ages until our own time. Inevitably, in the end, argument gives place to brute force. Inevitably, society accepts the primitive law that punishment and torture are, in the ultimate analysis, the most powerful instruments, not alone for forcing the individual to act contrary to his wishes, but also for preventing him rebelling against the existent rules of the governing body. It was familiarity with the truth of this concept which led the Inquisition to adopt torture as a means of securing confession; it was a realization of the force of this same concept which led the English government, in the Middle Ages, to practise torture in defiance of common law; it is the appreciation of this self-same concept which leads, in these ultra-civilized days, to war still remaining the final arbiter when the possibilities of every other conceivable type of negotiation have been exhausted.

The incorporation of any form of torture in a penological system, whether as a means of extracting confession, as in the Middle Ages, or as a form of punishment, as in most countries to-day, inevitably leads to its acceptance as a justifiable procedure by society generally, and involves a danger of its extension under suitable conditions. Just as familiarity with torture leads to approval of torture, so does the acceptance or ratification of torture lead to its justification.

[1] W. G. Sumner, *Folkways*, Boston, 1907, p. 238.

We see examples of this in the attempts, which modern society increasingly makes, to justify the torture of animals. The animal to-day is in the position of the negro in the West Indies a century ago. The negro in those days had no rights: he was weak, he was despised. The animal to-day has no rights: similarly it is weak, similarly it is despised. The negro was tortured a hundred years ago. The animal is tortured to-day. These facts are not admitted by society as reasons for persecution, nor is any justification of persecution essayed along these lines; but none the less precisely here lie the fundamental reasons for persecution and the possibility of justification being attempted. Thus it is contended—and the contention is supported by Biblical exegesis—that cattle were created by God to provide food for man; that butchers must live; that wild animals must be destroyed or they would overrun the earth and destroy man; that rabbits are pests which must be exterminated; that fox-hunting provides work for hundreds of horse-breeders, *et al.* All these excuses for the propagation of cruelty are possible only because society is *in a position to persecute animals.*

Some reflection of this attitude is, too, observable in relation to the persecution of those individuals who, in the spheres of morality, religion, and even pure intellect, are alien to normality or orthodoxy. The same measure of brutal treatment or persecution which would arouse the deepest resentment or indignation when applied to a kindred spirit or a close associate, if directed against one whose actions or opinions were viewed with abhorrence or disgust, would evince no words of protest, and might conceivably, were the circumstances sufficiently provocative, meet with active support. Thus the tolerance or approval of the most brutal persecutional measures accorded to criminals, to sexual perverts, to enemy aliens. The martyrdom of anyone who is associated with something out of tune with current thought or morality is not viewed with sympathy and is usually called by another and a harsher name. It is an inevitable result of mob psychology that the sympathy and tolerance of the masses is extended only to those near them in mentality as well as environment.

Mob Psychology in Relation to the Development of Torture

Once society began to practise torture, its development was certain. It matters little that any such practice was, in the beginning, restricted in its application to those guilty of certain crimes which, viewed in relation to the ethical and religious reactions of the time, were considered to be as monstrous as they were dangerous. The very fact that torture had been put into operation at all suggested the possibility of its extension; and further suggested to the leaders of society a method of dealing with their recalcitrant or rebellious members. Thus it not infrequently happened that the individuals who had been primarily responsible for the infliction of torture against certain members of society, found themselves, as a result of the development of persecution along unforeseen lines, and for unspecified purposes, among its next victims.

In the beginning torture was probably restricted to animals and to members of enemy tribes or races. A start having been made, the next steps were the extension in the quantity of subjects persecuted and developments in the technique of torture itself. The rule that the tolerated of to-day becomes the approved of to-morrow, applies to torture as well as to most things. And with toleration and approval of any specific form of persecution, in many cases, it ceases to rank as torture at all, but is accepted as a form of punishment or of penal procedure. This happened all through the ages. It happens to-day. It is for this reason that the *justification* of persecution has always been one of the *major forces* working against its abolition. The result of all this is that torture, in whatever country it is practised and wherever it is regarded as essential to the form of authority or government in vogue, must of necessity, if it is not to decline in its efficacy, be either continually increasing in its severity or extending in its scope. One of the greatest evils connected with torture is that whenever and wherever it is practised, and whatever be its objects, it must inevitably develop. The judges and executioners of the Middle Ages were compelled to be continually inventing new and more severe forms of torture. Thus by sheer tolerance, the brutal form of punishment practised in one decade became a commonplace method in the next.

The tortured individual is himself a potential torturer. The ill-treatment of animals by man is often to be found in conjunction with the ill-treatment of man by his fellowmen. A little over a century ago, in the British West Indies, the scavenging work was done by negro slaves guilty of some criminal offence or other. They worked in fetters and they were treated just about as inhumanly as one human being can be treated by another, and live. They were permitted to destroy every pig they found in the streets. This they looked upon as " great sport "; indeed they revelled in it, according to Mr. F. W. N. Bayley, who describes the following incident. It occurred in St. Vincent.

"I was one day standing at my window, gazing on these unfortunate beings at their work, when a pig passed the gang; before the poor animal had proceeded ten yards, a long pole, which they carry for the purpose, was immediately thrust into its side, and passed out beneath its belly; at that moment a woman, to whom the pig belonged, came out of her house, which was close by, and, seizing the animal's two legs, endeavoured to take it from the man. The enraged and savage brute immediately left his hold of the pike, and taking the other two legs of the pig, commenced pulling it in a contrary direction. The struggle lasted about five minutes, during which time the bowels and intestines of the animal were protruding in a most disgusting manner; and the females of the gang, *instead of turning away from the revolting scene before them, appeared to enjoy it like a delicious meal, and stood laughing at the despoiled owner.* At length the man gained the mastery, and having severed the head from the body, he stuck it on his pike, as if in triumph, and afterwards repaired to the market to make his bargain with the butcher."[1] (The italics are mine.—G. R. S.)

[1] F. W. N. Bayley, *Four Years' Residence in the West Indies*, 1830, p. 197.

CHAPTER III

SADISM AS A BASIC CAUSE OF TORTURE BY THE INDIVIDUAL

The Sadistic Concept of Torture

IT is futile to deny the existence of individuals who take a delight in the sight of suffering, or in the infliction of pain. Persons of this nature are often the leaders in scenes of mob violence. They are not necessarily sadists, but often they are.

It is important to distinguish between cruelty *per se* and sadism. The popular assumption, due largely to the loose way in which the term is now used in popular fiction and in newspapers, that sadism is a synonym for cruelty in any form, is a fallacy. Sadism is a sexological term, and, strictly speaking, it should never be employed apart from its sexual connotations. This widespread misuse detracts from the term's significance, and gives rise to a good deal of misapprehension.

The sadist, in most cases, either practises or delights in the witnessing of cruelty, but his pleasure is concerned exclusively with and is limited entirely to sexual excitation or relief. Cruelty, in any other circumstances, does not appeal to him. Moreover, the moment the sexual repercussion has spent itself he takes no further interest in the practice or expression of cruelty. In addition, the sadist usually expresses his cruelty along well-defined and restricted lines.

Now the individual who practises cruelty for any other purpose than sexual excitation is seldom motivated by such limitations. And for this reason he usually becomes consistently more and more cruel. Moreover he is cruel in a general and comprehensive rather than a limited and specialized sense. Whether his fundamental motive is primeval vengeance, or the lust for power, matters little. His appetite for cruelty has been created, and it may well prove to be an insatiable one. It is in this respect more perhaps than any other that the ordinary cruel person differs from the sadist.

14

For whereas the one is ever on the look-out for opportunities to practise his itch for cruelty, the sadist, after the satisfying of a biological need motivated in a peculiar form of psychopathological expression, becomes to all intents and purposes a normal individual, and may conceivably, apart from these sporadic indulgences in cruelty, be an ardent advocate of humanitarianism.

Sadism is not so abnormal a characteristic as one might well think. It is actually merely an extension or a development, along unilateral and obsessional lines, of a natural characteristic. There is a consistent and universal relationship between the sex act and pain in its purely objective sense. In the throes of erotic passion, however, the sensation which in any other circumstances would be characterized as pain, is not recognized as such. Any element of suffering is obliterated and subordinated by the pleasure associated with coitus. This is apparent in the sexual act as practised by many animals. It is evidenced in the fact that in numerous cases, and especially among races where sexual relations are of a more passionate nature than is customary in ultra-civilized society, the kiss becomes a love-bite. At the hands of her lover the female suffers treatment which, in other circumstances, would constitute rape of the most brutal kind.

This perfectly *normal* correlation between pleasure and pain, between cruelty and sexual expression, is the fundament of what in modern life is termed sadism, and which, through its association with the vicarious sexual aberrations of the psychopathologically motivated Marquis de Sade, has come to be looked upon as something monstrous beyond description. Sadism then, as we understand it to-day, is an extension of this basic sexual cruelty, which, partly through repression and partly as a result of environmental and sociological conditions, so often reaches an obsessional stage. In individuals who have not the faintest knowledge of the meaning of sadism, the sight of some cruel act occasionally arouses sexual excitation.

Sadism Developed by Public Exhibitions of Torture

Although it would be a gross exaggeration to say that the thousands of spectators who cheered the gladiatorial contests in the Roman amphitheatres were all sadists, there is little doubt that a considerable number of them were. In many other cases, too, the very fact of witnessing these exhibitions revived or developed sadistic tendencies.

The gratification of the mob, exemplified in the cheering of every act of cruelty, is in many cases but an expression of the lust for power, or of the pleasure derivable from vengeance exercised upon those who differ in biological, physiological or psychological fundamentals from existent society. It may or may not in the first instance be associated with sadism, but inevitably is there danger that an incipient tendency in that direction may be awakened or developed.

Coincidentally the sadist is inevitably attracted by all such scenes of persecution. Although there are sadists who, after taking part in or witnessing acts of cruelty, experience erotic excitation which must find relief in sexual intercourse, there are others, and I believe they are in the majority, who find they are able to secure sexual relief independent of actual coitus. They may find the act or the exhibition of cruelty itself provides all the sexual excitation expected or desired, thus forming a complete substitute for coition. Kürten, the Dusseldorf monster, belonged to this class of sadist. In his confessions to Dr. Berg he admitted " It was not my intention to get satisfaction by normal sexual intercourse, but by killing."[1] The actual torture or the witnessing of the torture may in itself induce ejaculation, or it may be followed by or associated with masturbation.

The position of woman is by no means so clear. Actually the popular idea that woman is less attracted by scenes of cruelty, and less inclined to practise cruelty, are both fallacies. The sadism of man is paralleled and often eclipsed by the sadism of woman. The difference, however, is that for the most part the sexual stimulation does not so much act as a substitute for coitus, or a causative factor in masturbation : it more usually induces a great development of eroticism manifesting itself in a desire to be subjugated by man. In this way it is almost always associated with masochism. It was Ovid who first pointed out that the spectacle of blood, as in the gladiatorial exhibitions of his time, led to the female

[1] Karl Berg, *The Sadist*, authorized translation by Olga Illner and George Godwin, Acorn Press, 1938, p. 111.

being in a state of mind in which she was extremely likely
to respond to the male's sexual overtures. It was this very
method which, according to Goncourt, was adopted by an
Englishman who had failed to overcome his young lady
friend's scruples—he induced her to witness a public execution in Paris.

At the same time, the effect of public exhibitions of
torture as a means of counteracting the evil potentialities
inherent in any form of sadism that has no opportunities for
securing relief, is manifest. It is an ironic commentary upon
civilization that just as prostitution may be looked upon as
a means of protecting respectable women; so may all public
exhibitions involving torture and cruelty be looked upon as
being the means of lessening the incidence of lust murders,
of lynchings, of animal torture, *et al*.

The *autos da fé* engineered by the Inquisition were
popular for the very same reason that, a thousand years
before, were the Roman gladitorial contests. The populace,
instead of rearing up in hot indignation at the cruelty, the
barbarity, and the inhumanity of burning alive the victims
of the Inquisition, cheered with gusto as the flames consumed the bodies of the martyrs.

Similarly with the public hangings at one time to be seen
in England, and which drew vast crowds; similarly with
breaking on the wheel, drawing and quartering,[1] whipping
at the cart's tail, and other methods of punishment inflicted
publicly.

What of sadism in these modern days when all such
public tortures are things of the past? Has sadism decayed
with the growth of humanitarianism?

I do not think so. In conformation with the change in
the life of the people has there been a change in the form of
sadism that manifests itself. More and more is vicarious or
subjective sadism subduing or replacing purely physical

---

[1] When Damien was executed in 1757 every available spot within eye-
reach of the scaffold was crowded with Parisian sightseers, who gloated
over the doomed man's sufferings. After having his hand burned off and
being subjected to the horrible torture of boiling oil and melted lead, for
hours, to the accompaniment of his piercing screams, the whip-goaded
horses dragged his limbs and body apart. Casanova, himself an eye-
witness, although compelled to turn his face away and stop his ears,
observed that his female companions " did not budge an inch."

sadism. And coincidentally with the decline in one form of mass cruelty, have there come into existence other forms of persecution : forms which perhaps are even more ecumenic than anything that was ever known in the past.

It may seem, at first glance, a far cry from the gladiatorial combats and gymnastic contests of ancient Rome to the circus performances and boxing matches of the present day, but fundamentally there is little if any essential difference. While the twentieth-century sadist is deprived of the sight of the murderer dying the death, he has every opportunity to revel in all the gory details of the crime which preceded the execution. And there still exists, in another sphere, the essentially emotional and surrogative cannibalistic orgy, celebrated regularly throughout Christendom, in which the drinking of blood and the eating of flesh solemnize a bloody sacrificial rite. Finally, there persists, in a hundred different ways, the torture of animals. In this one field, if in no other, the sadist is to-day enabled to gratify to the full extent of his desires, any form or degree of blood lust.

The Indulgence of Private Sadism

The contemplation, in connexion with sadism, of animal torture in modern life leads us inevitably to the consideration of private sadism. For even as regards animal torture, this is, in the tremendous main, exercised privately and under most effective forms of camouflage or euphemization.

Apart from and in addition to the presence of sadism which never actually functions in the shape of overt acts of torture or cruelty performed by the individual pervert, and which forms the bulk of existent sadism, there are in existence numerous sadists who cannot receive satisfaction in any vicarious or subjective way; in other words, they must themselves *inflict* acts of violence upon some human or animal subject. Individuals of this type are undoubtedly responsible for a lot of the cruelty which exists to-day.

There are so many ways in which active sadists are encouraged, by the remarkable apathy of society in relation to certain forms of cruelty, to indulge in their perverted appetites. They may, for instance, secure employment as keepers of animals or as workers on breeding establishments;

they may choose butchery as their trade; they may become warders in prisons or assistants in lunatic asylums. But, above and beyond all, they may adopt the easiest of all methods available for the indulgence of an appetite for sadism : that of acquiring animals for the express purpose of subjecting them to surreptitious torture.

I do not think there can be any doubt or question that a good deal of private or secret torturing of animals takes place in every civilized country. It is, of course, impossible even to guess at the extent of this type of cruelty, or at the forms it takes; but the figures relative to the convictions in the courts tell their own terrible story. And for every one such conviction I do not think I can be accused of the slightest exaggeration in assuming that there are a full hundred of which no one ever so much as hears.

The sadist may kill or maim as a complete substitute for coitus or he may kill or maim *during* sexual intercourse. Most cases of " pricking " are the work of sadists, and no doubt many of the " witch-prickers " of the Middle Ages were sexual perverts. It is noteworthy that there is a close connexion between the sight of the blood proceeding from the wounds and the sexual ecstasy of the sadist. Féré says " a large number of these perverts need effusion of blood. Some increase their pleasure by sucking the blood of the wounds they have caused."[1] Kürten, before his execution, admitted that in his case the *sight of blood* produced sexual excitement. " I saw blood come from her mouth and I had an orgasm."[2] Krafft-Ebing was of opinion that the " accidental sight of blood " might, in certain circumstances, put " into motion the performed psychical mechanism of the sadistic individual and awaken the instinct."[3]

Not all sadists kill or maim, however. Sadism being in part an expression of the will-to-power of the individual formulated specifically in sexual channels, may function in that form of persecution which takes shape in the imposition of disgusting tasks or moral humiliation. It is this form

[1] Ch. Féré, *The Sexual Instinct: Its Evolution and Dissolution*, University Press, 1900, p. 227.
[2] Karl Berg, *The Sadist*.
[3] R. V. Krafft-Ebing, *Psychopathia Sexualis*, authorized English adaptation of the twelfth German edition, by F. J. Rebman, New York, 1925, p. 86.

in particular which so often occurs, according to Féré, in women.[1]   Symbolical, vicarious or imaginary sadism occurs where the pervert secures sexual pleasure, often culminating in orgasm, through imagining sadistic scenes, witnessing executions and acts of cruelty, or even reading about such incidents.

Dr. Stekel has drawn attention to the cruelty inherent in modern therapeutics. He says : " Once in visiting a torture chamber I was struck with the similarity between instruments of torture and various medical apparatuses."[2] Modern massage is merely a rococo form of flagellation; the vapour bath,[3] as Dr. Stekel points out, gives rise to sensations somewhat similar to those of being buried alive; while psychoanalysis may easily become a sort of mental " third degree." " During the war tortures were made use of by over-patriotic physicians to extort admission of health! "[4] Finally, there is the possibility of operative treatment representing an expression of masochism on the part of the patient and of sadism on the part of the surgeon. " I know a case," says this same authority, " in which even the suturing of a wound was accompanied by ejaculation."[5]

[1] Ch. Féré, *The Sexual Instinct*, p. 148.
[2] Wilhelm Stekel, *Sadism and Masochism*, The Bodley Head, 1935, Vol. I, p. 436.
[3] The ancient Romans used their sudatories both as torture and execution chambers (cf. p. 242).
[4] Wilhelm Stekel, *op. cit.*
[5] Wilhelm Stekel, *op. cit.*

CHAPTER IV

THE PLEASURE PRINCIPLE IN MASOCHISM

The Submission to Torture

ALGOLAGNIA, or the pleasure principle in pain, takes two forms: sadism, or the ecstasy associated with the infliction or witnessing of pain; and masochism, or the eroticism induced by the suffering of pain or persecution. In masochism, as in sadism, this pleasure principle is limited to or intimately associated with sexual excitation. It may be accompanied by or it may form a substitute for coitus.

For the most part masochism is an individual affair. In its true psychopathological sense it is obviously not a phenomenon that can be induced in any ordinary way in masses of people. It takes a movement like the flagellation cult of the Middle Ages to arouse any such feelings on a wholesale scale.

Because of the existence of masochism, any wilful subjection to pain on the part of the individual is inevitably suspect. That, in the olden days, when submission to torture was common, the term masochism was unheard of does not alter the fact that in many instances such submission had a sexual content or basis. The masochist, too, often secures the acme of erotic pleasure from the fact that this pleasurable reaction follows immediately after the experiencing of pain, and by the well-known and almost universally applicable law of contrast the greater the antecedent pain the more intense the sexual pleasure correlated to it.

The most usual form which masochism takes is flagellation, and this very fact leads one to suspect that much of the so-called discipline indulged in by the saints and others connected with the Church had a masochistic fundament. The scourging of penitents might well have fulfilled a twofold purpose, enabling the priest to indulge a taste for sadism and the penitent a penchant for masochism.

Especially is it likely that this constituted the true explanation where the victim was a female, for in most cases of masochism the pleasure in punishment is experienced only where that punishment is inflicted by an attractive member of the opposite sex. There have been many scandals in Church history connected with the chastisement of penitents by confessors, notably the case where Father Girard flagellated the pretty Cadière girl; and the almost equally notorious instance in which the Franciscan monk, Cornelius Hadrien, was accused of having administered the discipline to naked girl pupils.

Although the connexion between religion and masochism has always been a marked one, largely because there are peculiar opportunities for its indulgence, the practice is by no means restricted to the Church. Most masochists seek sexual relief by paying prostitutes to " torture " them, just as many sadists employ prostitutes to suffer the infliction of minor forms of punishment. Thus Krafft-Ebing gives the case of a man who regularly visited a brothel where he " had himself bound hand and foot, and then flogged by the girl on the soles of his feet, his calves and buttocks ";[1] and Hammond instances the case of a young man who often visited a house of prostitution where he instructed three of the girls to tread upon his face and chest with their high-heeled shoes.[2]

Martyrdom and Masochism

In these days when religion has lost much of its power and appeal, when pain in its purely physical aspects is very much more dreaded than it was a few centuries ago, we cannot very well visualize the state of mind which enabled human beings to suffer severe punishment or persecution in the name of faith and glory. Just as the appeal to a future life of heavenly bliss has lost much of its one-time puissance, so, too, the dread of the tortures of hell has lost most of its potency, and there seems to be

[1] Krafft-Ebing, *Psychopathia Sexualis*, p. 143.
[2] W. Hammond, *Sexual Impotence in the Male*, 1883, p. 32.

nothing that religion has to offer modern man in a future life which would lead him to suffer avoidable persecution on earth.

It was largely the desire for atonement and the appeasement of a sadistic god that induced the people to inflict torture upon themselves. Self-flagellation was a mode of placating an angry deity. More, in many cases of female self-flagellation, it was a means of signifying subjection to the omnipotence of God.

But if one form of martyrdom has deteriorated, another has developed. Political or racial martyrdom has taken the place of religious martyrdom. The man who would scoff at the idea of sacrificing himself in the cause of a religious faith, will gleefully immolate himself to the moloch of patriotism. Such martyrdom is, of course, conditioned by the lack of free choice in the matter. It might well be said that the religious victim of the Middle Ages was no more free to reject martyrdom than is the twentieth-century political or racial victim in a position to reject the martyrdom imposed upon him in the name of patriotism.

All of which, although true, does not alter the fundamental fact that this patriotic martyrdom of to-day is, as was the religious martyrdom of the Middle Ages, conditioned and largely made possible by a form of symbolic masochism which is all the more potent in its influence and in its effects through the fact that it is not recognized as such by those members of society in whom it particularly functions.

The tendency to-day is towards an extension of psychological masochism on the part of society as a whole and in all countries, whether that society is governed by a tyrannous and sadistic dictatorship or an equally tyrannous and sadistic oligarchy; using the term sadistic here in its purely psychological and ideological significance and as a correlative of psychological masochism.

CHAPTER V

THE CAUSES OF WHOLESALE OR MASS TORTURE

Sacrifice in Relation to Torture

THE birth of the gods signified an advance from the concept of hatred as a subject concerned with purely private vengeance to a wider and more comprehensive system in which sacrifice was a potent factor. Sacrifice may be considered to represent the first step towards the use of torture not only as a religious but also as a patriotic embellishment. Into the mouths of the various deities were put demands for sacrifices. These sacrifices involved, in many cases, physical torture; and where the victim did not offer to immolate himself masochistically as a tribute to the omnipotence of the gods, they invariably involved psychological torture.

Sacrifice, whatever precise form it took, was a propitiatory act, designed to appease the anger of God, or to induce the granting of favours or indulgences. In accordance with the anthropomorphic conception of the Godhead, man interpreted the tastes of the deity on lines analogous to his own. It was perfectly natural that an anthropomorphic god should be conceded to possess carnivorous tastes and, by virtue of his superiority, anthropophagous tastes as well.

Whether animal sacrifice preceded human sacrifice is open to doubt. The evidence, such of it as is available, is conflicting. Possibly races varied in this respect. Possibly, too, deficiencies in the supply of human victims might lead, on the ground of expediency alone, to the substitution of animals.

So far as the evidence provided in the Bible is concerned, the sacrifice of the first-born seems to have represented the highest form which any propitiatory act could take. It was only in response to a command from Jehovah Himself that Abraham stayed the hand that was about to slay his son and instead offered up a ram.

In all contemporary cults, human or animal sacrifices, or both, formed part of the ritual, and the offering of the first-born seems to have been practised in many races. To Odin, the powerful god of the ancient Scandinavians, Aun, the Swedish king, in an attempt to secure the prolongation of his own life, sacrificed his nine sons; and to the same god, Earl Hakon, the Norwegian king, to secure divine help in his war upon the Jomsburg pirates, sacrificed his son.[1] Eusebius states that the Phœnicians sacrificed their children to Saturn. So, too, the Hindus and the Egyptians. The king of Mexico was continually waging war in order to secure captives for use as offerings to the gods: these sacrifices amounted to no fewer than fifty thousand human beings annually. Amurath, says Montaigne, sacrificed six hundred young Greeks to his father's soul.

Other races used as offerings enemies captured in war, but the supply in most cases was necessarily limited, and it was sporadic rather than regular, while the appetites of the gods apparently were omnivorous. To fill the gaps, criminals, slaves, aged persons of both sexes, the weak, the crippled, the abnormal, were sacrificed. In accordance with the ritual adopted by many races, the victim was tortured before death, or killed in a manner which entailed long and agonizing torment. Prescott says: " The Aztecs did not, like our North American Indians, torture their enemies from mere cruelty, but in conformity to the prescribed regulations of their ritual. The captive was a religious victim."[2]

With the development of civilization, the position did not change fundamentally, it merely crystallized into a more ecumenic and more powerful form of expression. The coming of Christianity, with its doctrine of charity and goodwill, did not, strangely enough, abolish torture and persecution. The Christians persecuted their opponents with all the rigour of the Romans. Indeed they borrowed the weapons

---

[1] T. W. Doane, *Bible Myths*, New York, 1882, p. 40.
[2] William H. Prescott, *History of the Conquest of Mexico*, 1843, Vol. III, p. 61.

and imitated the practices of their ancient enemies. Thus we read in Timothy, of Hymenaeus and Alexander, notorious heretics, being delivered unto Satan, in order that the terrible discipline to which they would be subjected, would teach them " not to blaspheme." And again we read in Galatians: " But there be some that trouble you, and would pervert the gospel of Christ. But though we, or an angel from heaven, preach any other gospel unto you than that which we have preached unto you, let him be accursed." Christianity, according to its promulgators, was the one true faith. All who professed any other doctrines were heretics and idolators. They were condemned, they were hated, and whenever opportunity offered, they were tortured until they saw the true faith; failing conversion or confession they were exterminated.

There are indications that human sacrifice continued to be practised in ancient Greece and Rome, despite the efforts of Tiberius and other emperors to put an end to it. In Europe during the Middle Ages sacrifices were common;[1] there are surreptitious cases even to this day.

In an ideological sense there is little distinction between religion and patriotism. The patriot, in any extreme sense, and in time of war or conditions which threaten war, is in much the same position as the religious fanatic. His obsessional interest in the cause of his own country or race engenders blind hatred for a rival or an enemy country or race. It is at such times that the danger of torture or persecution is particularly likely. It is in such circumstances that the most Christian-like individuals will be transformed into fiends clamouring for the blood of their opponents.

The Weak and the Despised

One of the major lessons of history is that the ultimate choice of any race, and, in the majority of cases, of any individual member of that race, rests between accepting the role of persecutor or persecuted. The story is a consistent one. The strong nation has been the persecutor, and coinci-

---

[1] The burying alive of a human being or an animal in the foundations of an edifice is a form of sacrifice (cf. p. 217).

dentally the respected, the admired and the successful. The weak nation, and likewise the weak individual in that nation, has been persecuted and despised. One might say with much truth that in the history of nations nothing succeeds like persecution. And further, one might just as truthfully say that the defeat of one form of persecution is only possible by the emergence of a stronger form. For this reason the world lives through a succession of persecutions, only the State, which, at any one time, is wielding tyrannous power, calls its persecutions by another and a far more mellifluous name.

The Romans tortured the Christians as long as their power lasted. The fall of Rome and the rise of Christianity saw the Christians persecuting every weaker religious sect with fine impartiality. The Jews, through thousands of years of history, have been consistently persecuted.

Minorities, of whatever nature, are persecuted. Here again history tells a consistent story. And it matters not at all what precisely is the nature of the minority. It may be a minority in a physical, an ethical, or an intellectual sense. The persecution is always present in some form or other, though it may not express itself in purely physical action. Psychological persecution in these days is far more effective, if for nothing but its insidiousness, than physical persecution.

The masses hate anything which they do not understand and at the same time cannot ignore, or which is repugnant to their wishes or tastes. They even hate those who tell the truth, because they do not want to know the truth. The burning of a great national newspaper during the war of 1914-18, for telling an unpalatable truth, was a gesture as psychologically significant as the burning of the witches in the Middle Ages. The persecution of John William Gott, in 1921, for his criticism of the Bible, was analogous to the persecution of Galileo, three hundred years previously, for affirming that the earth circumnavigated the sun. The weakness of a minority which is out of tune with the cerebration or psychology of the masses is a signal for the majority to turn and rend it. Because of this danger, all unpopular movements must work more or less surreptitiously, the degree of secrecy exercised being in direct ratio to the extent of their unpopularity.

State Domination and Power

The State has been quick to realize the virtues of persecution in the maintenance of power, and in the furtherance of economic, political and social aims. The power of the State is not only conditioned by the persecution, in various euphemized or psychological ways, of its own nationals, but in its exploitation of the persecuting powers of society against any dangerous rivalries, whether domestic or foreign. In its final analysis, the propaganda which every State utilizes to some extent all the time, and on certain occasions to a phenomenal degree, is the resuscitation or development of mankind's fundamental liking for persecution along definite lines and towards specific ends. The power of this incipient persecution is strikingly demonstrated in the way in which a mild-mannered man or woman can be transformed, almost overnight, into a human volcano spouting hate and savagery. We have had instances of this again and again. In the European war of 1914-18, every country concerned concentrated upon arousing the people to a state in which they were likely to inflict any form of physical cruelty upon such enemies as fell into their power.

CHAPTER VI

THE EFFECTS OF TORTURE

Paralysing Influence Upon the Individual

THERE have been a few notable instances where all the efforts of the tormentors have failed to break the will of their victims. In most of these cases the persons concerned have been religious fanatics who were prepared to suffer martyrdom in the service of their god rather than secure peace on earth, or they have been masochists who secured pleasure from experiencing physical persecution.

For every one such case, however, there must have been a full hundred instances where, whether through the fear of torture or during the actual experience of it, the prisoner confessed whatever he was expected to confess, even in circumstances where he knew such confession meant the virtual signing of his own death warrant.

This fear of torture was evidenced in the attempts that were made to escape the ordeal, even to the extent of committing suicide. So common were these attempts that in the days of the Roman gladiatorial contests, the criminals who were selected for fighting what was virtually a struggle in which they would be torn to pieces by wild beasts or by equally brutal human antagonists, were guarded with the utmost thoroughness in order to prevent them taking their own lives and cheating the public of its amusement.

During the time when the Spanish Inquisition was functioning at its mightiest, the horrors of the tortures to which its victims were subjected were sufficient to cause men to go to any lengths to prevent themselves falling alive into the clutches of the Holy Office. Similarly in the early days of America, when conflicts between Indians and whites were frequent, the settlers preferred to shoot their womenfolk and often themselves or one another rather than furnish the savages with material for torture.

In this fear of torture there is nothing calling for condemnation. No one realizing its true import, unless fortified by a love of martyrdom transcending all ordinary standards and bordering upon the psychopathological, could be blamed for expressing fear in the face of such a threat. It is not a matter of bravery. Torture destroys the roots from which bravery, or its negation, springs. In its worst stages, it transforms a human soul into a mass of pulsating flesh devoid of conscious cerebration.

The effects of torture are conditioned by the individual, and the extent and nature of the technique employed. Thus the very threat of torture will have a powerful effect in some and indeed most cases, while in others only the actual application of some form of punishment will prove in any way effective. Generally speaking, in its initial stages, or in its milder forms, torture destroys the will. In all its forms it injures the nerve power long before the stage is reached when consciousness fails.

Futility of Torture in the Securing of Confession or Evidence

We have seen that torture has always been accepted as the certain means of securing confession or evidence. When every form of persuasion or entreaty fails, the threat or the actual infliction of torture constitutes a trump card. Torture was used by savage races in all parts of the world to these ends. It was used by the ancient Romans. It was used throughout continental Europe during the Middle Ages. It was used in England in defiance of common law. It is used secretly in America to-day. Private individuals from the beginning of time have been accustomed to practise torture for these same express purposes. There is no doubt that, on occasion, they do so at the present time.

Now the evil in connexion with the use of torture for securing confession is that invariably it presupposes the guilt of the individual. The whole point of torture induced for this purpose is that the persecution *continues until the individual confesses* or succumbs under the ordeal, which in most cases merely means that the torture is suspended. All who had anything to do with the practice of torture must have been well aware that its effects in relation to the securing of evidence were unilateral, for the compelling reason that the purpose of torture was to extract a confession or an admission of guilt or to secure the information that was being asked for; that behind every act of torture was a gratuitous assumption of guilt or knowledge.

In the power of torture is existent its own negation. Its evil, from a penological and a psychopathological standpoint, lies in its power to elicit fiction in the name of truth; to compel the accused to condemn himself by false evidence of his own making.

It is impossible for the persecuted individual to be proved *innocent* as a result of the torture. So that for all practical purposes, and whichever way one looks at it, torture, for the purpose of securing confession, is an unnecessary procedure. Its sole object is to *justify* the persecution and punishment of the accused. It is not administered in any hope of securing justice. From the point of view of equity therefore the procedure is unjust; from the point of view of securing the truth it is ineffective. Confession when obtained need not be the truth. Two thousand years ago Cicero demonstrated its uncertainty.

All moral and ethical values are endangered under torture of any kind. It is for this reason that in so many cases the victim betrays friends, accomplices, and even close relatives under the pain of torture. He will confess anything that the inquisitors wish him to confess: he will sign any document that is put before him irrespective of its nature and content.

The truth of this was admitted by the inquisitors themselves. Von Spee, who was one of those who opposed the witch persecutions of the seventeenth century, mentioned that an inquisitor had boasted that if he could place the Pope on the rack, he would guarantee to induce him to plead guilty of sorcery. According to Scherr, it was this same Von Spee who said: " Treat the heads of the Church, the judges, or me, as you treat these unhappy ones (accused of witchcraft), subject any of us to the same torture, and you will discover that we are all sorcerers."[1] And Bernard Delicieux,

---

[1] Quoted by W. G. Sumner, *Folkways*, p. 241.

who was himself twice tortured by the Inquisition, and indeed died as a result of the treatment to which he was subjected, stated that Peter and Paul could have been proved guilty of heresy by the methods of the Inquisition.[1]   Heineccius relates the case of a German soldier, charged with theft, who was repeatedly put to the torture, and who alleged that his own friends were guilty of a number of murders and other crimes which had never been committed.   In 1793, the Parliament of Paris suspended two judges from their offices for having " ordered the execution of a man for the alleged murder of a woman, proved only by his own confession under torture—the woman being discovered alive two years after the execution of the supposed murder."[2]   In 1630, when the city of Milan was stricken with a plague, rumour had it that the pestilence was due to the activities of a body of persons called Untori, who secretly smeared the doors and walls of the houses with a deadly ointment.   The judges and the senate, affirmed Manzoni, secured convictions against several of these suspected individuals, on their own confessions, extorted by incredibly barbarous acts of torture.[3]

The efficacy of torture as a means of securing *convictions* (and no one can deny this efficacy) rests therefore in the fact that it leads to the conviction of the guilty and the innocent alike.   Its efficacy, and likewise its popularity, rest in the fact that it invariably provides the persecutors with a means of satisfying their call for vengeance.   Whenever and wherever torture has been in vogue the method adopted has been to continue the process until the victim confessed. The few cases where no confession was secured are negligible and do not invalidate the general statement that, in spite of any regulations or limitations respecting the severity or duration of the torments prescribed, the principle recognized, adopted and approved by judges and law officers was to continue the torture until its object was achieved.

These effects suggest that the Spanish Inquisitors and the French and English courts, in their adoption of torture, were far more concerned in finding victims to persecute or in

---

[1] H. C. Lea, *A History of the Inquisition of the Middle Ages*, Vol. II, p. 87.
[2] David Jardine, *On the Use of Torture in the Criminal Law of England*, 1837, p. 6.
[3] George Grote, *History of Greece*, 1850, Vol. VII, p. 274.

justifying their persecutions than in arriving at the truth; just as, in modern civilization, the law and the State are sometimes more concerned in securing convictions than in administering justice.

Psychological Effects on Society

Society from its very toleration or approval of torture stands in mortal awe of it. There is no surer way of developing the enmity of the community as a whole against a rival organization than the conviction of there existing a risk of persecution at the hands of that rival. In other words, the torturer, whether potential or actual, stands in fear and trembling at the possibility and prospect of being tortured himself. Although this may commend itself to some as a form of poetic justice, its effects are to extend and increase the potentialities for torture in all its forms and in all grades of society.

In the old days, fear of God's anger at the toleration of those who were worshippers of idols or heathen deities led to the torture of heretics in efforts at appeasement. The people concentrated on the persecution of others to ensure freedom from subjection to divine punishment themselves. Torture or be tortured has been, by implication, the unuttered battle-cry of humanity since man evolved as a consciously cerebrating anthropoid.

Certain it is that the example of the State is reflected in the attitude of society. This constitutes one of the major arguments against the use of torture in any penological system. It is owing to this fact that to punish brutality with an equal or an extra measure of brutality is indefensible. It is always evil. It cannot have anything but evil effects.

No one has a greater abhorrence of cruelty than I have—whether it be cruelty to human beings or to animals—but the contention that the only punishment for cruelty is the cat-o'-nine-tails suggests an entirely wrong approach to the problem with which we have to deal. It is impossible to hope for the abolition of torture so long as the State employs torture in its penal code. If it is wrong for an individual member of society to torture his fellows or animals, then it is wrong for the State to employ torture as a means of punishing the offender. The culprit could probably just as logically provide some form of extenuation or justification for his own act of cruelty.

It must be remembered that between the State and the component members of society there is of necessity the closest communion. It is impossible that the acts of the State as an official body should not influence the acts of its members as private individuals and vice versa. This intimate correlation between the State and its members is seen in the way in which the authorities, often enough, are compelled by force of opinion to instigate more severe forms of punishment. Thus it was the frantic clamourings of the people which were responsible for the passing of the clause in the Treason Act of 1842 providing whipping as a penalty for aiming a firearm at a sovereign; of the Garrotters Act of 1863; and of the provisions for the flogging of procurers and pimps in the Criminal Law Amendment Act of 1912. Any extension of punishment by the State, whether it has originated in a demand on the part of the public or in an official department of the State itself, leads to an extension of the practice of cruelty by private individuals. In this way the whole thing becomes a vicious circle.

PART TWO

THE HISTORY OF TORTURE

CHAPTER VII

TORTURE AMONG SAVAGE AND PRIMITIVE RACES

The Transition from Torture as a Religious Rite to Penal Torture

THERE is scarcely for the finding a savage or primitive race which does not employ torture either in its religious rites or its code of punishment. The nearness to animal behaviourism, which is a characteristic of savage life, is responsible for a crudity and a barbarity which appal modern civilization. Because of this fundamental approximation to nature, the tortures adopted by these savage tribes lack the ingenuity and subtlety of those originated by civilized and semi-civilized races.

In many parts of the world the tormenting of those captured in war was looked upon and accepted as inevitable. Often such captives were sacrificed to the gods. The acceptance by so many races of the necessity for human sacrifice (cf. Chapter V), led to the widening of the criminal code in the race itself on the one hand, and the continual excursions into enemy country on the other, in efforts to secure a plenitude of victims to assuage the thirst for blood put into the mouths of the gods. So inevitable were torture and death looked upon by members of enemy tribes that in many cases they would not allow themselves to be taken alive. The Aztecs of Mexico invariably sacrificed any captives to the god Tezcatepoca. And the manner of their death was a horrible one. The captive was stretched on his back at full length upon the sacrificial stone. His arms and legs were firmly held by priests. The executioner, a scarlet-robed official, using a sharp-edged instrument, slit open the breast of the victim, inserted his hand through the wound, and tore out the warm and palpitating heart. Sometimes, as a variation in the procedure, the arms and legs were methodically cut off before the heart was removed.

In Peru, says Picart, the Antis tribe sacrificed prisoners of distinction only, ordinary persons being executed on the spot and without ceremony. The victim to be sacrificed was stripped naked, tied securely to a stake, and then bits of flesh were hacked or slashed from various parts of the body with knives made of flint stone ground very sharp. The breasts, buttocks, thighs, calves, and other fleshy parts were first attacked, much in the manner in which the Chinese executioner proceeds in the torture known as the " Death by the Thousand Cuts " (cf. page 105). The sacrificial and magical elements were, however, of outstanding importance and significance in this particular Antis rite: men, women and children dipped their fingers in and smeared their persons with the blood of the victim. Nursing mothers daubed this sacrificial blood upon the teats of their breasts, allowing their babies to imbibe it with the milk.

Torture is rarely absent from the theosophic, initiatory and other rites adopted by savage tribes. The callous attitude of primitive man towards bloodshed, the lack of sympathy for suffering, and the phlegmatic reaction to death itself, are all in accord with the exhibition of stoicism in circumstances of danger or suffering. In some cases this stoic attitude, or bravery, is deliberately induced. The young men are not only inured to hardship and danger, but they are subjected to certain specific ordeals designed to inculcate fortitude in the face of most agonizing pain. The slightest sign of cowardice in the course of the ordeal, or initiation, as it is termed, would be greeted with scorn by the onlookers, and the young man would never again be able to hold up his head. Probably he would be banished from the tribe for ever. Although, in most cases, the initiate is forced to undergo the ordeals, because of the inevitable results of any refusal, he becomes for all practical purposes a willing party, and virtually therefore the torture amounts to self-torture.

After Picart.

TORTURE AND SACRIFICE OF PRISONERS BY THE AZTECS

After Picart.

"SLICING TO DEATH"

A SACRIFICIAL RITE OF THE ANTIS TRIBE

(See Text, page 36.)

The Place of Torture in Initiatory Rites

The forms which the initiatory rite takes are many, and the suffering involved may be of a relatively mild variety involving no actual risk to life itself, or it may reach such a degree of severity that a considerable proportion of the initiates fail to survive the test. An example of the first type is the flogging rite practised by the Indian tribes of Guiana. According to Brett:

> "The young men and boys, fantastically adorned, were ranged in two parallel rows facing each other, each holding in his right hand the Maquarri from which the dance takes its name. The Maquarri is a whip, more than three feet long, and capable of giving a severe cut, as their bleeding legs amply testified. They waved these whips in their hands as they danced, uttering alternate cries which resembled the note of a certain bird often heard in the forests. At some little distance from the dancers were couples of men lashing each other on the leg. The man whose turn it was to receive the lash stood firmly on one leg, advancing the other; while his adversary, stooping, took deliberate aim, and, springing from the earth to add vigour to his stroke, gave his opponent a severe cut."[1]

Of a far more serious nature are the rites of initiation involving mutilation of the genitals which are practised by the Australian Blacks, and which apply to both sexes on attaining puberty. Although circumcision, whether practised in infancy or at puberty, can scarcely be termed torture, the mutilations employed so universally among the aborigines of Australia, Polynesia, Borneo and other places, certainly entail an amount of suffering and pain, often for protracted periods, which can be described by no other word. Similar mutilations, in other parts of the world, rank as punishments; and even among the races adopting them as religious rites these same operative measures are sometimes featured in the penological code. According to Czekanowski, among the Azandeh race, the punishment for adultery

[1] W. H. Brett, *The Indian Tribes of Guiana*, 1868, p. 154.

consists of the removal of the exterior genitalia and the amputation of both hands.[1]

The mika operation of the Australian Blacks consists of incising the male sexual member, so as to expose and open the urethra, from the scrotum to the glans penis. The operation is performed on the attainment of puberty, and no anæsthetic is used. The patient is forcibly held down by assistants, while the operator, with a knife or sharp flint, cuts into the urethral channel, extending the opening thus made by forcibly tearing the tissue apart with his fingers. The suffering and pain involved are tremendous, and owing to the total lack of aseptic conditions the operation is not devoid of danger to life itself.

The sexual mutilations practised upon the girls of many races are cruel and barbarous. The commonest of these is known as infibulation. It is adopted by the natives of East Africa and Abyssinia. At puberty, the clitoris and the labia minora, and sometimes the labia majora as well, are cut or hacked off with the aid of a dull knife. The operator is usually an old woman.

Of all initiatory rites ever practised by savages, however, those adopted by the North American Indians probably ranked as the most terrifying, involving excruciating and diabolical torture. The procedure varied in different tribes, but that adopted by the Mandans appears to have been the most pitiless and sanguinary. Previous to the actual ordeal the young man was emaciated by fasting. The procedure, says Catlin, was as follows:

"The initiate placed himself on his hands and feet. An inch or more of the flesh of each shoulder, or each breast, was taken up between the thumb and finger by the man who held the knife in his right hand, and the knife, which had been ground sharp on both edges, and then hacked and notched with the blade of another, to make it produce as much pain as possible, was forced through the flesh below the fingers, and being withdrawn, was followed with a splint or skewer, from the other, who held a bunch of each in his left hand, and

[1] Felix Bryk, *Circumcision in Man and Woman*, translated by David Berger, American Ethnological Press, New York, 1934.

CLUBBING A CRIMINAL TO DEATH IN THE SANDWICH ISLANDS
From an old engraving.

After Catlin.

INITIATORY TORTURE RITES OF THE MANDANS
(See Text, page 38.)

was ready to force them through the wound. There were then two cords lowered from the top of the lodge (by men who were placed on the lodge outside for the purpose), which were fastened to these splints or skewers, and they instantly began to haul him up; he was thus raised until his body was suspended from the ground where he rested, until the knife and a splint were passed through the flesh or integuments in a similar manner on each arm below the shoulder, below the elbow, and below the knees. Each one was then raised with the cords, until the weight of his body was suspended by them, and then while the blood was streaming down their limbs, the by-standers hung upon the splints each man's appropriate shield, bow and quiver, etc."[1]

As if this, in itself, did not involve enough in the way of torture, the victim was then gradually raised by means of the ropes until the weights swung clear from the ground, thus ensuring that not only the weight of the man's body but also that of the various impedimenta attached to his limbs were thrown upon those parts to which the ropes were attached. So great was the strain upon the flesh where the skewers were inserted that it was lifted from the surrounding tissue at these points in pinnacles of six to eight inches in height. And so, in a state of such agonizing pain as makes one shudder even to visualize, these initiates continued to hang in the air, covered with their own gore, biting back every suspicion of a groan in their efforts to emerge triumphant from this supreme test of hardihood and courage. They were, says Catlin, " appalling and frightful to look at." When those in authority were satisfied, they ordered the bodies to be lowered to the ground, where they lay apparently lifeless, coming round in their own good time.

One might well imagine that such an ordeal was enough to satisfy the most exacting of disciplinarians. But no, this did not represent the end of the initiate's sufferings. There was yet another test to be endured. It was known as " the last race," or, in the language of the tribe, " *Eh-ke-nah-ka-nah-pick*." Each of the young men was put in charge of

---

[1] Geo. Catlin, *Letters and Notes on the Manners, Customs and Conditions of the North American Indians*, 1841, p. 170.

two older athletic warriors. One of these escorts, as they might well be called, stood on the right side and the other on the left side of the initiate, grasping the loose end of a broad leather strap which was wrapped around each wrist. To his flesh at various points were attached, with skewers, several heavy weights. At a given signal, the two escorts started running around a large ring, dragging with them the young man in their charge. Round and round, the various initiates, dragged by their escorts, continued in procession, the weights pulling at the flesh until it came out in great, ugly, bleeding lumps. The process continued until the victim fainted through loss of blood and exhaustion.

A curious form of torture, according to Greenwood, was adopted as an initiatory rite by the Mandrucu tribe of Amazonian Indians. To look at, the instruments employed in this particular ordeal appeared remarkably innocent. They consisted of two cylindrical cases fashioned out of palm-tree bark, measuring about a foot in length, and stopped at one end. They were for all the world like a pair of huge and crudely made gloves, and it was as gloves they were used. The initiate thrust his hands into the cases, and, followed by a procession of onlookers, which in fact amounted to all the available members of the tribe, started upon a tour of the village or camp, stopping at the door of every wigwam to execute a sort of dance. These " gloves " were, however, by no means so innocent as they seemed, and the dance their wearer performed was more real than mimic. For each gauntlet contained a collection of ants and other insects, all selected for their venomous, biting capacities. And, says Greenwood, " what with the heat engendered within and the blazing sun playing without the bark gloves, the wretched hands seem literally a furnace."[1] The " ordeal of the venomous gloves," in very truth, was something to be dreaded.

Punishment by Torture

Turning from these initiatory modes to the infliction of torture purely as a means of punishment for various crimes and offences, we are struck with the universality of the practices employed in various parts of the world. Because

[1] James Greenwood, *Curiosities of Savage Life*, 1863, pp. 95-6.

of the nearness to death or severe injury which may be classed as a normal characteristic of savage life, and because of the callousness and indifference to human suffering thus generated, even the infliction of capital punishment is either carried out in a terribly cruel manner involving prolonged agony, or is preceded by torture.   In the Sandwich Islands criminals who are sentenced to death are either beaten with a club until life is extinct or strangled with a rope.   For those crimes where the death sentence is not pronounced, punishment assumes some form of mutilation.   For instance, where a native belonging to the ordinary classes is convicted of being on terms of intimacy with a chief's wife, the punishment prescribed is that his eyes should be put out.   The procedure is described by Arago :

"I have not seen it executed myself, but the poor wretch with whom Gaimard and myself conversed in the presence of M. Rives, told us how it was executed upon him.   Two men held him by the feet, two more by the arms, and another by the hair of the head, whilst a sixth, who was the executioner, gave him a violent blow with his fist over each eye, and almost at the same instant plunged his forefinger into the lachrymal angle, and pulled out the ball; the other eye was taken out in the same manner, yet we could scarcely perceive a cicatrice under the lower eye-lid."[1]

For sheer barbarity, few savages have ever surpassed the North American Indians.   The sanguinary, splenetic and ferocious punishments inflicted not only upon prisoners of war, but also upon those in their own tribes guilty of crimes and misdemeanours, have never been exceeded.   In the long and terrible struggle between the pioneer whites and the native Indians, which raged throughout the eighteenth century and well into the nineteenth, death by torture was an everyday occurrence.   The tearing out of the eyes and the placing of red-hot embers in the sockets; various forms of mutilation, and burning to death over a slow fire, were customary methods.   During the period from 1846 to 1852

[1] J. Arago, *Narrative of a Voyage Round the World*, 1823, Vol. II, p. 139.

it is estimated that in Texas alone two hundred whites were put to death by torture every year. A frequent practice was to tie a captive to a tree, and day by day to cut away a limb or a portion of the flesh until ultimately death mercifully supervened.

The Choctaws, one of the most barbarous of the tribes of American aborigines, were peculiarly ingenious in their methods. Before scalping their expiring victims, these savages stripped them naked, pinioned their arms, and tied a strong grape-vine, which acted as a rope, about their necks. The other end of the vine was fastened to the top of the war-pole. In this way the prisoner could run around the pole over a considerable area of ground, much in the way that a bear could run around in the old days when bear-baiting was an English sport. Then, says Greenwood:

> " The women make a furious onset with their burning torches; his pain is soon so excruciating that he rushes from the pole with the fury of the most savage beast of prey, lashes them with the trailing vine-rope, and bites and kicks and tramples on all he can catch. The circle immediately fills again either with the same or fresh persons; they attack him on every side—now he runs to the pole for shelter, but the flames pursue him. . . . Should he sink or flag under the torture, they pour over him a quantity of cold water till his spirits recover, and so the like cruelties are renewed until he falls down and happily becomes insensible to pain."[1]

The Indians who were captured by enemy tribes and subjected to various tortures bore their sufferings with a stoicism for which the ordeals described in the earlier part of this chapter acted as preparatory torments, and which were no doubt ordained to this end. For a " brave " to groan or supplicate was to disgrace not only himself but the tribe of which he was a member. Not all the whites whose unfortunate lot it was to be made prisoners by the Redskins could be expected to show such stoicism and fortitude. But some did. And of those of whom we have any authentic record none is more remarkable than the case of Father Jean de Brébeuf, who was one of that brave company forming the

[1] James Greenwood, *op. cit.*, pp. 35-6.

From Moore's *Martyrology*, 1809.

TORTURE OF ROASTING ALIVE

Jesuit mission to the Hurons in Canada. He was captured by the Iroquois in 1649 and was put to death by torture. For stark horror the record of the sufferings which this missionary had to endure before he died is probably un-rivalled in all history. It was undoubtedly an instance where the powerful physique and iron constitution of the victim were to be regretted purely because they caused him to have to endure suffering and agony which long before would have killed or rendered insensible a weaker man.

To start with, de Brébeuf's hands were chopped off. His flesh, at many and different parts of the body, was pierced with pointed iron instruments of various kinds. Tomahawks made red-hot were suspended around his neck, so that every turn of the head was a torment; while a belt composed of bark smeared with resin and pitch was tied around his body and set alight. These various tor-ments, in all their severity, were such as would neither kill nor render unconscious a strong man. They were specifi-cally designed to ensure a gruesome lingering death and to provide prolonged entertainment for the savages who capered around their prisoners—other members of the mission, as well as a number of Hurons, were captives too and were being treated in similar fashion. But de Brébeuf, we are told, endured these agonies staunchly. More, he lifted up his voice and preached to his persecutors. They retaliated by seizing burning brands from a fire and thrusting them into his mouth. Even this could not stop the flow of eloquence. They proceeded to further out-rages and mutilations, eventually silencing him for all time by cutting off his lips. Then, over his body, they flung, again and again, buckets of boiling water. They cut pieces of flesh from his limbs and trunk, avoiding any part likely to prove fatal, roasted them in the fire and ate them there and then before his eyes. The sands of life were running low by this time, but before death actually came, they managed to amputate his feet and to tear off his scalp.[1]

---

[1] For a full narrative of the life and martyrdom of this heroic missionary, I would refer the reader to *The Travels and Sufferings of Father Jean de Brébeuf*, edited by Theodore Besterman, Golden Cockerel Press, 1938; to which work I am indebted for the salient details contained in the above account.

CHAPTER VIII

TORTURE IN ANCIENT GREECE AND ROME

Torture of Free Citizens

IN the statement so often repeated by various writers that
torture (*quæstio*) in Greece and Rome was rigidly restricted to slaves, we see another example of the way in
which historians and others have been misled through the
restriction of the term to the mode of securing confession.
In Greece, for example, although torture for the purpose
of obtaining testimony or confession was never applied to
free citizens, it was used as a means of punishment applicable to all classes. Aristophanes alludes to the wheel
being frequently employed for this purpose.[1] The rack,
too, was in regular use. Among other free-men, Antiphon
was racked to death. According to Polybius, the tyrant
Nabis used an infamous instrument of torture shaped like
a woman (anticipating the "Virgin Mary" of the
Spanish Inquisition and the *Jungfernkuss* of mediæval
Germany) in which the victims were clutched until they
paid tribute in money. (See Chapter XXII.)

In Rome the free-man was not, in any ordinary circumstances, liable to torture as a means of extorting confession.
The exception to this rule was in the case of anyone
accused of treason. The subjection to torture of those suspected or accused of this particular crime was first justified
by Arcadias Charisius. Gibbon implies that the extension
of legal torture to cases of treason virtually annulled the
principle by which the free-man was supposed to be
exempt from the *quæstio* except in these supposedly rare
cases of treason, because it was a comparatively easy
matter to bring a variety of offences into this somewhat
elusive category. Treason, says Gibbon, "included any
offence that the subtlety of lawyers could derive from an
hostile intention." The rank of the accused individual did

[1] *Lysistrata.*

44

not save him, for it was contended that in regard to treason all were on an equal footing. This same waiving of all rights to exception on account of official position or noble birth applied in the case of anyone accused of sorcery or witchcraft.

In regard to certain other crimes also, the free-man could, with some exceptions, be subjected to torture. A woman accused of poisoning her husband could be put to the *quæstio*; so, too, could anyone who, in giving evidence, betrayed inconsistency. In the reign of Severus, one guilty of adultery could be tortured; under Maximus the *quæstio* was applicable in cases of incest; and under Constantine to sorcery and magic. The most notable of the exceptions, in relation to all crimes except the above mentioned ones of sorcery and treason, applied to the aristocracy, to priests, to pregnant women, to soldiers, and to children below the age of fourteen years. Torture was restricted, however, to those actually accused of the crimes concerned; it was not applicable to witnesses, and it could not be applied to a prisoner before the actual time of trial. And it is noteworthy that anyone bringing a charge of treason against another individual, and failing to substantiate such a charge, could himself be subjected to the *quæstio*.

Turning to the use of torture as a means of punishment, we find that its use was widespread. In some cases it constituted the whole of the punishment; in others it was but a part of it, preceding banishment or the death penalty. Under the Republic, private individuals were empowered to torture debtors, confining them in private prisons and subjecting them to any form of torture short of causing death, until the debts were paid. Offences against the Church in particular were punished with torture of the utmost severity. By the express order of Justinian anyone guilty of insulting a priest or a bishop in a church could be tortured. In some cases mutilation was the prescribed punishment. In the early days, the feet and hands were often amputated *in toto,* but Justinian tempered the severity of this law, restricting it to the amputation of one hand only. In accordance with the Theodosian Code, anyone convicted of heresy could be flagellated with a whip the thongs of which were weighted with lead (*contusus plumbo*). Apart from those guilty of this particular crime, of certain other offences against the Church, and of adultery, which was punished by flogging and the amputation of the nose, whipping was not inflicted upon free-men. It was the punishment of the slave: a mark of dishonour and degradation so profound that the average Roman preferred death to scourging.

The Torture of Slaves

In Greece and in Rome the torture of slaves was accepted as their lot and destiny. Scarcely a voice was raised against it. Even the philosophers were in favour of it. Aristotle, for one, expressed his approval. Plato, in presenting his concept of Eutopia, admitted the necessity of one law for the free-man and another law for the slave. He subscribed to the common and popular doctrine of flogging the slave for an offence which, in the case of a free-man, deserved only censure; of putting the slave to death where the free-man would be let off with a fine.

The slaves in ancient Greece were at first confined to those captured in warfare or during marauding expeditions. The nation had realized that the forcing of enemies to perform all the degrading and humiliating tasks of life was a far better proposition than executing them or confining them in dungeons. The principle of slavery, once it had been put into practice, appealed to the populace. More and more did people applaud the notion of having distasteful work performed by someone who could neither refuse to do the tasks set them, nor could command anything in the way of remuneration beyond their bare keep. It was natural that as the supply of captives became insufficient, eyes should be cast upon other means of securing fresh and additional recruits. Criminals or offenders were pressed into service. Until Solon stopped the practice, anyone who owed money and could not pay the debt became automatically the slave of his creditor. Then came the traffic in mankind. Slaves were bought and sold like cattle. In the notorious slave-market of Athens they were

exposed in all their nakedness—men and women both—
and sold to the highest bidder.

As it was recognized in Roman law that so far as a slave
was concerned the best and in most cases the only way in
which the truth could be secured was by torture, and as,
additionally, the owner was vested with very nearly absolute
power, the life of a slave, often enough, was punctuated by
continual punishments of the most cruel and brutal nature.

All of which does not mean there were no State regulations respecting torture. There were many such regulations.
But these were in respect of those modes of punishment
apart from and in addition to the private tortures to which
every slave was liable to be exposed; an owner being entitled
to punish any slave in his possession for any offence, real or
imaginary, and to any extent he decreed. The State regulations were restricted to offences coming within the jurisdiction of the courts. For instance, whether the slave was
accused of a crime or whether he was merely a witness (with
certain exceptions) he could be tortured for the purpose of
eliciting the truth. Where a husband charged his wife with
adultery, the slaves of the husband, of the wife, and of the
wife's father, could all be subjected to torture in order to
extract evidence. Generally speaking, however, no slave
was allowed to give evidence against a master. Exceptions
to this general rule were concerned with charges of
treason.[1]

The property right of the owner in the slave affected the
matter of torture by any other authority than his own. It
was a reasonable argument that the after-value of a slave
might, as a result of judicial punishment, be seriously im-
paired. Thus, where a slave was tortured against the will
or without the express consent of his master, security was
given to the owner for the cash value of the slave. In the
event of an accusation being brought against a slave by someone other than his master, and this accusation being proved
to be false, the owner of the tortured slave was entitled to
secure recompense from the accuser for the damage sustained
up to double the value of the slave.

The nature of the torture and its extent rested with the

---

[1] Adultery, coining, and frauds concerning the revenue were looked
upon as coming under the heading of treason.

judge. Only when all other proofs had been duly submitted and examined could torture be resorted to. In the case of an accusation, when all evidence had been presented, and the only remaining point to secure conviction was confession, torture could be ordered. If this torture failed to secure a confession, despite the evidence against the accused being strong and wellnigh complete, the judge was empowered to order its repetition. He could give such an order again and again, there being no limit fixed to the number of repetitive tortures where the occasion was deemed to warrant them. Unlike a free-man, a slave was denied the right of appeal, though his master possessed this right. While any such appeal was under consideration the accused was confined in prison but he could not be subjected to torture in any form.

ROMAN *FLAGELLUM*

The coin depicts a contest between gladiators

Of the forms of judicial torture employed, the rack (*equuleus*) was perhaps the principal, as well as the earliest, being referred to by Cicero. Compression of the arm by means of gradually tightening cords was frequently used to induce witnesses to give evidence. Slaves were continually punished by flagellation. Whips of various types were used. The terrible Roman *flagellum*, made of thongs of ox-leather, cut into the flesh like a knife. According to Horace, the sadistic cruelty and vindictiveness of some judges led them to order floggings which were so excessive, and continued so long, that the executioner often enough, through sheer exhaustion, was obliged to desist before the sentence was completed. Many slaves died under the whip. For lesser crimes there was the *scutica*, a whip consisting of thongs of parchment; while for minor offences, the *ferula*, a flat strap of leather, was used. Apart from sentences given in the courts, slave-owners used the whip daily and for all manner of offences. Nor were there in force any regulations respecting these private punitive measures either as regards the severity of the punishment or the type of whip to be used. Slave-drivers exercised their ingenuity in devising more terrible instruments of correction than any used by the courts. The thongs were knotted with bones and pieces of metal; sometimes lead balls, cruel hooks or spikes were affixed to the ends. Ladies who could not wield the whip themselves hired the public executioner or compelled other slaves to flog their servants.

Apart from flogging, the forms of punishment to which slaves were subjected were numerous, and although not all these punitive measures could justifiably be called tortures, the majority, indubitably and without any straining of the truth, were flagrantly cruel and brutal. Slaves who attempted to escape and were caught, were often branded upon the forehead. So were thieves. In other cases, they were suspended by the hands, with weights attached to their feet, and in this position whipped until near to death. The iron collar and the manacles were in common usage. For certain forms of theft one hand was hacked off at the wrist.

Where the sentence was death, crucifixion ranked as the most common method of execution. A slave condemned to death by crucifixion was compelled to wear the *furca*, a collar in shape something like a letter V. The *furca* was fixed over the back of the neck, the ends resting on the shoulders. The criminal's hands were bound to his thighs. In this fashion he was marched to the place of execution, while all the way *carnifices*, walking behind, beat him with cudgels or flogged him with whips.

Under Constantine a slave guilty of seduction, or an accessory to the crime, was put to death by burning or the pouring of molten lead down the throat.

The Roman women, we are told, had certain of their young male slaves made into eunuchs, for purposes of sexual pleasure and to avoid the risk of parentage; a procedure which was considered to exhibit a marked advance in every respect on the practice of the Scythian women, who, says Montaigne, " put out the eyes of all their slaves and prisoners of war, that they might have their pleasure of them, and they never the wiser."[1]

---

[1] Montaigne's *Essays* (Charles Cotton's translation), 1711, Book III, Ch. V, p. 110.

The Roman Gladiators

Of all the tortures which flourished in the mighty days of Rome, nothing approached in fiendish ingenuity and in horror those to which the gladiators were compelled to submit as a means of providing entertainment for the populace. The gladiatorial exhibitions of ancient Rome have acquired a degree of celebrity and a reputation which exist to this day. Much of their brutality has been covered up or purposely obliterated in the passage of time, and to the average Englishman or American of to-day they rank as evidence of the sport-loving qualities of the Romans of old. Their true nature is rarely commented upon.

In these exhibitions men were matched to fight against wild beasts and against one another. The gladiators, about whom an aura of glamour has been woven, contrary to popular opinion, were not willing contestants, longing for an opportunity to show their strength, skill and bravery. They were not even paid contestants. They were captives, criminals, offenders, *et al.*, who had been sentenced to death. The gladiatorial exhibition was their prescribed mode of execution. It was just as surely a method of execution as if they had been hanged or shot. It differed only from other forms of execution in being infinitely more cruel, in involving for the condemned man tortures indescribable in their nature and extent. The notion even that the man thus forced to take part in this fight to the death had a slender chance of escaping with his life is a fallacy. He had no such chance. His death, in some horrible form, and to the accompanying cheers of the spectators, was a certainty. Little wonder that the authorities, to avoid being deprived of their sadistic pleasure, had to exercise the most strict watch and to take all manner of precautions, to ensure that the condemned man did not commit suicide before the time came for him to feature in a gladiatorial display. Often, despite every precaution, he did commit suicide. One such notable instance occurred when Symmachus ordered a number of prisoners to fight in honour of his son. They strangled one another to escape the destiny which he had designed for them.[1]

[1] Quoted by W. G. Sumner, *Folkways*, p. 572.

Almost every type of savage animal was used in the amphitheatres. Lions, bears, leopards, tigers, panthers and wolves were pitted against men in fights to the death. The human fighter was hopelessly handicapped from the start. In many cases where wolves or mad dogs were their opponents the men were tied to stakes just as, a thousand years later, bears and bulls were tied to furnish pleasure for English audiences. Some faced certain death bravely, putting up the best fight they could. Others, of weaker or softer calibre, refused to enter the arena, in which case they were whipped until they changed their minds, or they were flung to the waiting animals, neck and crop. When the supply of criminals or captives ran short, slaves were purchased to take their place. The vast audiences which gathered regularly in the amphitheatres were not to be deprived of their amusement.

Occasionally women were forced to fight in the arena. Nero, master sadist of them all, we are told, gloated over such exhibitions. According to Martial, on one occasion a woman was mangled by a lion. The same authority instances a case where a robber was nailed to the cross, and in this position was ripped to pieces by a bear. In all cases the manner of death was frightful to witness. With scarce an exception, before the end came, the victims were begging to be granted the favour of a quick execution.

CHAPTER IX

THE PROGRESS OF TORTURE

The Attitude of the Church

THE pagan gods were merciless, revengeful, unjust and cruel.
Yahveh, the God of Israel, according to the wealth of testimony provided in the Old Testament, for sheer cruelty,
terrorism and frightfulness, surpassed belief. Those who
displeased Him He massacred in thousands; He smote the
Israelites "with a very great plague";[1] He approved the
punishment of derelictions of duty and petty offences by such
tortures as stoning to death and burning alive.

It was not unnatural that the ecclesiastical authorities,
in punishing offences committed by the people, should be
inspired by the example of the god they worshipped and
feared. And further, in particular reference to those crimes
which were specifically directed against God and His commands, was it natural they should be especially concerned
in following divine example and instruction. Thus heresy
and blasphemy, in particular, being likely to anger God, were
punished with the utmost rigour. Moreover, as regards all
crimes, the primitive concept of vengeance, put into the
mouth of Yahveh, as in the days of the pagans the same
concept was put into the mouths of a miscellany of deities,
represented the keynote and fundament of every form of
punishment.

The development of religion from its basic anthropomorphic sun-worship into a trinitarian Godhead, with a
visualized heaven in which there was to be a future perpetual
sinless life, had its effects upon the concept of punishment.
Death was never looked upon as annihilation. Punishment
upon this earth was viewed with something approaching
resignation by the person who was assured of a life free from
persecution in another and far better world. It was due to
this firm conviction that the martyrs bore their persecutions

[1] Numbers xi. 33.

52

with a stoicism which in these days, when the Christian faith lingers in an emasculated state, is almost incomprehensible.

The Christian Approach

The Hebrew policy of retribution, as we have already noted, was adopted by the early Christians. The humanitarianism of Jesus, as expressed so repeatedly in the Gospels, has conveyed an impression that Christianity was mightily concerned with the negation of all cruelty. The belief is fallacious. The concept of vengeance lived. We read in St. Matthew: " The Son of man shall send forth his angels, and they shall gather out of his kingdom all things that offend, and them which do iniquity; and shall cast them into a furnace of fire; there shall be wailing and gnashing of teeth."

To a very big extent the Christian Church adopted the Roman law of torture in regard to treason, applying it to heresy, which they construed to be " treason against God."[1] It also adopted the principle of confiscation of all property owned by those guilty of heresy;[2] a policy peculiarly dangerous to society as a whole in view of the Church's perpetual need of funds and the opportunities afforded by such a measure for securing such funds.

The ecclesiastical authorities condemned every faith outside Christianity as demonology; they averred, in a crescendo of denunciation, that the worship of pagan and heathen deities angered the true Christian trinitarian Godhead; that wherever a heretic reared up his ugly head there was danger to the whole neighbourhood through God's anger being directed towards the inhabitants of this particular spot. Lecky says: " It is not surprising that the populace should have been firmly convinced that every great catastrophe that occurred was due to the presence of enemies of the gods."[3] Nor is it to be wondered at that when once the public discovered a heretic in their midst they looked upon him as we to-day should look upon a leper; that in their mortal

---

[1] *Crimen læsæ majestatis divinæ.*
[2] The term heresy included analogous or associated offences, notably blasphemy.
[3] W. E. H. Lecky, *History of European Morals*, 1869, Vol. I, p. 437.

terror they clamoured for his immediate extermination.

The result of all this was that heresy, "the crime against God," was considered by all to be the most terrible offence conceivable, meriting the severest punishment and calling aloud to heaven for vengeance. To prove the guilt of any-one suspected of heresy was a matter of vital necessity,

Tortures of the Middle Ages as depicted in
ULRIC TENGLER'S *Layenspiegel* (1511)

transcending in importance anything else. To secure this proof, by the extraction of a confession from the accused party, was a case where, it was held, the end justified any measures. Once anyone was suspected of heresy the public waited neither for guidance nor authority from Church or State. They took the law into their own hands. They tortured the suspect until a confession was secured, and then without more ado burned him at the stake. The fact of an individual being accused of heresy was sufficient to ensure his martyrdom. Often enough the wish was father to the thought. It only required the occurrence of something in the nature of a catastrophe for the people to form the conclusion that there was a heretic in their midst. Once such a conclusion was reached, they searched the district diligently until someone was unearthed who, in accordance with the elastic interpretation of which heresy was capable, could be accused of the crime.

The penalty of burning may be said therefore to have been devised in the first place, not by the State, but by the public. Here, as in so many cases, mob law anticipated or suggested State law. Similarly, the Inquisition was rendered possible by the public approval of the torture of persons suspected of heresy. The Inquisition was not, in its early stages at any rate, the detested and abhorred tyrannous establishment that certain historians would have us believe; to the contrary, it was approved by the public. In many instances it may truly be said that the Inquisition saved suspected heretics from an even more evil fate.

Once the populace had started the campaign against heresy, the Church took control and organized the crude efforts of the rabble into a definite system of persecution, which came to its head in this powerful Holy Inquisition, with the activities of which we shall deal in another chapter.

The notion, however, that the Catholic Church held a monopoly of the art of persecution may, to members of the Protestant faith, have been a comforting thought, but it by no means represented the whole truth. It was merely that the activities of the Inquisition, because of their extent, their consistency and their unexampled rigour, eclipsed all the other forms of torture that were in progress during the Middle Ages. It was owing to the Inquisitions being known and celebrated as places of torture, and the spectacularity of the *autos da fé*, that these particular operations overshadowed all others; and so far as history is concerned have sufficed to relegate to the background every other contemporary form of persecution.

While the Church persecuted the followers of all rival faiths deemed to show possibilities of becoming powerful

competitors of Christianity, they disapproved of judicial
torture. St. Augustine denounced it, contending that should
the accused individual " be innocent, he will undergo for an
uncertain crime a certain punishment, and that not for
having committed a crime, but because it is unknown
whether he committed it." In 384 a synod at Rome
denounced the use of torture by civil courts.[1] And at all
times the Church attempted, not always with success, to
secure the exemption of the clergy from submission to the
quæstion in all cases except those tried by the ecclesiastical
courts.

The Persecutions Suffered by the Waldenses

About the middle of the seventeenth century the members of the sect known as the Waldenses, who had settled
in the valleys of the Piedmont to escape persecution in their
native countries, were accused of heresy.

On January 25, 1655, under the sanction of the Duke
of Savoy, Andrew Gastaldo, doctor of civil laws, issued the
following order:

> " That every head of a family, with the individuals of
> that family, of the reformed religion, of what rank,
> degree, or condition soever, none excepted, inhabiting
> and possessing estates in Lucerne, St. Giovanni, Bibiana,
> Campiglione, St. Secondo, Lucernetta, La Torre, Fenile,
> and Bricherassio, should, within three days after the
> publication thereof, withdraw out of the said places.
> . . . This to be done on pain of death, and confiscation
> of houses and goods, unless within the limited time they
> turned Roman-catholics."

The result of this edict was the commencement of a
rigorous campaign of persecution conducted by the Catholics
in the district and by the troops.

> " The armed multitude," says an eye-witness, " fell
> upon the Waldenses in a most furious manner. Nothing
> now was to be seen but the face of horror and despair;
> blood stained the floors of the houses, dead bodies be-

[1] Lea, *Superstition and Force*, Philadelphia, 1878.

strewed the streets, groans and cries were heard from
all parts. Some armed themselves, and skirmished with
the troops; and many, with their families, fled to the
mountains. In one village they cruelly tormented 150
women and children, after the men were fled; beheading
the women, and dashing out the brains of the children.
In the towns of Villaro and Bobio, most of those that
refused to go to mass, who were over fifteen years of age,
they crucified with their heads downwards; and the
greater number of those under that age were strangled."

The soldiers, in particular, exercised their lust for cruelty
in a most diabolical manner. Mutilations of every possible
form preceded the *coup de grâce*; in many cases, no final
blow was given, the maimed victims being left to die of
starvation or bleed to death. Isaiah Garcino was literally
minced; Mary Raymondet had the flesh sliced from her
bones piece by piece until she died in frightful agony.
Giovanni Pelanchion was tied by one leg to the tail of a
mule and dragged through the streets of Lucerne, the mob
pelting his body with stones. Ann Charbonierre was trans-
fixed upon a stake and left to die slowly. Others were
suspended from trees and beams with iron hooks piercing
their abdomens. Holes were bored in Bartholomew
Frasche's heels, ropes were passed through the open wounds,
and in this way he was dragged to the dungeon where he
died.

A favourite torture was to place small bags of gunpowder
in the mouths of the victims and then set fire to them.
Daniel Rambaut had his fingers and toes amputated in
sections, one joint being cut off each day, in an effort to
induce him to embrace the Roman faith. Burning at the
stake, drowning and suffocation were common methods of
execution.

Sara Rastignole des Vignes, for refusing to repeat Jesus
Maria, had a sickle thrust into the lower part of her abdomen. Another young woman, Martha Constantine, was
raped and then killed by cutting off her breasts.

" A servant of Jacopo Michalino of Bobio," says
Morland, " received divers stabs with a dagger in the

soles of his feet, and in his ears, by the hands of one
Gulielmo Roche, a famous massacrer of Lucerna, and
another called Mandolin, who afterwards cut off his
privy members, and then applied a burning candle to the
wound, frying it with the flame thereof, that so the blood
might be stopt, and the torments of that miserable
creature prolonged. This being done to their mindes,
they tore off his nayls with hot pincers, to try if they
could by any means force him to renounce his religion.
But when nothing would do, they tied one of his legs
to the Marquis of Lucerna's mule, and so dragged him
along the streets, till such time as he had almost ended
his painfull life; and then binding his head about with
a cord, they strained and twisted the same with a staff
until they wrung his head from his body."[1]

Children were cut to pieces, decapitated and killed in
various ways before the eyes of their parents. Mary
Pelanchion was stripped naked and hung head downwards
from a bridge over a river, and in this position made a target
for the soldiers to fire at. Cypriania Bastia, on being commanded to renounce his religion and accept the Popish faith,
said: " I would rather renounce life, or turn dog," to which
a priest answered, " For that expression you shall both
renounce life and be given to the dogs." Bastia was thrown
into prison, and when deprivation of food had brought him
near to death, he was pitched into the road and left there to
be devoured by wild dogs.

Jacopo di Ronc, a schoolmaster of Roras, was stripped
to the skin, had his nails torn off with red-hot pincers, and
holes bored through his hands. A rope was then tied around
his middle, and by this he was led through the streets of
Lucerne, with a soldier-guard marching on each side. Alternately, as the procession moved along, one of these guards
sliced off a bit of the victim's flesh with a sword, and the
other struck him with a bludgeon, both of them crying,
" Wilt thou yet go to mass? "

As a result of these continual persecutions and murders,
the towns and villages of the Piedmont valleys were almost

---

[1] Samuel Morland, *The History of the Evangelical Churches of the
Valleys of Piedmont*, London, 1658, Book II, p. 341.

From Moore's *Martyrology*, 1809

TORTURES OF THE PROTESTANTS IN THE PIEDMONT VALLEY
DURING THE SEVENTEENTH CENTURY

depopulated. Those who were not actually exterminated on the spot, for the most part, after escaping to the mountains, died of starvation, or fell victims to disease.

The Persecutions Suffered by the Quakers

In 1646 George Fox founded the Society of Friends. The movement met with much success. In a few years it became a serious menace to the established Church. Then began a series of persecutions designed to discourage the securing of new recruits, and to cause the abandonment of their project by Fox and his immediate followers. In the reign of Charles the Second the Star Chamber got to work in dead earnest. The Quakers, as the followers of this new cult were dubbed, were imprisoned in hundreds, their goods were confiscated, they were oppressed and hounded in every way short of actually putting them to death, and there is little doubt that a good many of them were surreptitiously tortured.

In the face of such travail, some of the leading lights of the movement, despairing of making any progress in their own country, turned hopeful eyes westwards towards the virgin fields of America. In the July of 1656, Mary Fisher and Ann Austin, Quakers both, with hope and faith big in them, braved the perils of the three-thousand-mile voyage and reached Boston. But their hopes were dashed at the outset. They stepped right out of the frying-pan into the hottest of fires. They were met, not by a brass band and the welcoming obeisance of men and women panting to embrace a new and novel faith, but by a mob of infuriated citizens clamouring for their blood. Mary and Ann were seized, they were " stripped stark naked, in such an immodest manner as modesty will not admit to mention," says a chronicler, they were whipped at a cart's tail, and packed, bag and baggage, on to the ship that had brought them, with threats of what would happen if they ever dared to again sully the soil of New England with their heretical feet.

Though these two women had been the first Quakers actually to set foot on American soil, they had not been alone in their determination to found a colony of Friends in the New World. Others were on their way, and altogether a sizable band of them managed to reach Boston during the years of 1656 and 1657. They preached their gospel in this town and that, they secured many recruits; they threatened the very security and existence of the Church. And so, the New England Puritans, under the leadership of Governor Endicot, embarked upon a campaign of persecution that was characterized by some of the most cruel acts that the history of religious intolerance has to show. Both men and women were whipped unmercifully, branded, mutilated and imprisoned. Many were put to death; many more were sold as slaves to the plantations.

> "Mary Tomkins and Alice Ambrose were cruelly ordered to be whipped at a cart's tail through eleven towns at one time, ten stripes apiece on their naked backs, which would have amounted to 110 in the whole, and on a very cold day, they were stripped and whipped through three of the towns (the priests looking on and laughing) and through dirt and snow, sometimes half leg deep, till Walter Barefoot, of Salisbury, got the warrant and discharged them."[1]

Lydia Wardel was stripped from the waist upwards, tied to a fence-post, "with her naked breasts to the splinters of the posts, and there sorely lashed, with twenty or thirty cruel stripes."[2] Ann Coleman was whipped within an inch of her life, the knots of the whip splitting her breasts. Edward Wharton was flogged so severely that, it was testified, "peas might lie in the holes that the knots of the whip had beat into the flesh of his arms and back; and his body was swelled, and very black from the waist upwards."[3] Thomas Newhouse was stripped and fastened to a gun-wheel, where he was given ten stripes, and then on three separate occasions whipped at the cart's tail.

And so the tale of persecutions goes on. The complete account of it would need a volume in itself. Let us close with the narration of the treatment meted out to William

---

[1] John Whiting, *Truth and Innocency Defended Against Falsehood and Envy*, 1702, p. 108.
[2] George Bishop, *New England Judged by the Spirit of the Lord*, 1703, p. 377.
[3] *Ibid.*, p. 442.

Brend, as Bishop gives it in his gory catalogue of the sufferings endured by these Quakers.

" The gaoler put him into irons, neck and heels, lockt so close together, as there was no more room between each, than for the horse-lock that fastened them on; and so kept him in irons for the space of sixteen hours (as the gaoler himself confessed) for not working; and all this without meat, whilst his back was torn with the whipping the day before, which did not satisfy the bloodthirsty gaoler, but as a man resolved to have his life, and by cruelties to kill him, he had him down again the next morning to work, though so many days without meat, his back beaten, his neck and heels bruised, by being bound so long together, because he could not bow to his will; yet he laid him on with a pitch'd rope twenty blows over his back and arms, with as much force as he could drive, so that with the fierceness of the blows the rope untwisted and his arms were swollen with it : presently after this, the gaoler having either mended his old, or got a new rope, came in again; and having haled him downstairs with greater fury and violence than before, gave his broken, bruised, and weak body fourscore and seventeen blows more, foaming at the mouth like a madman, and tormented with rage; unto which great number he had added more blows, had not his strength and rope failed him, for now he cared not what he did do : and all this, because he did not work for him, which he could not do, being unable in body and unfree in mind. So he gave him in all 117 blows with a pitch'd rope, so that his flesh was beaten black, and as into a jelly, and under his arms the bruised flesh and blood hung down, clodded as it were in baggs, and so into one was it beaten, that the sign of one particular blow could not be seen."[1]

The Growth of Judicial and Penal Torture in Europe

Practically every European State practised torture for extorting confessions of guilt in all cases of criminal trials, adopting the principle embodied in the old Roman code. At

[1] *Ibid.*, pp. 65-6.

first the whole matter of procedure was in a most amorphous state, but as time went on, and the ingenuity of man added to the variety of methods adopted, certain rules and regulations were enacted and carried out with some thoroughness.

The development of judicial torture seems to have kept pace, almost in fact step by step, with the elaboration of torture as an ecclesiastical weapon. The courts of Europe and the Inquisition were using torture at the same time, and there is little doubt that the attitude of the one influenced the attitude of the other. Even in countries where the Inquisition had no power, its methods were adopted in the civil and ecclesiastic courts.

Towards the close of the thirteenth century judicial torture flourished in Italy as strongly as it did in the days of the Cæsars. Gradually it spread into other countries, with the result that by the birth of the seventeenth century there was scarcely for the finding a European State (Scandinavia appears to have been the one exception) where torture was not looked upon as a necessary part of criminal procedure. In Germany, in France and in Spain, judicial torture became incorporated in the regular penal system.

The success of torture was the reason for its development and extension. The old Roman rule that it should be resorted to only in cases where the evidence was sufficient to indicate the guilt of the accused and his confession or admission was alone wanting, was disregarded. Mere suspicion of complicity in a crime was a sufficient excuse for the application of torture. On an accusation, unsupported by any evidence whatever, being made by any one individual against another, the accused or the suspected person was liable to be seized and put to the *quæstion*. Prevarication, silence, unexplained absence, and even pallor, says Lea,[1] were all considered to sanction the use of torture. The system was extended to include witnesses as well. When two witnesses presented opposing or conflicting evidence, they were both tortured in the presence of each other until agreement was reached. Indeed full power was given the judges to order torture as they thought fit, and there seems no reason to believe that the majority of them erred on the side of leniency or mercy.

[1] H. C. Lea, *Superstition and Force*, p. 439.

In France, by the closing years of the fourteenth century, the records of the Châtelet of Paris show that "torture had virtually become the rule and the main reliance of the tribunal, for the cases in which it was not employed appear to be simply exceptional."[1] Even the admission of guilt did not always ensure freedom from this ordeal, for if the crime was not of sufficient magnitude to warrant a capital sentence it became customary to torture the culprit into admitting a more serious offence. Thus Fleurant de Saint-Leu, on January 4, 1390, charged with stealing a silver buckle, after admitting under torture his guilt, was again tortured in an effort to induce him to confess the commission of other crimes, but although nothing further was extorted, he was executed just the same.[2] And Marquerite de la Pinele, for stealing a ring, after additional torture failed to extract admissions of other offences, was buried alive.[3] The length of time during which this method of repetitive torturing continued to be practised is indicated by the fact that Beccaria was denouncing the system in 1764. Even Farinacius, the seventeenth-century procurator-general to Pope Paul V, and author of *Praxis et Theoricæ Criminalis*, one of the most complete works on torture ever written, stated that the *quæstion* was admissible for the discovery of crimes other than those with which the prisoner was charged or of which he was suspected.

In all countries the punishments employed for various kinds of offences and crimes involved torture. Capital punishment, in itself, was usually preceded by torture. Thus in France and Germany, murderers had portions of their flesh pinched off with red-hot pincers and their right hands burnt away, before execution. In other cases, the form which the death penalty took (e.g., breaking on the wheel, burning alive, flogging with the *knut*, and partial hanging followed by quartering) amounted to death by torture.

[1] *Ibid.*, p. 441.
[2] *Ibid.*, p. 443.
[3] *Ibid.*, p. 444.

CHAPTER X

THE HOLY INQUISITION

The Birth and Development of the Holy Office

THE Inquisition was a court of justice or tribunal founded by the Roman Catholic Church for the express purpose of suppressing and eradicating heresy. The war on heresy antedated the Inquisition by a thousand years, and, as we have seen, heretics were hounded without mercy from the time when Christianity was born. In the year of grace 382 an Act was passed by which anyone convicted of heresy was to be executed. Then, with Christianity firmly established, for some centuries the persecution of the heretics by the Church itself was not so blatant, so thorough or so merciless. Anyone guilty of the crime, for it continued to rank as a crime, was excommunicated, and in most cases the Church was content to let it go at that. Sometimes, probably as a result of sporadic campaigns, heretics were much more severely handled, and even on occasion condemned to death.

As time went on, however, and as a result of leniency, and other factors, various heretical cults gained strength, and even threatened to become rivals of Christianity itself, the ecclesiastical leaders came to the conclusion that sterner measures were essential. In particular, the activities of the heretical sect known as the Albigenses, roused the Roman Church to vigorous action. The result was the beginning of a war of extermination. Innocent III conceived a scheme, or accepted the rough-and-ready idea of it from some other party, for dealing with all those who had the temerity to rebel against the Church. The result was the founding, in the first half of the thirteenth century, of the Holy Inquisition, with Dominique as the first Inquisitor-General.

Once initiated, the Inquisition set about its task in grim earnest. Its aim was to rid the country of heresy by destroying the cancer, root and branch. Spies were appointed and were soon at work everywhere. The slightest suspicious remark was sufficient for the individual uttering it to be haled before the court. Witnesses lied glibly and with gusto, not only because of their hatred of supposed heretics, but also to placate the officials of the Holy Office.

The first Inquisition was established at Toulouse in 1233. Five years later another court was opened at Aragon. The movement spread rapidly. In Germany, in Holland, in Spain, in Portugal, in France, courts were established and proceeded merrily in the war, deliberate and concerted, against heresy in all its forms.

These courts, in many cases, were magnificent structures. Often they were palaces. The Inquisition of Portugal, for instance, contained four courts, each of which was some forty feet square. The chief inquisitor had his own set of apartments, which were spacious and elegant. Around the huge courtyard were a number of magnificent salons and chambers, which the royal family, members of the court, and a number of other dignitaries, during an *auto da fé*, occupied for the purpose of observing the executions.

What a contrast these magnificent chambers and apartments presented to the dungeons or cells which housed the prisoners. There were some three hundred of these dungeons; dark, damp and small. The only accommodation provided was a miserable apology for a bedstead, a urinal, wash-hand basin, two pitchers, a lamp and a plate. The prisoners were given poor and scanty food, they were forbidden to speak or make any kind of noise, and punished severely for any breach of the regulations. Torres de Castilla, in describing the Portuguese Inquisition of Goa, says the places allocated to the prisoners were the

" dirtiest, darkest and most horrible that can possibly be, into which the rays of the sun never penetrate. The kind of noxious air that must be breathed may be imagined when it is known that a dry well in the middle of the space where the prisoners were confined and which is always uncovered, is used as a privy, the emanations from which have no other outlet for escape than a small opening. The prisoners live in a common privy."

The Examination of the Accused

The procedure was much the same in all the Inquisitions. The prisoner was often kept for months in one of the dungeons before he was examined. This was probably part of a carefully thought out scheme to wear down his powers of resistance. On being brought before the tribunal, the accused was asked to speak the truth, and to promise to conceal the secrets of the Holy Office. Acceptance implied that the examination would proceed; refusal meant a return to the dungeon and probably the infliction of some form of punishment. In the case of the examination being continued, a number of questions were put by the president of the tribunal and the prisoner's answers were recorded by a clerk. In a few days, the accused was again brought before the tribunal for further examination. He was asked to confess his crimes against the Holy Office, and led to believe that the inquisitors possessed evidence and that they had secured witnesses who were prepared to testify against him. He was not allowed to know either the nature of the evidence or the identity of the witnesses. Continued resistance and denial of guilt led to the inquisitors adopting sterner measures.

Inside the Torture Chamber

Torture was introduced for the express purpose of extracting confession, being authorized by Pope Innocent in a Bull issued in 1252. The inquisitors reduced torture to something approaching a fine art, and in the process showed the possession of much psychological knowledge and insight, the procedure being nicely calculated to wear down the resistance even of the strongest minded and most powerfully built man. First, the accused was threatened with torture, which threat, in itself, had often the desired effect. If this failed to extort confession, he was conducted to the torture chamber and shown the instruments used. This torture chamber was well designed to afflict all except those possessing nerves of iron, with horror, dread and despair. It was usually an underground apartment, devoid of windows, and lighted with nothing better than a couple of candles. The

From Moore's *Martyrology*, 1809.

THE TORTURE CHAMBER OF THE INQUISITION SHOWING THE METHODS USED

executioner was an extraordinary, awesome apparition. Clothed from head to foot in a black garment, with his head and face covered, except for two eye-holes, with a black cowl, he presented a most diabolical and satanic appearance.

Should the sight of the torture chamber, its impedimenta and the executioner, fail to have the desired effect, the prisoner was stripped to the buff, and his hands bound.

"The stripping," says Limborch, "is performed without regard to humanity or honour, not only to men, but to women and virgins, the most virtuous and chaste of whom they have sometimes in the prisons. For they cause them to be stripped, even to their very shifts, which they afterwards take off, forgive the expression, even to their pudenda, and then put on their strait linen drawers."[1]

When the accused was all prepared for the infliction of torture, again were the questions repeated, and in the event of the prisoner continuing to deny his guilt, the actual torments began.

The main tortures employed by the Inquisition were the pulley, the rack, and fire. There were also various modifications and extensions of these, as well as a number of lesser persecutions, all of which will be described in detail in another part of this work. (See Chapter XIX.)

It is important to note, however, that the whole inquisitorial system, from the moment anyone was unfortunate enough to fall into its clutches, until released by banishment or death, constituted one long torment. "In many cases," says Lea, "torture and prolonged imprisonment, in the foulest of dungeons, doubtless produced partial derangement, leading to the belief that he had committed the acts so persistently imputed to him."[2]

Punishment of a severe nature, and often in itself amounting to torture, was inflicted for the slightest breaches of the regulations. Says Torres de Castilla, writing of the Inquisition of Lisbon,

[1] Philip a Limborch, *The History of the Inquisition*, 1731, p. 219.
[2] H. C. Lea, *A History of the Inquisition of the Middle Ages*, Macmillan, New York, 1906, Vol. III, p. 506.

" should anyone commit a fault he is flogged in a most cruel manner. They strip him naked and lay him on the ground with his face downwards, and in this position he is held by several men while others flog him most unmercifully with cords stiffened by being dipped in melted pitch, which brings away flesh at every stroke until the back is one large ulcer."

It may be stated here, however, that the tortures were of such a nature that few failed to confess. This applied to the innocent just as much as to the guilty. The few that remained silent and continued to protest their innocence until unconsciousness sealed their lips, were carried back to their cells. When some amount of recovery had been made, another appearance before the tribunal followed, with more threats, and, if no confession were made, further tortures. And since, as a rule, confession meant life imprisonment or death, the majority either suffered this penalty or died as a result of the tortures they endured.

Among the cases on record where, in spite of every effort of the inquisitors, the victim's lips remained sealed, is that of Tomás de Leon, who, at Valladolid, on November 5, 1638, was racked until his left arm was broken. More remarkable still was the case of Florencia de Leon, who underwent three forms of torture, the *balestilla*, the *mancuerda*, and the *potro*, and yet remained silent; while Engracia Rodríguez, at sixty years of age, despite having one arm broken and a toe torn off in the *balestilla*, refused to confess.[1] On the other hand, many confessed at the very threat of torture, even though they were well aware that confession meant being sentenced to death. Gilles de Rais was one such. He admitted the whole category of sadistic crimes with which he was charged.

At every examination there was present either an inquisitor or a commissioner of the Holy Office. The decision as to the nature and degree of the torture to be inflicted was left to the discretion of the tribunal. No one, other than the judges, the registrar and the executioners, were allowed in the chamber while the torture was in progress. The walls

[1] H. C. Lea, *A History of the Inquisition of Spain*, Macmillan, New York, 1906.

of the apartment were lined with heavy quilts to prevent the screams and cries of the prisoner being heard outside. Any confession made during the process of torture, which confession was duly recorded by the registrar, had to be ratified by the prisoner later. If he retracted this confession and refused to sign the document he could be again tortured. This repetition of torture was given in the code of Torquemada issued to the Spanish Inquisition in 1484, and similar codes were in force in other Inquisitions. In no other circumstances, it was stated, could torture be repeated. The rule, however, proved of little practical use in conditioning or restricting the persecutions to which prisoners were subjected once they became inmates of the dungeons. The inquisitors tortured their victims again and again, but instead of calling these fresh torments repetitions, they described them as *continuations* of the same torture.

An instructive example of this was furnished by the case of Maria de Coceicao, a young lady residing in Lisbon, who was charged with heresy and ordered to be tortured on the rack. So severe were the torments that, unable to endure them longer, she confessed. Later, when called upon to ratify her confession, she refused to sign the document they had prepared. Her ground for refusal was that any confession she had made had been forced from her during the terrible ordeal to which she had been subjected. The inquisitors thereupon ordered her to be again racked. Once again she confessed. On recovery, she was again requested to sign the confession, and again she refused, stating that if they repeated the torture a hundred times " as soon as I am released from the rack I shall deny what was extorted from me by pain." A third and last time did the executioners do their fell work with the rack; but on this occasion she did not even confess, and refused to answer a single question. Changing their tactics, the inquisitors ordered her to be publicly whipped through the streets and banished for ten years.

The duration of the torture varied considerably according to the regulations in force in the different courts. Philip III issued a Bull limiting it to one hour. Often the victim became unconscious long before the stipulated time. In any such case an examination was made by a physician in order to ascertain whether the condition was real or simulated. In accordance with the physician's verdict the torture was suspended or continued. Even so, there are numerous cases on record where the torture was continued for far longer periods than it would appear were countenanced in the regulations. Lea says it often lasted two or even three hours.[1] He instances a case where one, Antonia Lōpez, at Valladolid, in 1648, was tortured continuously from eight till eleven o'clock, leaving him with a crippled arm. The poor fellow tried to commit suicide by strangling himself. He died in his prison within a month.[2]

The Auto da Fé

A confession having been secured, the penalty was then decreed. Punishments in the less serious cases were whipping, imprisonment, the galleys, and banishment; those of a graver nature called for death either by burning at the stake or by strangling. The capital sentence did not necessarily mean that the prisoner would escape the ordeal in the torture chamber by confessing at the very threat of persecution. The death sentence was looked upon as an *additional* punishment.

The doomed prisoners, at a certain specified time, were led in procession to the place of execution. The ceremony was known as the *auto da fé* (Act of Faith) or gaol delivery. These *autos da fé* were not held at any regular times, or even annually, but in accordance with the discretion of the Holy Office. They might be held at intervals of one year, or every two, three or four years. The ceremony, which always took place on a Sunday, was the occasion of a gathering of all the populace. The victims were to be burned to death in public or otherwise punished.

> "The victims who walk in the procession," says Dr. Dowling, in his *History of Romanism*, "wear the *san benito*, the *coroza*, the rope around the neck, and carry in their hand a yellow wax candle. The *san benito* is a penitential garment or tunic of yellow cloth reaching down to the knees, and on it is painted the picture of

[1] H. C. Lea, *A History of the Inquisition of Spain.*
[2] *Ibid.*

TORTURE OF A NATIVE GIRL IN TRINIDAD
(See Text, page 149.)

AN AUTO DA FÉ

the person who wears it, burning in the flames, with figures of dragons and devils in the act of fanning the flames. This costume indicates that the wearer is to be burnt alive as an incorrigible heretic. If the person is only to do penance, then the *san benito* has on it a cross, and no paintings or flames. If an impenitent is converted just before being led out, then the *san benito* is painted with the flames downward; this is called ' *fuego resuelto*,' and it indicates that the wearer is not to be burnt alive, but to have the favour of being strangled before the fire is applied to the pile. Formerly these garments were hung up in the churches as eternal monuments of disgrace to their wearers, and as the trophies of the Inquisition. The *coroza* is a pasteboard cap, three feet high, and ending in a point. On it are likewise painted crosses, flames and devils. In Spanish America it was customary to add long twisted tails to the *corozas*. Some of the victims have gags in their mouths, of which a number is kept in reserve in case the victims, as they march along in public, should become outrageous, insult the tribunal, or attempt to reveal any secrets. The prisoners who are to be roasted alive have a Jesuit on each side continually preaching to them to abjure their heresies, and if anyone attempts to offer one word in defence of the doctrines for which he is going to suffer death, his mouth is instantly gagged."[1]

On arrival at the place of execution, where a large scaffold had been erected, prayers were offered, and a sermon preached in which the Inquisition was praised and heresy bitterly condemned. If the prisoner were prepared to accept and to die in the Catholic faith he had the privilege of being strangled first and then burnt. In the event of him electing to die a Protestant or a member of any other heretic cult, he was roasted alive. And now let Dr. Geddes, who was himself the horrified spectator of the *auto da fé* held at Madrid in 1682, take up the tale.

" The officers of the Inquisition, preceded by trumpets, kettle-drums and their banner, marched on the

[1] Quoted by James Gardner in *Faiths of the World*, 1858, Vol. I, pp. 267-8.

30th of May, in cavalcade, to the palace of the great
square, where they declared by proclamation that on
the 30th of June the sentence of the prisoners would be
put in execution. There had not been a spectacle of
this kind at Madrid for several years before, for which
reason it was expected by the inhabitants with as
much impatience as a day of the greatest festivity and
triumph. When the day appointed arrived, a prodigious number of people appeared, dressed as splendid
as their respective circumstances would admit. In the
great square was raised a high scaffold; and thither,
from seven in the morning till the evening, were
brought criminals of both sexes; all the Inquisitions
in the kingdom sending their prisoners to Madrid.
Twenty men and women out of these prisoners, with
one renegade Mahometan, were ordered to be burned;
fifty Jews and Jewesses, having never before been imprisoned, and repenting of their crimes, were sentenced to a long confinement, and to wear a yellow cap;
and ten others, indicted for bigamy, witchcraft and
other crimes, were sentenced to be whipped and then
sent to the galleys: these last wore large pasteboard
caps, with inscriptions on them, having a halter about
their necks, and torches in their hands. On this solemn
occasion the whole court of Spain was present. The
grand inquisitor's chair was placed in a sort of tribunal
far above that of the king. The nobles here acted the
part of the sheriffs' officers in England, leading such
criminals as were to be burned, and holding them when
fast bound with thick cords; the rest of the criminals
were conducted by the familiars of the Inquisition.

" At the place of execution there are so many stakes
set as there are prisoners to be burned, a large quantity
of dry furze being set about them. The stakes of the
Protestants, or, as the inquisitors call them, the professed, are about four yards high, and have each a small
board, whereon the prisoner is seated within half a
yard of the top. The professed then go up a ladder
betwixt two priests, who attend them the whole day
of execution. When they come even with the afore-
mentioned board, they turn about to the people, and

the priests spend near a quarter of an hour in exhorting them to be reconciled to the see of Rome. On their refusing, the priests come down, and the executioner ascending, turns the professed from off the ladder upon the seat, chains their bodies close to the stakes, and leaves them. Then the priests go up a second time to renew their exhortations; and if they find them ineffectual, usually tell them at parting, that 'they leave them to the Devil, who is standing at their elbow ready to receive their souls, and carry them with him into the flames of hell-fire, as soon as they are out of their bodies.' A general shout is then raised, and when the priests get off the ladder, the universal cry is: 'Let the dogs' beards be made!' (which implies, singe their beards). This is accordingly performed by means of flaming furzes, thrust against their faces with long poles. This barbarity is repeated till their faces are burnt, and is accompanied with loud acclamations. Fire is then set to the furzes, and the criminals are consumed.

"The intrepidity of the twenty-one men and women in suffering the horrid death was truly astonishing; some thrust their hands and feet into the flames with the most dauntless fortitude; and all of them yielded to their fate with such resolution that many of the amazed spectators lamented that such heroic souls had not been more enlightened. The near situation of the king to the criminals rendered their dying groans very audible to him; he could not, however, be absent from this dreadful scene, as it is esteemed a religious one, and his coronation oath obliges him to give a sanction by his presence to all the acts of the tribunal."

Influence of the Inquisition

It was only to be expected that in every country where the Inquisition existed, or, in other words, in every country where the Roman Catholic religion flourished, any one who had the temerity to flirt with heresy in any form, lived continuously under the shadow of a terror. It is axiomatic that cruelty begets cruelty, persecution begets persecution.

The inquisitors, gorged with their inhumanity, developed a degree of callousness rarely rivalled in the annals of civilization. So wide was the interpretation of the term heresy that the free expression of opinion in all Catholic countries, for the five hundred years of the Inquisition's tyranny, may be said to have been inexistent. It was bad enough as regards spoken opinion; it was a hundred times worse in relation to the written word. Every book that came from the press was scrutinized minutely with the express object of finding some passage which might be interpreted as being against the principles or interests of the Catholic faith. The censorship of books took three forms: (1) complete condemnation and suppression; (2) the expunging of certain objectionable passages or parts; and (3) the correction of sentences or the deletion of specific words. A list of the various books condemned upon any of these three heads was printed every year, after which anyone found to be in the possession of a volume coming under section (1) or an unexpurgated or uncorrected copy of a volume coming under section (2) or (3) was deemed guilty of a crime and liable to severe punishment. The author and the publisher of any such book often spent the remainder of their lives in the dungeons of the Inquisition.

In a considerable number of instances charges were deliberately faked against individuals who, in some way or other, had incurred the enmity of the inquisitors or of high and powerful authorities, ecclesiastical or otherwise, connected with the Church. The vast power of the inquisitors, and particularly their authority to order prisoners to be tortured, enabled them to secure a conviction with ease against anyone against whom they had a grudge. For this reason, Catholics as well as heretics, were in danger. The very fact of having a charge brought against one, and of being summoned to the Inquisition, was sufficient to strike abject terror into the bravest man or woman. For few who entered the doors of that hall of torment emerged whole in mind and body. If they escaped with their life, they were, with rare exceptions, maimed, physically or mentally, for ever.

The power and security of the Inquisition were strengthened and solidified by the grip of terror which it secured upon the people. Whatever anyone dare think, he could not, without running the risk of being incarcerated, give voice to any criticism or disparagement of the Holy Office. To the contrary, everyone chanted its virtues and praised its fairness. Even those—the few there were—who were released from its clutches, either kept rigid silence respecting the treatment that had been meted out to them or otherwise glorified the institution. Says Dellon, in his account of the Inquisition at Goa, written in 1788:

" Those who have thus escaped the fire by their forced confessions, when they are out of the prison of the Holy Office, are strictly obliged to publish that they were treated with much goodness and clemency, since their life was preserved to them, which they had justly forfeited. For if a man who having confessed himself guilty, should afterwards presume to justify himself after his enlargement, he would be immediately accused, arrested, and burnt at the first *Act of Faith*, without any hope of pardon."

Many of the inquisitors were sadists. Many were libidinous monsters. They took such women as they wanted, on trumped-up charges of heresy, and kept them for the rest of their days as mistresses. When the French troops captured the city of Aragon, Lieutenant-General M. de Legal ordered the doors of the Inquisition to be opened, and the prisoners, numbering some 400, to be released. " Among these were sixty beautiful young women who appeared to form a seraglio for the three principal inquisitors." One of these ladies had a remarkable story to tell. She related it to the French officer who later became her husband, and to M. Gavin, the author of *A Master Key to Popery*. I reproduce the account in her own words.

" I went one day, with my mother, to visit the Countess Attaras, and I met there Don Francisco Tirregon, her confessor, and second inquisitor of the Holy Office. After we had drank chocolate, he asked me my age, my confessor's name, and many intricate questions about religion. The severity of his countenance frightened me, which he perceiving, told the countess to inform me that he was not so severe as he looked. He then caressed me in a most obliging manner, presented his hand, which I kissed with great reverence and modesty; and, as he went away, he made use of this remarkable expression, ' My dear child, I shall remember you till the next time.' I did not, at the time, mark the sense of the words; for I was inexperienced in matters of gallantry, being, at that time, but fifteen years old. Indeed, he unfortunately did remember me; for the very same night, when our whole family were in bed, we heard a great knocking at the door. The maid, who laid in the same room with me, went to the window, and inquired who was there. The answer was, the Holy Inquisition. On hearing this I screamed out, ' Father! Father! Dear father, I am ruined for ever!' My father got up, and came to me to know the occasion of my crying out; I told him the Inquisition were at the door. On hearing this, instead of protecting me, he hurried me downstairs as fast as possible; and, lest the maid should be too slow, opened the street door himself; under such abject and slavish fears are bigoted minds! As soon as he knew they came for me, he fetched me with great solemnity, and delivered me to the officers with much submission.

" I was hurried into a coach, with no other clothing than a petticoat and a mantle; for they would not let me stay to take anything else. My fright was so great, I expected to die that very night; but judge my surprise, when I was ushered into an apartment, decorated with all the elegance that taste, united with opulence, could bestow. Soon after the officers left me, a maid-servant appeared with a silver salver, on which were sweetmeats and cinnamon-water. She desired me to take some refreshments before I went to bed; I told her I could not, but should be glad if she could inform me whether I was to be put to death that night or not. ' To be put to death! ' exclaimed she, ' you do not come here to be put to death, but to live like a princess, and you shall want for nothing in the world, but the liberty of going out; so pray don't be afraid, but go to bed and sleep easy; for to-morrow you shall see wonders within this house; and as I am chosen to be your waiting-maid, I hope you'll be very kind to me.'

There follows a long discursive account of the manner in which, through the medium of this servant girl Mary, Don Francisco sent to his latest victim elegant clothes, valuable presents, and personal messages, both polite and endearing, and an invitation to have dinner with him, which, acting on Mary's advice, the young lady accepted. Don Francisco informed her that, because of certain accusations which had been made against her in connexion with matters of religion, the Inquisition had pronounced sentence of burning alive "in a dry pan, with a gradual fire," but that he, out of respect for her family and pity for her, had managed to stop the execution of the terrible sentence, at any rate, for the present. The man made it plain, however, and Mary made it additionally plain, that there was only one way of escaping death, and that anyone other than a born fool would take it. Probably acting under instructions from Don Francisco, Mary went further and, after securing a promise of absolute secrecy from the already terrified young lady, offered to show her the implements of torture. And so the next morning, before anybody was stirring,

"taking me downstairs, she brought me to a large room, with a thick iron door, which she opened. Within it was an oven, with fire in it at the time, and a large brass pan upon it, with a cover of the same, and a lock to it. In the next room there was a great wheel, covered on both sides with thick boards; with a little window in the centre, Mary desired me to look in with a candle; there I saw all the circumference of the wheel set with sharp razors, which made me shudder. Mary then took me to a pit, which was full of venomous animals. On my expressing great horror at the sight, she said, ' Now, my good mistress, I'll tell you the use of these things. The dry pan is for heretics, and those who oppose the holy father's will and pleasure; they are put alive into the pan, being first stripped naked; and the cover being locked down, the executioner begins to put a small fire

into the oven, and by degrees he augments it, till the
body is reduced to ashes. The wheel is designed for
those who speak against the Pope, or the holy fathers
of the Inquisition; for they are put into that machine
through the little door, which is locked after them, and
then the wheel is turned swiftly, till they are all cut to
pieces. The pit is for those who contemn the images,
and refuse to give proper respect to ecclesiastical persons;
for they are thrown into the pit, and so become the food
of poisonous animals.

"We went back again to my chamber, and Mary
said that another day she would show me the torments
designed for other transgressors; but I was in such
agonies at what I had seen, that I begged to be terrified
with no more such sights. She soon after left me, but
not without enjoining me strict obedience to Don Francisco; 'for if you do not comply with his will,' says she,
'the dry pan and gradual fire will be your fate.' The
horrors which the sight of these things, and Mary's
expressions, impressed on my mind, almost bereaved me
of my senses, and left me in such a state of stupefaction
that I seemed to have no manner of will of my own.

"The next morning Mary said, 'Now let me dress
you as nice as possible, for you must go and wish Don
Francisco good morrow, and breakfast with him.' When
I was dressed, she conveyed me through a gallery into
his apartment, where I found that he was in bed. He
ordered Mary to withdraw, and to serve up breakfast
in about two hours' time. When Mary was gone, he
commanded me to undress myself, and come to bed to
him. The manner in which he spoke, and the dreadful
ideas with which my mind was filled, so terribly
frightened me, that I pulled off my clothes, without
knowing what I did, and stepped into bed, insensible of
the indecency I was transacting: so totally had the care
of self-preservation absorbed all my other thoughts, and
so entirely were the ideas of delicacy obliterated by the
force of terror."

After the seduction of the girl, she was introduced to the
other young ladies, numbering fifty-two in all, the eldest of

which was about twenty-four years, who formed the seraglio. And for three days, gorgeously upholstered, living in the most luxurious apartments, eating and drinking the finest products of the land, she lived the life of a queen. Then, after an evening of gaiety, the girl was taken to a small, dungeon-like room, in which was another young lady. Mary, who was her conductor on this occasion too, said, " This is your room, and this lady your bed-fellow and companion," and immediately went away. Then . . . but let the narrator resume her story:

" My perplexity and vexation were inexpressible; but my new companion, whose name was Leonora, prevailed on me to disguise my uneasiness from Mary. I dissembled tolerably well when she came to bring our dinners, but could not help remarking, in my own mind, the difference between this repast and those I had before partook of. This consisted only of plain common food, and of that a scanty allowance, with only one plate, and one knife and fork for us both, which she took away as soon as we had dined. When we were in bed, Leonora, upon my solemn promise of secrecy, began to open her mind to me. ' My dear sister,' she said, ' you think your case very hard; but, I assure you, all the ladies in the house have gone through the same. In time you will know all their stories, as they hope to know yours. I suppose Mary has been the chief instrument of your fright, as she has been of ours; and I warrant she has shown you some horrible places, though not all; and that, at the very thought of them you were so terrified that you chose the same way we have done to redeem yourself from death. By what hath happened to us, we know that Don Francisco hath been your Nero, your tyrant; for the three colours of clothes are the distinguishing tokens of the three holy fathers. The red silk belongs to Don Francisco, the blue to Don Guerrero, and the green to Don Aliaga; and they always give those colours (after the farce of changing garments, and the short-lived recreations are over) to those ladies whom they bring here for their respective uses. We are strictly commanded to express all the demonstrations of joy, and to be very merry for three days, when a young lady first comes amongst us, as we did with you, and as you must now do with others; but afterwards we live like the most wretched prisoners, without seeing anybody but Mary, and the other maid-servants, over whom Mary hath a kind of superiority, for she acts as housekeeper. We all dine in the great hall three days in a week; and when any one of the inquisitors hath a mind for one of his slaves, Mary comes about nine o'clock, and leads her to his apartment. Some evenings Mary leaves the door of our chambers open, and that is a token that one of the inquisitors hath a mind to come that night; but he comes so silent that we are ignorant whether he is our patron or not. If one of us happens to be with child, she is removed into a better chamber till she is delivered; but during the whole of her pregnancy she never sees anybody but the person appointed to attend her. As soon as the child is born it is taken away, and carried we know not whither; for we never hear a syllable mentioned about it afterwards. I have been in this house six years, was not fourteen when the officers took me from my father's house, and have had one child. There are, at this present time, fifty-two young ladies in the house; but we annually lose six or eight, though we know not what becomes of them, or whither they are sent. This, however, does not diminish our number, for new ones are always brought in to supply the place of those who are removed from hence; and I remember, at one time, to have seen seventy-three ladies here together. Our continual torment is to reflect that when they are tired of any of the ladies, they certainly put to death those they pretend to send away; for it is natural to think that they have too much policy to suffer their atrocious and infernal villainies to be discovered, by enlarging them. Hence our situation is miserable indeed, and we have only to pray that the Almighty will pardon those crimes which we are compelled to commit.' "

This description, the narrator continues, proved to be a true one. Eighteen months were to elapse before the French officers opened the doors of the Inquisition, and during this

From Moore's *Martyrology*, 1809.

ROCHUS BURNT AT THE STAKE BY ORDER OF THE INQUISITION

(See Text, page 81.)

period, while eleven of the inmates disappeared in the mysterious manner mentioned by Leonora, nineteen new girls entered, making the total number at the moment of deliverance no fewer than sixty.

Victims of the Inquisition

Precisely how many people were burned to death, and how many were tortured and allowed to die in the dungeons, it is impossible to say. Many statements have been made regarding the number of executions. But it is more than likely that none is accurate. Where the historian does not underestimate, the probability is that he exaggerates. Llorente, the Roman Catholic writer, who for years acted as secretary to the Spanish Inquisition, estimates that from 1481 to 1517, that is during a period of less than forty years, 13,000 persons were burnt alive, and 17,000 were condemned to different forms of punishment. These figures are probably under rather than over the true mark. The triviality of the offences for which punishments, and often death, were incurred was instrumental in causing the total number of persecutions to be so immoderately large. A glance at the records shows the trifling nature of these offences and the severity of the punishments meted out to the offenders.

Rochus, a carver of St. Lucar, Spain, for defacing an image of the Virgin Mary rather than sell it to an inquisitor for a mere trifle, was burnt at the stake. The keeper of the prison at Triano, Spain, for showing kindness to the prisoners in the castle, was sentenced to 200 lashes and six years labour as a galley slave. A woman servant in the Inquisition, for granting favours to the captives, was whipped in public and branded on the forehead. Ferdmando, a Protestant schoolmaster, for teaching the principles of his faith to his pupils, was first tortured, and then burnt. Another Protestant, named John Leon, and some Spaniards of the same faith, on endeavouring to escape to England, were captured by agents of the Inquisition, tortured, starved, and finally burnt. For refusing to take the veil and turn nun, but instead taking up the Protestant faith, a young lady was condemned to the flames.

Christopher Losada, an eminent physician of his day, for

professing the tenets of Protestantism, was racked and burnt. A monk of the monastery of St. Isidore, Seville, who turned Protestant, was tortured and burnt. A Protestant writing-master of Toledo, who had decorated the walls of a room in his house with a reproduction of the ten commandments in full,[1] in his own handwriting, was burnt at the stake at Valladolid in 1676. At the same court, Martin-Juan de Salinas was sentenced to 200 lashes for bigamy.

An Englishwoman, married to a man named Vascon-cellos, and living in Madeira, in 1704, was charged with heresy and sent to the Inquisition of Lisbon. For nine months and fifteen days this woman, for a crime of which she steadfastly claimed to be innocent, was kept in a dungeon, on nothing but bread and water, and no better sleeping provisions than a damp straw-bed. In attempts to extort confession she was whipped on several occasions with knotted cords; her breast was burnt with a red-hot iron in three different places and the wounds left to heal themselves. Finally, she was conveyed once again to the torture chamber and commanded by the executioner to sit in a fixed chair, to which she was bound with cords in a way which prevented the slightest motion. Her left foot was then bared, and an iron slipper, which had been put in the fire until it was red-hot, was fixed on her naked foot, where it remained until the flesh was burnt to the bone. The woman fainted. She was then flogged so fiendishly that her back from the shoulders to the waist was one mass of torn flesh. They then threatened to put the red-hot slipper on her right foot. Unable to endure any further torments she signed the paper they held in front of her.

Jane Bohorquia, a lady of noble family living at Seville, for conversing with a friend about the Protestant religion, was seized and imprisoned. She was pregnant at the time, but immediately after the birth of the child, and while still in a lamentably weak state, she was racked with such severity that the flesh was cut through to the very bones and blood gushed from her mouth. A week later she died. In this case, as on many another occasion, it was reported that she had been found dead in prison, no official mention being

---

[1] The Papists omitted that part of the second commandment forbidding the worship of images.

made of the torture to which she had been subjected. The report read: "Jane Bohorquia was found dead in prison; after which, upon reviewing her prosecution, the Inquisition discovered that she was innocent. Be it therefore known, that no further prosecutions shall be carried on against her, and that her effects, which were confiscated, shall be given to her heirs at law."

The allegation that death was due to an accident or to illness was a favourite method employed by the inquisitors when the torture inflicted had proved fatal and the case was one where it might conceivably be difficult to justify such extreme cruelty. Thus at Valladolid, in 1623, one Diego Enríquez, had an "accident" and died in hospital.[1]

There is the case of Isaac Martin, an English Protestant, at Malaga, in 1714. Because of his name, he was accused of being a Jew. Martin was seized and taken to the Inquisition at Granada for trial. He was locked up in a dungeon and given these instructions: "You must observe as great silence here as if you were dead; you must not speak, nor whistle, nor sing, nor make any noise that can be heard; and if you hear anybody cry, or make a noise, you must be still, and say nothing, upon pain of 200 lashes." After a long imprisonment, punctuated by several audiences with the chief lord inquisitor, Martin was convicted of heresy, and sentenced to receive 200 lashes through the streets of Granada and to be banished from Spain. As Isaac Martin is one of the few who suffered torture at the hands of the inquisitors and was in a position to tell the truth, let him give the tale of his sufferings in his own words.

"The next morning about ten of the clock, I was brought downstairs, the executioner came in with ropes and a whip. He bid me take off my coat, waistcoat, wig and cravat. As I was taking off my shirt, he bid me let it alone, he would manage that. He slipp'd my body through the collar, and ty'd it about my waist. Then took a rope and ty'd my hands together, put another about my neck, and led me out of the Inquisition, where there were numerous crowds of people waiting to see an

[1] H. C. Lea, *A History of the Inquisition of Spain.*

English heretic. I was no sooner out, but a priest read my sentence at the door, as followeth: 'Orders are given from the Lords of the Holy Office of the Inquisition, to give unto Isaac Martin 200 lashes, through the public streets. He being of the religion of the Church of England, a Protestant, a Heretic, irreverend to the Host, and to the Image of the Virgin Mary, and so let it be executed.' Knowing what was to be done to me, I was not so frightened as when they blind-folded me. The sentence being read, the executioner mounted me upon an ass, and led me through the streets, the people huzzahing, and crying out, an English Heretic! Look at the English Heretic, who is no Christian! and pelting me. The cryer of the city walked before me, repeating aloud the sentence that was read at the door of the Inquisition, the executioner whipping me as I went along, and a great many people on horseback, in ceremonial robes, with wands and halberts following."[1]

There is, too, the remarkable case of Francisco Moyen. At the age of twenty-nine, this Frenchman, who was then living at Potosi, was seized by the Inquisition and charged with heresy. He was sent to Lima for trial. In those days, travel in South America was a lengthy process. The journey was a long one and, in consequence, it was not until the March of 1752 that Moyen, after undergoing incredible hardships and privations, was handed over to the Inquisition at Lima. He was tried as a heretic and sentenced to 200 lashes and ten years imprisonment. In 1754, with the aid of the candle supplied at supper-time, he set fire to his cell door in the hope of being able in this way to effect his escape. The scheme failed and for the remainder of his term of imprisonment, he had to eat his meals in darkness. The man was shackled for the whole of these ten interminable years, and his condition may be judged from the fact that, in view of the malignant ulcers with which the ankle was covered and the fear that gangrene might set in and deprive them of their prey, the inquisitors ordered the shackle to be removed from the affected foot. On the 6th April, 1761,

---

[1] John Marchant, *A Review of the Bloody Tribunal or The Horrid Cruelties of the Inquisition*, Perth, 1770, p. 121.

Moyen was released and banished from the country, a mere caricature of a man.

The Inquisition respected neither rank nor station. Rich or poor, peasant or nobleman, it was God help anyone who fell into its hands. One of the most illustrious of the many victims was no less a personage than Don Carlos, the eldest son of Philip the Second, and heir-apparent to the crown. Appalled at the excesses committed, in the name of God, by the Popish hierarchs, Don Carlos, on more than one occasion, when among his friends and acquaintances, declaimed against the methods of the inquisitors. The matter came to the ears of the Holy Office and the prince was arrested. That the power of a king was less than that of the Spanish Inquisition Philip was well aware; and his thorough realization of this, added to the fact that he was not over fond of his son, caused him to make no real effort at interference. Don Carlos was found guilty of heresy and condemned to death. Owing to his rank, one concession was granted him—the choice of the manner of his death. He decided to have a vein opened and bleed to death.

CHAPTER XI

TORTURE IN GREAT BRITAIN AND IRELAND

The Rise of Judicial Torture in England

ENGLISHMEN have always been, as they are to-day, inclined to boast that torture has never been practised in their country. The statement is an erroneous one. It is based upon and is due to the fact that torture has never been legally recognized by the common law of England. Apart, however, from the many cases where, in defiance of common law, and with the authority of the reigning monarch, torture was repeatedly used both to extract confession and to obtain evidence; persecution, as I have been at some pains to point out (cf. Chapter I), has always existed. However it may have been disguised, euphemized or justified under the name of punishment or as discipline, torture it has remained nonetheless. And in this respect, all through the ages, torture in England has been applied in full measure.

The Anglo-Saxons, like all other contemporary races, were callous and cruel. Servants were slaves in all but name, and were beaten and ill-used by their masters and mistresses. On the slightest provocation they were loaded with fetters, kept without food, and often scourged to death.

Long before the Roman conquest there are indications that mutilation was a common form of punishment, and that brutal floggings were inflicted for trivialities. At the time of the invasion, according to Milton, " the Roman wives and virgins hang'd up all naked, had their breasts cut off, and sow'd to their mouths, that in the grimness of death they might seem to eat their own flesh."[1]

In the early days, trial by ordeal, which, in some forms, such as the cold-water and hot-iron tests, represented forms of torture, was common. But as these practices declined, and in course of time were abolished, offenders refused to

---

[1] John Milton, *The History of Britain*, 1777, Book II, p. 78.

accept any alternative forms of trial. When brought before the court they pleaded neither guilty nor not guilty, but maintained a silence which threatened to balk every effort of justice, as it was impossible to convict an accused person who remained mute.

To deal with cases such as these the punishment known as *peine forte et dure* was brought into use. Here, in particular, we have a form of punishment which did not, according to English common law, constitute torture, but which in reality was as barbarous a method of persecution as anything used in the Spanish Inquisition. Thumb-tying was widely adopted as a means of inducing prisoners to plead or witnesses to give evidence; and the "pricking" of those suspected of witchcraft was frequently adopted in the Middle Ages. These practices were forms of torture, but they were not *recognized* as such. This reasoning, which was nothing but rank sophistry, seems to have been unconditionally accepted by the people, for apparently few raised the slightest remonstrance or protest.

When it came to the use of the rack, however, judges recognized there was no way in which this could be described as anything other than torture, and as torture was prohibited by common law, they had to set about finding some way of justifying the use of the *quæstion* in special circumstances. They solved their problem by making it possible for torture to be employed in circumstances where a special licence was granted by the reigning monarch or by some body, such as the Privy Council or the Star Chamber,[1] whose authority superseded common law.

In the year 1310 we find a royal warrant being issued to authorize the torturing of the Templars. In 1468, Sir Thomas Coke, Lord Mayor of London, was tried and found guilty of treason, upon evidence provided by a single witness, which evidence was secured by torture. As time went on

---

[1] The Court of the Star Chamber was formed in the reign of the eighth Henry. It consisted of two chief justices and the Privy Council, and it was established for the purpose of considering important cases and those involving legal problems of more than ordinary gravity or complexity. This Court, however, quickly abused its power. It became unjust, prejudiced and tyrannical. As a result of orders given by the Star Chamber there were inflicted some of the most brutal tortures that ever disgraced English justice. The Court was abolished in 1640.

the use of torture became more frequent. In fact, although
it is probable that torture in some form or other and under
other names, was employed widely from the beginning of
English history, references to its use in the earlier years are
remarkably scanty, but during the fifteenth, sixteenth and
seventeenth centuries, the evidence is abundant. In the
opinion of no less an authority than Jardine, torture was
"always used in all grave accusations at the mere discretion
of the King and the Privy Council."[1]   A few instances may
be given.

> "On the 9th June, 1555, letters were written to the
> Lord North and others, to put such obstinate persons as
> would not confess to the torture, and there to order them
> at their discretion; and a letter was written to the lieuten-
> ant of the Tower to the same effect."[2]

> "On December 28, 1566, a letter was addressed by the
> Privy Council to the Attorney-General and others, that:
> where they were heretofore appointed to put Clement
> Fisher, now prisoner in the Tower, in some fear of
> torture. Whereby his lewdness and such as he might
> detect might the better come to light, they are requested,
> for that the said Fisher is not minded to feel some touch
> of the rack.—Council Register. Eliz. MSS."

In 1571, Queen Elizabeth issued a Letter of Warrant to
Sir Thomas Smith and Dr. Wilson "for putting two of the
Duke of Norfolk's servants to the rack."[3] Samuel Peacock,
suspected of treason, was tortured on a warrant issued by the
Privy Council. At Newgate Sessions, on October 14, 1660:

> "George Thorely, being indicted for robbery, refused
> to plead, and his two thumbs were tyed together with
> whipcord, that the pain of that might compel him to
> plead, and he was sent away so tied, and a minister
> persuaded to go with him to persuade him; and an hour

---

[1] David Jardine, *On the Use of Torture in the Criminal Law of
England*, 1837.
[2] Bishop Burnet, *The History of the Reformation*, Oxford, 1829.
[3] *Notes and Queries*, May 20, 1916.

after he was brought again and pleaded.   And this was said to be the constant practice at Newgate."[1]

At the Stafford Assizes, in the March of 1674, a murderer, who refused to plead, was sentenced to the *peine forte et dure*.   The Scavenger's Daughter, invented by Sir William Skevington, a lieutenant of the Tower, in the reign of the eighth Henry; the rack;[2] the iron gauntlets, the boots, and other instruments of torture, were in constant use.   The loathsome dungeon known as "Little Ease," which, in 1604, was the subject of a government inquiry; and the even more terrible place of torment known as the "dungeon among the rats," in which it was admitted that "flesh had been torn from the arms and legs of prisoners during sleep by the well-known voracity of these animals," were seldom unoccupied.   Flogging, which did not rank as a form of torture at all, was an everyday occurrence.

It would appear that judicial torture reached its greatest ecumenity in the reign of Elizabeth.   "In the latter part of her reign," says Hallam, "the rack seldom stood idle in the Tower."[3]   There is some dispute as to whether or not Guy Fawkes was actually put on the rack, but at any rate he was *threatened* with torture, and probably some preliminary steps were taken to induce his confession.   Certainly all was ready, the order having been issued : "If he will not otherwise confess, the gentlest tortures are to be first used on him, and so on, step by step, to the most severe, and so God speed the good work," and we have the assertion of King James himself that the rack was shown to Fawkes.

Judicial Torture in Scotland and Ireland

In the sixteenth and seventeenth centuries torture was much more commonly resorted to in Scotland than in England, and especially in relation to those accused of sorcery and witchcraft.   The King and the Privy Council were both empowered to order it at their discretion.   Thus in

[1] *A Report of Divers Cases*, collected by John Kelyng, 1708, p. 27.
[2] The rack, according to tradition, was first introduced into the Tower in the reign of Henry VI, by the Duke of Exeter, hence its colloquial name, the "Duke of Exeter's Daughter."
[3] Hallam, *Constitutional History*, Vol. I, p. 201.

1596, James VI ordered Edinburgh rioters to be tortured. In 1650, Parliament authorized the use of torture in the case of Colonel Sibbald.

Indeed there were many notorious and celebrated cases. In the year 1590, Dr. Fian "was put to the most severe and cruell paine in the worlde, called the bootes." In 1600, one Rhynd, on a charge of participation in the Gowrie House conspiracy, was put to the torture. In 1689, the alleged murderer of the Lord President Lockhart was tortured to induce him to divulge the identity of his accomplices. In 1615, a Jesuit named John Ogilvie, charged with treason, "was convoyit to Edinburgh, and ther keepit in strait waird, and a gaird of men, be the space of eight dayis, with small sustentation, and *compellit and withhaldin, perforce, from sleep,* to the great perturbation of his brayne, and to compell him *ad delirium*!"[1]

The instruments employed appear to have been more varied than in England. The rack, the caspicaws, or caschie-lawis, the witch's bridle, thumbscrews, the boot; the pilnie-winkis, were all in frequent use. And D'Archenholz in his *Picture of England* (1790) indicates that *peine forte et dure* was not unknown in Scotland.

Turning to Ireland, we find remarkably few instances of judicial torture on record. In 1583, in Dublin, an Irish priest named Hurley, suspected of treason, when brought before the Lord Justices, Archbishop Loftus and Sir H. Wallop, remained mute. On applying to London for instructions, the Irish council was told to put him to the torture in order to induce him to speak. As no rack was available, "hot boots," in which, according to some accounts, melted resin was poured, were applied, and Hurley confessed.[2] Sometimes offenders were taken to London, for torture in the Tower, presumably on the ground of its better equipment for the purpose. There was an instance in 1581, when Myagh was removed to the Tower by command of the Lord Deputy. By 1615, the Dublin authorities apparently had procured a better set of torturing implements, for there is a record of one O'Kennan being racked in that city.

---

[1] Robert Pitcairn, *Ancient Criminal Trials in Scotland*, Edinburgh, 1833, Vol. III, p. 332.
[2] J. A. Froude, *History of England*, 1863.

Torture in the Guise of Punishment

For every case of torture practised for the purpose of extorting confession or evidence, there must have been hundreds of instances where it was adopted as a means of punishment. The fact that it was rarely described as torture does not affect the point. The punishment may have been partly in the form of torture or wholly in that form. Torture often preceded death. But rarely was it admitted that anyone sentenced to death, however brutal or horrible the manner of execution might be, had been subjected to torture.

The most frequent form of punishment involving torture was flogging, and of death by torture, burning. Branding and mutilation were also common minor punishments. The horrible, and already noted, *peine forte et dure* survived until 1772. The tortures to which those accused of witchcraft were subjected will be considered in another place (cf. Chapter XII).

The criminal records abound with cases of torture in the guise of punishment. Thus in 1556, Andrew Drummond, convicted of forgery, was sentenced " to be publickly led with his hands tied behind his back to the market-cross of the burgh of Edinburgh, and there to have his right hand struck off and fastened on a pole: and thereafter to be banished from the kingdom for life."[1] For a similar offence, on May 5, 1558, at Edinburgh, David Fethye had his right hand amputated.[2] On December 10, 1549, for setting fire to a house, Isobella McFerlane was sentenced " to be branded on the cheek." On March 8, 1615, James Boyle, Johnne Hammiltoun and Adame Moffet, were scourged through the town of Edinburgh, and burned with a hot iron upon the cheek.[3] On July 30, 1618, for stealing a purse, Johnne Broune was burnt on the cheek; and on November 10, 1636, some Egyptians, described as " vagabonds and thieves," were convicted and sentenced as follows: " the men to be hangit, and the weomen to be drowned: and that suche of the

---

[1] Robert Pitcairn, *Ancient Criminal Trials in Scotland*, 1833, Vol. I, p. 388.
[2] *Ibid.*, p. 403.
[3] *Ibid.*, Vol. III, p. 358.

weomen as hes children to be scourged throw the burgh of
Hadinton and brunt of the cheeke."[1]

Burning at the stake was a form of execution for certain
other crimes besides witchcraft.   Thus on September 17,
1605, Johnne Jak (alias Scott) for the horrible crime of
bestiality was bound to a stake and burnt alive along with
the mare which was his partner in the crime.

Although breaking on the wheel was comparatively rare,
there have been instances where death in this terrible form
has been inflicted.   On April 30, 1591, Johnne Diksoun, for
parricide, was executed in Scotland in this way.   And there
is an entry in Robert Birrel's *Diary* which reads: " Robert
Weir broken on ane cart-wheel, with ane coulter of ane
pleuch, in the hand of the hangman, for murdering the
Laird of Warriston, quhilk he did, 2 Julii 1600."

Torture was not confined to the punishment of crime by
the State.   Not infrequently the people took the law into
their own hands and tortured individuals against whom
they had private grudges.   Not infrequently did sadists and
others perform crimes in which torture was a predominating
feature.   Only the most flagrant cases, and such as resulted
in criminal prosecutions, as a rule came to the notice of the
public—the thousands of others have remained unknown or
if known the responsible parties were never discovered or
apprehended.

For evidence, we are therefore compelled once again to
consult the criminal records.   In 1598, James Crawfurd,
Magnus Andersoune and Johnne Andersoune were charged
with the torture of Margaret Gairner.   The girl, it appears,
was suspected of having stolen a purse of money from
Crawfurd and in their endeavours to induce a confession, the
precious trio forced the girl's fingers into the "bores or
perforations through which harrows are thrust" causing
much tearing and laceration.   They then burnt her upon the
back, the shoulders, and under the armpits with red-hot
tongs, and left her bound and helpless, without food or
drink, for two days.[2]

Few accounts of torture recounted in a British court,
however, have ever equalled that which was disclosed when

[1] *Ibid.*, Vol. III, p. 595.
[2] Pitcairn's *Trials*, Vol. II, p. 45.

certain members of the clan McFarlane were, in the year
1623, charged with and convicted for the murder of George
Buchanan. It appeared that a feud between the two clans
was the primary cause of the crime. Coming across one of
the Buchanans early in the morning, several members of the
McFarlane clan seized him and bound him to a tree trunk.
This occurred about eight o'clock, and from thence until ten
at night, at intervals of an hour each, they gave him " three
cruel strokes with a dirk in such parts of his body as was not
to bring present death." Finally they killed him, stripped
his body of all its clothing, cut his throat, removed his
tongue and killed his four dogs. One dog's tongue they cut
out and put in the murdered man's mouth, and Buchanan's
tongue they placed in the dog's mouth. This grim record
of posthumous cruelty and barbarity is not yet ended.

" Nocht content heirwith, bot the forther to satisfie
their inhuman and barbarous crewaltie upon the naked
corpis, they slitt up his bellie, tooke out his whole intrallis, and pat thame in ane of the dogis belleis, eftir
they had opnit the dogis bellie and tane out his intrallis,
quhilkis they pat in the gentilmannis bellie: and so left
him lyand naked, and the foure deid dogis aboue him;
quhair he lay aboue the eard the space of aucht dayis
thaireftir, or he was found."[1]

In Ireland there were lots of instances where private
individuals, singly or in gangs, tortured their fellows. But
nothing in Irish history, for sheer bloodiness and savagery,
equalled the wave of terror which swept certain parts of the
island when, in 1642, the Irish Papists wrecked their vengeance on the English Protestants. In a pamphlet[2] published
in London in 1689, the story in all its ghastly horrifying
tragedy is recounted. There seems to be no form of crude
torture that human ingenuity could conceive, which was not
used upon men, women and children of the hated faith, in
the glorious name of religion. In Kilkenny an Englishwoman was beaten into a ditch, where she died; her child,
about five years old, they ripped up abdominally, letting

[1] *Ibid.*, Vol. III, p. 548.
[2] *A Relation of the Bloody Massacre in Ireland.*

out her guts. "One man they forced to mass, then they wounded him, ript his belly, took out his guts, and so left him alive." With fiendish cruelty they pricked, stabbed and mangled in every part but where a wound would prove immediately fatal, men and women of all ages, leaving them to wallow in their own blood and starve to death. They plucked out men's eyes, or cut off their hands. Some they buried alive; some they stoned to death; others they pushed into fires feet foremost and slowly roasted them. They hung up women who were big with child, ripped open their bellies so that the infants dropped out, throwing these living babies to wild dogs. They took the twelve-year-old child of one, Thomas Stratton, and boiled him in a cauldron; while another youngster had his backbone broken and was left in the fields to die slowly.

"In the town of Sligo, all the Protestants were first robbed of their estates, then cast into gaol, and about midnight were all stript naked, and were then most cruelly and barbarously murdered with swords, axes, skeins, &c. Some of them being women great with child, their infants thrust out their arms and legs at the wounds, after which execrable murders, these hell-hounds laid the dead naked bodies of the men upon the naked bodies of the women, in a most immodest posture; where they left them till the next day to be looked upon by the Irish, who beheld it with great delight."

Even this does not exhaust the catalogue of torture. They forced women to hang their own husbands, mothers to drown their own children and maidens to execute their own parents.

From Moore's *Martyrology*, 1809.

TORTURES INFLICTED ON THE PROTESTANTS, BY THE IRISH PAPISTS,
IN 1642

CHAPTER XII

THE PERSECUTION OF THE WITCHES

The War Upon Demonology

IN the history of persecution, the torturing of the wizards and witches through many centuries of civilization represents one of the biggest blotches upon the face of Christianity. Sorcerers and magicians, real and suspected, had to endure not only the persecution of the Inquisition, representing all the accumulated hatred of the Catholic faith, but they had to endure the persecution of the Protestants as well. Of no avail was it for them to flee from the Catholic ridden countries of continental Europe to seek refuge in Protestant England, for here they were not one whit better off. As worshippers of the devil they had the whole civilized world against them.

The peculiar beliefs and superstitions attached to or associated with witchcraft caused those who were suspected of practising the craft to be extremely likely to be subjected to tortures of greater degree than any ordinary heretic or criminal. More, certain specific torments were invented for use against them. Thus it was held that witches were secretly marked by the devil, and the search for these marks, in itself, led to a form of torture being devised that was restricted to those accused of sorcery. Thus, too, the application of the water ordeal to witches long after this form of persecution had ceased to be employed in the trial of any other type of offender (cf. Chapter XXIII).

Although there had been sporadic attacks on witches from the time of Noah, it was not until towards the end of the fifteenth century, when Pope Innocent VIII issued his notorious bull which specifically mentioned sorcerers and witches as enemies of the Christian religion who must be rooted out and exterminated, that the witch persecutions in grim earnest and on a wholesale scale really began. Henrich Kraemer and Johann Sprenger were appointed as inquisitors charged with carrying the war against witchcraft in North Germany to a successful conclusion. These Dominican monks, who were, I strongly suspect, sadists masquerading as fanatical Christians, were the joint authors of that remarkable work on witchcraft entitled *Malleus Malificarum*.

Thus was inaugurated, on the continent of Europe, a long campaign against sorcery and magic in all their forms; a campaign marked by the seizure and handing over to the Inquisition of many thousands of men and women whose only crime was the practice of a form of religion differing from Christianity in certain slight details, and the practice of various forms of magic on a par with the spiritualism, clairvoyance, levitations, trance speaking, *et al.* of our own enlightened days.

Many and varied were the punishments which these unfortunate men and women, most of whom were innocent of the charges made against them, were compelled to undergo. They were whipped or beaten, in an endeavour to induce them to confess the crimes with which they were charged. If whipping failed, other tortures were applied. Huguet Aubry, after being imprisoned for nearly a year, and tortured on many occasions, was thrown into a river and suspended from a tree; Le petit Henriot, after imprisonment and torture, had his feet burnt to such an extent that he became a cripple for life.[1] Confession ensured being burnt alive; failure to confess meant lifelong incarceration, or a succession of tortures which eventually ended in death.

The Mark of Satan

Although confession was deemed desirable, it was not always considered necessary in order to ensure conviction. In many cases, evidence provided by witnesses was sufficient in itself. The presence of the devil's mark alone was enough. It was generally recognized that, of these devil's marks, there were two kinds: visible and invisible. The visible marks were well known and easily discoverable, being moles, warts, birth-stains, supernumerary teats, and

[1] H. C. Lea, *A History of the Inquisition of the Middle Ages*, Vol. III, p. 532.

various spots or cicatrixes of unusual or abnormal appearance. It was in an effort to find these marks that the witch was stripped naked and had all her hair shaved off. As regards the invisible marks, it would appear that these might well have baffled every kind of search. But the witch-finders were nothing if not ingenious. They held that there was one characteristic which any invisible badge of the devil invariably possessed: the flesh at the precise point where the mark existed was insusceptible to pain and would fail to bleed even if punctured by the sharpest implement. If there existed on any part of the skin surface a spot that did not bleed when cut, then need one seek no further for evidence that the woman was a witch. In his learned treatise on witchcraft, King James I said that the absence of blood was an infallible sign.

Whenever, therefore, a woman was accused of witchcraft the "bleeding test" was made. A long thin needle was used, and the witch-finder (who was usually paid by results) systematically prodded all parts of the body in order to discover a spot that failed to yield blood or until the accused woman ceased to cry out in pain. The test was usually successful. It was successful because the torture occasioned by this continuous prodding was of such a degree of severity that either the woman, in order to put an end to it, ceased to give any indication of experiencing pain; or, because, as a result of long continued torture, her body had become insensitive to pain and her mind was in a daze.

In the 1785 edition of Beccaria's notable *Essay on Crimes and Punishments,* there is a notable description of such a trial. I reproduce it here.

"In the year 1652, a country woman, named Michelle Chaudron, of the little territory of Geneva, met the Devil in her way from the city. The Devil gave her a kiss, received her homage, and imprinted on her upper lip, and on her right breast, the mark which he is wont to bestow upon his favourites. This seal of the Devil is a little sign upon the skin, which renders it insensible, as we are assured by all the demonographical civilians of those times.

The Devil ordered Michelle Chaudron to bewitch two young girls. She obeyed her master punctually, the parents of the two girls accusing her of dealing with the Devil. The girls being confronted with the criminal, declared that they felt a continual prickling in some parts of their bodies, and that they were possessed. Physicians were called, at least men that passed for physicians in those days. They visited the girls. They sought for the seal of the Devil on the body of Michelle, which seal is called, in the verbal process, the Satanical mark. Into one of these marks they plunged a long needle, which was already no small torture. Blood issued from the wound, and Michelle testified, by her cries, that the part was not insensible. The judges not finding sufficient proof that Michelle Chaudron was a witch, ordered her to be tortured, which infallibly produced the proof they wanted. The poor wretch, overcome by torment, confessed, at last, everything they desired.

"The physicians sought again for the Satanical mark, and found it in a little black spot on one of her thighs. Into this they plunged their needle. The poor creature, exhausted and almost expiring with the pain of the torture, was insensible to the needle, and did not cry out. She was instantly condemned to be burnt, but the world beginning at this time to be a little more civilized, she was previously strangled."

Witch-Hunting in Britain

In England, much the same methods were adopted, and although there was never at any time a branch of the Inquisition, or anything resembling it, in operation, the persecution of the witches was pursued with a degree of rigour equalling anything attempted on the Continent. Indeed, as regards the discovery of witches by "pricking," that arch-fiend Matthew Hopkins excelled the lot of them. Hopkins was a lawyer, a native of Suffolk, and the author of *The Discovery of Witches,* a publication which, although a smaller and more restricted affair altogether, might well, in a supplementary sense, have been bracketed with the *Malleus Malificarum* itself. From 1644 to 1647, he operated throughout the eastern part of England, searching everywhere for witches and tracking to their doom all of whom he could hear. The success of his efforts may be judged by the fact that he was responsible for the death of over two hundred women in this three years' period. His method was to search the suspected witch for the devil's mark, a search which he pursued with such thoroughness, it was said, that no one ever escaped. The dice were loaded against them, for, as it transpired after his death, this cunning sadist held a trump card. He possessed a specially constructed blunt-ended needle, fixed in a wooden handle. The needle, on being pressed against the flesh, telescoped into the handle, giving the impression that it had penetrated the flesh to the hilt without drawing a cry or a drop of blood from the accused. When all else failed, Hopkins had recourse to this trick.

This practice of " pricking," as it was called, was widely adopted in Scotland. The " prickers " were in great demand, travelling from town to town in their search for witches. In 1749, John Kincaid, the most cele-brated " pricker " of his day, was engaged by the magis-trates of Newcastle for this purpose; the terms of engage-ment being that, in addition to his travelling expenses, he should receive twenty shillings for every conviction. On Kincaid's arrival the bellman was sent through the town calling for informers. As a result thirty women were arrested and dragged to the town hall, where they were subjected to the " pricking " test. Twenty-seven of them were convicted.

The system obviously lent itself to abuses. Those women who could secure the money would gladly pay the informers to escape accusation, or the " pricker " to find them " innocent."

Often torture was applied to the suspected witch in order to secure a confession independent of and usually before any search was made for the devil's mark. Brand[1] quotes from a rare tract entitled *News from Scotland* (1591) a passage which states that a suspected witch was tortured with

[1] John Brand, *Observations on Popular Antiquities*, 1813.

" the pilliwinckes upon her fingers, which is a grievous
torture, and binding and wrenching her head with a
cord or rope, which is a most cruel torture also, they
upon search, found the enemy's mark to be in her fore-
crag, or forepart of her throat, and then she confessed
all. In another the Devil's mark was found upon her
privates."

Iron collars, and a contrivance known as the witch's
bridle, were used to induce confession, often in conjunction
with deprivation of sleep. In many cases several forms of
torment were tried one after another until success was
achieved. An outstanding example of this was the case of
Doctor Fian (alias John Cunningham) suspected of being a
sorcerer. The following account is taken from the pages of
Pitcairn's *Criminal Trials* (1833):

" To make him confesse, hee was commanded to have
a most strange torment, which was done in this manner
following. His nailes upon all his fingers were riven and
pulled off with an instrument called in Scottish a Turkas,
which in England wee call a payre of pincers, and under
everie nayle there was thrust in two needels over even
up to the heads. At all which torments notwithstanding,
the Doctor never shrouke anie whit; neither woulde he
then confesse it the sooner, for all the tortures inflicted
upon him. Then was hee, with all convenient speede,
by commandement, convaied againe to the torment of
the bootes, wherein hee continued a long time, and did
abide so many blowes in them, that his legges were crushed
and beaten together as small as might bee; and the bones
and flesh so bruised, that the bloud and marrow spouted
forth in great abundance; whereby, they were made un-
serviceable for ever."

Despite the failure of these terrible tortures to elicit any
confession, the accused was adjudged guilty. He was
strangled and his body burnt.

In England the last trial of anyone for witchcraft was
in 1712. The jury found the accused, Jane Wenham, guilty
and sentenced her to death, a sentence which was afterwards

repealed through the efforts of the judge, who had vainly endeavoured to induce the jury to discharge the prisoner. The last execution in Scotland, according to official records, was in 1722, though Captain Burt, in his *Letters from the North of Scotland,* affirms that a woman was burnt in 1727.

CHAPTER XIII

TORTURE IN CHINA, JAPAN AND INDIA

Judicial Torture in China

OF all the countries in all the world China has perhaps acquired a reputation for being the one place in which torture is more universal and takes stranger, more cruel, and more revolting forms than it does in any other part of the civilized and uncivilized globe. Much of this reputation is due to the description, in books of fiction, of forms of torture which have originated largely in the fertile imaginations of sensational novelists. It is true that as regards methods practised privately for purposes of revenge, in order to elicit information and from purely sadistic motives, torture, *in any country,* sometimes assumes most bizarre forms, and it is impossible, of course, to secure any reliable information or evidence as to the precise nature or extent of such practices. But as regards those tortures authorized by the Chinese authorities for purposes of inducing confession, as forms of punishment, or modes of execution, it is doubtful if they exceeded either in their elements of the bizarre or in their brutality, the methods adopted for similar purposes in many reputedly more civilized countries.

For forcing reluctant witnesses to speak, or criminals to confess, compression of the fingers or ankles was a favourite practice. Semedo describes the apparatus used as a kind of rack:

"For the feet they use an instrument called *Kia Quen.* It consisteth of three pieces of wood put in one traverse, that in the middle is fixt, the other two are moveable, between these the feet are put, where they are squeezed and prest, till the heel-bone run into the foot: for the hands they use also certain small pieces of wood between the fingers, they call them *Tean Zu,* then they straiten them very hard, and seale them round about with paper, and so they leave them for some space of time."[1]

Sir George Staunton, in his authoritative work on the *Penal Code of China,* written a century and a half later than Semedo's book, also refers to the use of these instruments of torture.

If the first application fails to elicit the truth, it is lawful to repeat the operation a second time.   These particular forms of torture, at the time of which Staunton wrote, at any rate, were used especially in cases of robbery and homicide.   They were not applicable, however, to criminals under fifteen years of age or over seventy; to the diseased or the crippled.   It is also worthy of note that, with rare exceptions, the ankle torture was reserved for male culprits, and the finger torture for females.

A more rigorous measure was beating with the bastinado, a terrible instrument of correction.   According to Semedo " They do many times die of the bastinadoes they receive."[2]

Methods of Punishment

Fornication by a monk merited the most severe punishment, according to Picart.   A hole was bored with a hot iron through his neck, and one end of an iron chain measuring some 60 feet in length, was put through this hole and secured.   Stark naked, the culprit was then led by the chain through the streets of the city.   Every time he attempted to lay hold of the chain in order to ease the pain caused by its dragging weight upon the open wound, another monk, walking behind and carrying a heavy whip, used this instrument with telling effect upon the fornicator's back. This procession continued until the victim had collected a specified sum of money for the monastery to which he was attached.[3]

For the punishment of a number of offences, notably those deemed to be minor ones, a peculiar kind of pillory has been used for centuries.   It is variously termed the

---

[1] F. Alvarez Semedo, *History of China,* London, 1655, p. 143.
[2] *Ibid.,* p. 141.
[3] B. Picart, *Religious Ceremonies,* 1737, Vol. IV, p. 230.

cangue, the *tcha,* or *kea.* The best description which I
have come across is that given by Semedo, who terms this
pillory the " punishment of *kian hao.*" I give the account
in the author's own words:

" It is a great thick board, four or five palmes
square, with a hole cut in the middle of it about the big-
ness of a man's neck. This they fasten about their
necks, and to it are hung two scrolls of paper of a hand's
breadth, wherein are written his fault, and the cause of
his punishment; they serve also to show that the board
hath not been opened; and so with these great boards
about their necks, these poor wretches are brought out
every day and exposed to shame in the public streets, for
fifteen, twenty or thirty days, according as they are
adjudged by their sentence, whose greatest rigor is that
during all that time these boards are not taken off their
necks, neither night nor day."[1]

This punishment is usually preceded with a severe beating with the bastinado, which leaves the culprit in a weak
and pitiable condition. As from the nature of the pillory
it is impossible for the wearer to reach his mouth with his
hands, he is dependent absolutely for food and drink upon
the kindness of others. Those with neither relatives nor
friends are in sore danger of dying through exhaustion or
starvation.

At the time of which Semedo writes it was the invariable
custom to secure all prisoners at night. The gaolers were not
content with the fact that criminals were locked up in the
prisons and that guards were within easy reach. The
prison bed was made of planks. At the bottom of the bed
was a heavy piece of timber in which were holes through
which the prisoner's feet were pushed, the apparatus then
being clamped in such a way that it was impossible to draw
them out again. His hands also were manacled and a
heavy iron chain drawn tightly across his chest. In this
manner he was secured so thoroughly to his bed that it was
out of the question for him to so much as turn over.

Flagellation with the bamboo has always been the most

---

[1] F. Alvarez Semedo, *History of China,* p. 141.

After Picart.

TORTURE OF THE CHAIN—AN ANCIENT CHINESE PUNISHMENT
(See Text, page 103.)

From Macartney's *Embassy to China*, 1796.

CHINESE PUNISHMENT OF THE TCHA
(See Text, page 104.)

frequent form of punishment. The culprit is laid down with his face to the floor, and in this position is beaten lightly but persistently upon the naked buttocks. The monotonous regularity of the blows soon begins to have its effect. Sir Henry Norman, who witnessed the punishment being given, says:

> " After a few more minutes of the dactylic rap-tap-tap, rap-tap-tap, a deep groan broke from the prisoner's lips. I walked over to look at him, and saw that his flesh was blue under the flogging. Then it became congested with blood, and whereas at first he had lain quiet of his own accord, now a dozen men were holding him tight."[1]

The same observer mentions a peculiar form of Chinese torture known as " kneeling on chains." The criminal is suspended by means of a cord fastened to the thumbs and big toes, in such a manner that his knees, with the whole weight of his body behind them, rest upon a small coiled chain, " with sharp-edged links."[2] The suffering is of an intense nature and one can well imagine that, apart from its use as a method of punishment, admissions of guilt are often secured in this way.

Capital Punishment in China

The methods of execution are strangulation, decollation, and the terrible death known as " Torture of the Knife " or *Ling-chy,* often described as the " Death by the Thousand Cuts,"[3] and occasionally more extravagantly as " Cutting into ten thousand pieces." It is also referred to in China as execution by the " slow process " or by the " slicing process," and is usually reserved for the punishment of parricide. According to the various accounts given by travellers, the precise technique adopted in this form of execution varies in different parts of China.

[1] Henry Norman, *The People and Politics of the Far East,* Fisher Unwin, 1895, p. 221.
[2] *Ibid.,* p. 223.
[3] Many victims of the atrocities connected with the Communist fighting in South-West China during 1927-8, were executed in this way. (Cf. p. 269.)

In some instances death may come quickly; in others it may be unduly delayed, according to the luck of the victim, or, more likely, the secret instructions given to the executioner. There is a basket, covered with a cloth or other material, in which is a collection of knives. Each of these knives is marked with the name of some portion of the body or some limb. The executioner pushes his hand under the cloth into the basket and draws out a knife at random. He then proceeds to cut off whatever limb or part of the body is indicated on the knife. It has been stated that the relatives of the condemned man bribe the executioner to "find" as speedily as possible the knife destined to be plunged into the heart.

There seems ground for the belief that the technique already described has been largely if not entirely displaced by a method of execution in which no element of chance is allowed to interfere with the infliction of one of the most frightful forms imaginable of death by torture. No basket with its multiplicity of marked knives enter into it. A single keen bladed instrument is used, and the slicings, cuttings, hackings and amputations proceed slowly step by step through the whole ghastly allotted course.

It is this method which is described by Sir Henry Norman, who says the criminal is secured upon a rough cross, and the executioner, "grasping handfuls from the fleshy parts of the body, such as the thighs and the breasts," slices them off. The "joints and the excrescences of the body" are next cut away one by one, followed by the amputation of the nose, the ears, the toes and the fingers. "Then the limbs are cut off piecemeal at the wrists and the ankles, the elbows and knees, the shoulders and hips. Finally, the victim is stabbed to the heart and his head cut off."[1]

Torture in Japan

The courts of Japan, like those of China, recognized torture as a legitimate means of eliciting the truth from criminals, from those who were accused or suspected of offences, and from witnesses who were reluctant to give evidence or to tell the truth.

[1] *Ibid.*, p. 225.

TORTURE OF DEATH BY THE THOUSAND CUTS

From a Model in the possession of the Wellcome Historical Medical Museum, London.

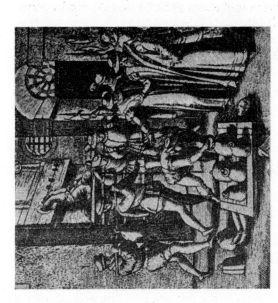

PEINE FORTE ET DURE OR PRESSING TO DEATH
(See Text, page 155.)

From an Engraving in *Theatrum Crudelitatum Haereticorum*, 1592.

During the notorious Tokugawa regime, which flourished from 1652 until the middle of the nineteenth century, says Murdoch, four different forms of torture were employed. The most frequently adopted of these methods was flagellation. A special whip was used for the purpose. It was made of three strips of split bamboo, bound together.   It made a formidable weapon, the sharp edges of the bamboo cutting into the flesh like knives.   It was applied to the shoulders and the buttocks, and anything up to 150 strokes could be given.   "Hugging the stone" was another method. Heavy weights of stone or other material were piled upon the victim's knees while he knelt upon a number of sharp-edged, three-cornered flints.   In the third method of torture, the prisoner's arms and legs were bound so tightly with rope that his life was endangered. He was kept in this position until the signs of approaching death manifested themselves.   In the fourth torture the prisoner's wrists were bound with the utmost tightness behind his back.   He was then suspended from a hook in the ceiling. All his weight resting upon the wrists, the cord gradually sunk into the flesh, cutting it to the bone.   If one torture failed to produce satisfactory results, another method was tried, allowing the prisoner to rest a day or two in the meantime.[1]

Judicial torture was abolished in Japan in 1873.   Actually, however, there is every probability that here, as elsewhere, the practice is by no means extinct.   Longford states that years after its abolition by the Japanese

> " the present writer had every reason to believe that torture was still and not rarely used in local police offices, while it is notorious that it was freely used with pristine severity on alleged rebels, both in Korea and Formosa, often on persons who were entirely innocent.   I knew, from unquestionable authority, of many instances in Formosa."[2]

[1] James Murdoch, *A History of Japan*, revised and edited by Joseph H. Longford, Kegan Paul, 1926.
[2] Joseph H. Longford in his revised edition of the late James Murdoch's *History of Japan*, Kegan Paul, 1926, Vol. III, p. 338n.

A Terrible Campaign of Religious Persecution

The seventeenth century was marked in particular by a long record of torture and persecution rivalling anything known in the history of any race. An effort was made to drive out of the country all those professing Christianity. Every method practised by the ancient Romans, and almost every method known to the Inquisition of Spain, appear to have been called into use. Men, women and children were stripped of all coverings and thrown into the rivers and the sea. Placed on horseback, they were driven through the streets while boiling water was continually thrown over them. In the hot springs with which certain volcanic regions of Japan abound, the victims were immersed again and again until they were literally boiled to death. At Nagasaki, in the September of 1622, we learn that fifty Christians were burnt alive. Others had their bodies torn apart, each leg being harnessed to an ox, and the animals being driven in opposite directions.

This account, grim though it be, does not exhaust the lengths to which, in the blessed name of religion, these persecutors were prepared to go. But let me give the rest of the terrible story in the words of a contemporary chronicler.

" They forced the women and more tender maids to go upon their hands and feet, bowing, supporting and dragging them naked in the presence of thousands through the streets; that done, they caused them to be ravished and lain with by Russians and villains, and then throwing them so stript and abused, into great deep tubs full of snakes and adders, which crept by several passages into their bodies, suffered them to perish unspeakable miseries in that fearful manner. They thrust hurds into the mothers privities, and binding the sons about with the same combustible matter, thrust and forced them, as also the fathers and daughters, to set fire to each other, whereby they underwent unconceivable torments and pains: some they cloathed with sods, and poured hot scalding water continually upon them, tortured them in that manner till they died, which dured

two or three daies, according to the strength of the party;
hundreds of them being stript naked, and burnt in the
foreheads that they might be known, and driven into the
woods and forests, all men being commanded by proclamation, upon pain of death, not to assist them with
either meat, drink, clothing or lodging; many more put
into pinfolds upon the sea-shore, and kept there half
their time dry and half wet, being every tide overflown
by the sea; but these were permitted to eat and drink,
to keep them longer alive in their misery, which lasted
ordinarily ten or twelve daies.   These bloody executioners put out the parents eyes, and placing their little
children by them, pinched and plagued them whole days
long, enforcing them with tears of blood to call and cry
to their helpless fathers and mothers for an end of their
sufferings, which had no period but with their lives,
whilst their woeful parents, unable to assist either their
children or themselves, did often die in their presence,
whom they could not see for grief or sorrow.   All these
miseries, too long and too many to relate, were born by
the poor Christians with constancy to a miracle; except
some few, who not able to resist the bitterness of these
torments abandoned their faith, for some relaxation from
pain.   Once a year they precisely renewed their inquisition, and then every individual person must sign in their
church-books, with his blood, that he renounces Christianity; and yet all would not do, for many hundreds
of Christians are found every year, and destroyed with
variety of torments.   At last they found a more hellish
and exquisite way of torturing than before; they hung
these sufferers by the heels, their heads in pits, which
to give the blood some vent, they slash lightly cross-
wayes (but they do that now no more) and in this posture they live several daies, ten or twelve, and speak
sensibly to the very last: the greatness of this torment
surpasseth all other, being beyond all humane strength
to suffer and be undergone, but by such who are ex-
traordinarily strengthened from above.   This extremity
hath indeed (by reason of its continuance) forced many
to renounce their religion; and some of them who hung
two or three daies, assured me that the pains they en-

dured were wholly unsufferable, no fire nor no torture
equalling their languor and violence."[1]

Japanese Methods of Punishment

The fundamental principle of Japanese judicial punishments, as of those pertaining to all Oriental nations, from
time immemorial to the present day, is that of " an eye for
an eye and a tooth for a tooth."   The reformation of the
prisoner forms no basic part of their system of penology.
Corporal punishment, inflicted with the wicked bastinado,
plays a major role.

The methods of execution have always been numerous.
Crucifixion was largely used for regicides.   The " death
dance " was sometimes adopted, the condemned man being
enveloped in a thick, tight-fitting garment made of reeds
and other inflammable material.   A light was applied and
the criminal, compelled by the terrible agony he was enduring, leaped and danced about until movement was no
longer possible.

Those who were privileged to be allowed to avail themselves of death by suicide, or *hari-kari,* usually did so.
According to the Japanese code, death is preferable to dishonour, and suicide is preferred to death at the hands of
another.   The committing of *hari-kari* condoned any and
every crime.   Taking the disembowelling knife in his hand,
the condemned criminal ripped open his own bowels with
two swift deep cuts in the form of a cross.

Another terrible form of execution is known as the
" execution of twenty-one cuts," in which the prisoner is
literally hacked to pieces, the art of the executioner consisting of managing to slice away limb after limb and
piece after piece, before the twenty-first stroke acts as a
coup de grâce.   It bears a very close resemblance to the
Chinese " Torture of the Knife."

The rebel chief, Mowung, was executed in this
manner, and the following account is from the pens of
two eye-witnesses of the event.

[1] Francis Caron and Joost Schorten, *A True Description of the Mighty
Kingdoms of Japan and Siam,* translated from the Dutch by Roger Manley,
London, 1671, pp. 66-9.

" With superhuman command of self, the unhappy
Mowung bore silently the slow and deliberate slicing-
off—first of his cheeks, then of his breasts, the muscles
of upper and lower arms, the calves of his legs, etc. etc.,
care being taken throughout to avoid touching any immediately vital part. Once only he murmured an
entreaty that he might be killed outright—a request, of
course, unheeded by men who took a savage pleasure in
skilfully torturing their victim."[1]

Torture in India

In no country in the world was torture more widespread than in India before and at the time of the English
occupancy. It was practised as a punishment for a very
large number of offences, religious and civil. Mutilations
were common. We learn from Forbes that for blasphemy
it was customary to cut out the tongue. Grose instances
the case of a Malabar woman having her breasts cut off by
order of the Queen of Attinga. The woman had appeared
in the presence of the queen with her breasts uncovered.

Ordeals of fire, water, poison, the balance, and boiling
oil, were employed in the trial of accused persons (see
Chapter XXIII), especially on the Malabar coast. According
to Forbes, the custom was so firmly incorporated in and
recognized as part of the life of the people that it received
the sanction of the British government.

Corporal punishment, apart from its use as a means of
castigation for offenders of all kinds and classes, was used
with or without legal sanction by all who employed servants. Parents used the bastinado and the whip on their
children. From long practice, those using the bastinado
acquired remarkable proficiency in wielding it, and in
selecting the most sensitive parts at which to strike. The
elbows, the ankles, the shins, and even the scrotum were
included among these.

The stocks, forcibly bending back the fingers, branding
with hot irons, immersion in water to the point of drown-

[1] R. Mounteney Jephson and Edward Pennell Elmhirst, *Our Life in
Japan*, London, 1869, p. 33.

ing, deprivation of sleep, dipping the hands and feet in boiling oil, starvation, and all the category of torments used in England and the continental countries were in regular use. There are indications that the rack, the wheel and other tortures used in Europe by the Inquisition were at one time employed.

According to Percival (*Ceylon,* p. 124) at the time of the seizure of Colombo by the English, both a rack and a wheel were discovered in the prison.' These and other forms of torture were used for the punishment of criminals and slaves. At one time, too, in Ceylon, a favourite mode of execution adopted by the Dutch was to break the criminal's thighs with an iron club previous to giving the death stroke.

In addition to all these methods of torture, there were also used many specific methods peculiar to India, indicated by environmental conditions : thus driving the prisoner up and down for hour after hour in the broiling sun; tying him to a tree and smearing his face with honey to attract red ants; imprisoning, by means of a cloth covering or a cage, on some sensitive part of the body, such as the armpit, the breast, and, in women, the pudenda, a biting insect (e.g. the carpenter beetle or the poollah) and leaving it to gnaw the victim's flesh—a form of torture producing unendurable agony. Sometimes a prisoner was chained to the rear of a cart and forced to run for long distances during the hottest part of the day. Or a piece of strong but thin heated wire was wound around one arm, or both arms, sometimes in several places, after which cold water was applied continually to induce contraction and consequent sinking into the flesh. Another diabolically ingenious method was to tie two criminals together by their hair, so that practically every movement made was productive of pain.

The Terrible KITTEE and Other Indian Tortures

The *kittee* was an instrument of torture in regular use. It bore some relationship to the thumbscrew so popular at one time in England and Scotland. Con-

---

[1] In Ceylon judicial torture was abolished in 1799.

structed of wood, and resembling somewhat a household
lemon-squeezer, various sensitive parts of the body, such
as the hands, the feet, the ears, the nose, the breasts of
women and the exterior genitals of men, were squeezed
between the two plates until the victim could stand the
terrible agony no longer or, as often happened, he fainted
under the strain. It often caused permanent disablement.
A variation of the *kittee* consisted of two boards, between
which the hands or feet of the prisoner were compressed,
sometimes by the executioner standing upon the upper
board, and sometimes by heaping heavy weights upon it
and leaving the victim to suffer for hours at a stretch.

Another favourite torture was termed *anundal*. It
would appear to be of purely Eastern origin. The nearest
approach to it among European methods was the Scavenger's Daughter. But with this Oriental method no
appliances, other than ropes or cords, were required.
Anundal consisted of compelling the victim to remain for
a considerable length of time in a most unnatural or abnormal, and consequently painful, position. The ingenuity
of the executioner was given full play. The head of the
prisoner would be forced down and tied to his feet by
means of a rope or belt passed around his neck and under
the toes. Or one leg would be forced upwards to the
uttermost extent and fastened to the neck, compelling the
victim to stand in this agonizing position. Or the arms
and legs, forcibly interlaced to the point almost of dislocation, were bound so as to be immovable. In other cases
heavy stones were fastened to the victim's back, which was
often stripped naked, the sharp edges cutting into the
flesh. In each variety of punishment it frequently happened that the executioner would sit astride of the culprit's
body at frequent intervals in order to increase the torment,
and in almost every case the torture was practised under
the powerful rays of the Indian sun.

In the Report of the Commissioners for the Investigation of alleged cases of torture in the Madras Presidency,
presented to Parliament in 1855, reference is made to the
use of *anundal* by government officials in the collection of
land revenue. Vencatachella Rajaulee, in conjunction with
his father, were put to torture in order to compel payment

of an extraordinary assessment of ten rupees. Both men were " placed in *anundal*, their legs tied together, and their heads tied to their feet in a stooping posture; their hands were tied behind them, and stones placed upon their backs; in which posture they were made to stand from six in the morning until noon. It will hardly be matter of surprise that the father died the following month." In another instance, a Ryot named Singuriah, " who refused to pay the sum of one rupee four annas (2s. 6d.) had his hands tied behind his back and his head bound to his feet with a coir rope, for two hours."

A third most popular method was known as *thoodasavary*. It involved the use of no apparatus. It could be practised on the instant and on the spot by a strong policeman. Usually two or three policemen participated in the job, which was practically equivalant to what, in these days, in England and America, is known as " beating up." The prisoner was manhandled by his tormenters, who pulled him about by the ears, the nose, the hair, or by bunching together the soft flesh in various parts of the body. Often, in the process, the moustache or some of the hair of the head was pulled out by the roots.

Another form of torment which, although not apparently in itself particularly painful or dangerous, in reality, through its long continuance, produced " intolerable agony," consisted of forcing the prisoner to adopt a squatting attitude in which his posterior touched the floor. In this position, his arms were forced " under and inside the thighs," and he was compelled " to take hold of his ears, one with each hand." Any attempt to move by a fraction from this posture was the signal for a blow from the guard continually on the watch.

All these methods were used by tax collectors and others for inducing the payment of dues and debts, as well as for eliciting confessions and securing evidence in criminal cases. Occasionally, too, ingenious and sadistic officials used lesser known forms of torture to effect their purpose. An account of such an incident taking place at Tattah, in the seventeenth century, is given by Forbes.

" The collector of customs was a Hindoo of family,

wealth and credit.   Lulled into security from his interest at court, and suspecting no evil, he was surprised
by a visit from the vizier, with a company of armed
men, to demand his money; which being secreted, no
threatenings could induce him to discover.   A variety
of tortures were inflicted to extort a confession; one
was a sofa, with a platform of tight cordage in network,
covered with a chintz palampore, which concealed a
bed of thorns placed under it: the collector, a corpu-
lent banian, was then stripped of his jama, or muslin
robe, and ordered to lie down on the couch: the cords
bending with his weight, sunk on the bed of thorns;
those long and piercing thorns of the baubul or forest
acacia, which being placed purposely with their points
upwards, lacerated the wretched man, whether in
motion or at rest.   For two days and nights he bore the
torture without revealing the secret; his tormenters
fearing he would die before their purpose was effected,
had recourse to another mode of compulsion.   When
nature was nearly exhausted, they took him from the
bed, and supported him on the floor, until his infant
son, an only child, was brought into the room; and
with him a bag containing a fierce cat, into which they
put the child, and tied up the mouth of the sack.   The
agents of cruelty stood over them with bamboos, ready
at a signal to beat the bag, and enrage the animal to
destroy the child: this was too much for a father's
heart! he produced his treasure."[1]

Another curious method, at one time common on the
Malabar coast, of inducing the payment of fines or of
punishing crimes, is described by the same authority.
The chief of the tribe, who carried out the torture in person, fixed a sharp pointed stone on the crown of the victim's head.   On top of this he placed a much larger and
heavier stone, which he proceeded to bind firmly and
tightly by a strap or rope carried under the chin.   Continued refusal to pay the sum demanded or to confess (and
in the case of punishment for a crime, the severity of the
offence) indicated the binding of additional heavy stones

[1] James Forbes, *Oriental Memoirs*, 1813, Vol. II, p. 429.

one upon the other, causing continually increasing pressure upon the small sharp stone, which ultimately caused a most painful death.

Other ingenious tortures and the manner of their application were referred to in the Report (already mentioned) concerning torture in the Madras Presidency. Let us glance at a few of them.

> "Verasawmy Naidoo and Iyeppa Naidoo were tortured by the application of a rope tightly wound round the thighs, so as to force the blood into the feet, which causes great pain."

At Syadoorgum (a village in the Cuddalore district), one Soobapatha Pillay was "tied by the legs, and hung up with his head downwards." While in this position, powdered chilli was forced into his nostrils and a strong belt was passed around his waist and tightened. The details of this torture are, it is added, "too revoltingly indecent to be referred to."

> "Murshid Aly Khan, who became Newab of Bengal in 1718, made defaulting zemindars drink buffalos' milk mixed with salt, till they were brought to death's door by diarrhœa."

A curious form of execution, involving torture preceding death, was the practice of having the criminal trampled to death by an elephant. The following account of such an execution, at Baroda, in 1814, culled from a Bombay journal, appears in *The Percy Anecdotes* (Vol. VIII, pp. 26-7):

> "The man was a slave, and two days before had murdered his master, brother to a native chieftain, named Ameer Sahib. About eleven o'clock the elephant was brought out, with only the driver on his back, surrounded by natives with bamboos in their hands. The criminal was placed three yards behind on the ground, his legs tied by three ropes, which were fastened to a ring on the right hind leg of the animal.

At every step the elephant took, it jerked him forwards, and eight or ten steps must have dislocated every limb, for they were loose and broken when the elephant had proceeded five hundred yards. The man, though covered with mud, showed every sign of life, and seemed to be in the most excruciating torments. After having been tortured in this manner about an hour, he was taken to the outside of the town, when the elephant, which is instructed for such purposes, is backed, and puts his foot on the head of the criminal."

Torture of School Children

There is evidence to the effect that torture was still rampant in India in the nineteenth century. So deeply steeped in the social and penal life of the community was it that even the children attending the village schools in Bengal were persecuted. According to the Rev. J. Long of Calcutta, in 1869, hoisting boys to the ceiling by means of a pulley, placing them in sacks with stinging nettles, and the application to the naked body of nettles dipped in water were favourite modes of inflicting punishment. These may rank as minor torments, seeing they did not endanger life or limb, but tortures they were nevertheless.

Some Bizarre Forms of Torment

In Hahhed's *Code of Gentoo Laws* we read:

"If a sooder listens to the Vedas of the Shaster, then heated oil shall be poured into his ears; and arzeez and wax shall be melted together, and the orifices of the ears shall be stopped up therewith."

In fact, there seems strong grounds for believing that the majority of the tortures employed so lavishly in the seventeenth century were used just as merrily in the nineteenth, together with certain new forms which the ingenuity of sadistic tormenters had discovered.

Thus the bull's-hide torture, in which the prisoner,

tightly bound hand and foot, was sewn up in the newly flayed hide of a buffalo. As the hide slowly dried, it gradually shrunk, causing a prolonged and agonizing death. Somewhat similar, but even more terrible, was the sheep-skin torture, practised so largely by the Mahrattas. The warm and well-stretched skin of a freshly killed sheep was wrapped as tightly as possible around the nude body of the criminal, and sewn firmly in this position. The culprit, in this queer garment, was then exposed to the full power of the tropical sun. As the hide gradually dried and contracted it drew with it the flesh of the prisoner. Speedily putrefaction set in, and this coupled with hunger and thirst, brought death at last, but not until the victim had lived through æons of torment.

In the torture of the rope, a cord or rope was tightened around the abdomen and various other parts until circulation was impeded. Pieces of flesh were plucked out with pincers; and women's breasts were twisted and mutilated with the same tool. A variation of *kittee* consisted of compressing the chest between two bamboo rods, one of them being placed under the shoulders and the other across the chest of the victim. In this position two powerful men exerted pressure at the ends of the uppermost bamboo. Similarly the fingers were crushed between bamboo rods. In other cases the four fingers of one hand were bunched and tied tightly together with strong cord. Bamboo splints or iron wedges were then hammered between the fingers. Another favourite method was to tie the criminal securely, lay him on his back on the ground, and then place stones, weights, etc., upon his chest—in other words, the old *peine forte et dure* cropping up again in India one hundred years after its disuse in Europe.

According to a writer in the *Spectator* (December 23, 1893) a Persian prince, within living memory, "bricked-up brigands in a wall with their heads exposed for the vultures to eat." And, says the same authority, "under the old Burmese *régime*, on the 'testimony of an eye-witness,' the children of traitors were pounded with heavy pestles in wooden mortars."

CHINESE TORTURE : TEARING THE LIMBS

CHINESE TORTURE : SAWING A WOMAN IN TWO

THE TORTURE OF SLAVES IN THE WEST INDIES, MAURITIUS AND THE UNITED STATES OF AMERICA

The Traffic in Human Beings

THE torture of the negro slaves in the British West Indies, in the cotton-growing states of North America, and in many another part of the world, represents a major disgrace to civilization. That the British government, for so many generations, upheld this terrible treatment of human beings, ranking them with dogs and cattle, is a scar that will ever remain. In a bitter attack upon this disgraceful and pernicious trade and the men who engaged in it, Mr. Stephen said:

> "Why Shylock, raging for his pound of flesh, was a merciful man compared with Britons in the West Indies, who set their inventions to work to 'find reasons' to indulge themselves in the pleasure of whipping innocent men, women and children, their own dependants, and entitled to look up to them for protection!"

The American slave trade goes back to the time of Christopher Columbus. It may be questionable whether or not the explorer and adventurer was responsible for the introduction of syphilis into Europe, but there is no manner of doubt respecting the part he played in the traffic in human flesh. He seized hundreds of the natives inhabiting the West Indian islands, transported them to Spain, and sold them to the highest bidders in the market-place of Seville.

The settling of the whites in the West Indian islands led to the demand for cheap labour to work on the plantations. It was to Las Casas that occurred the bright idea of importing negro slaves from Africa. In 1563, the first English importation of African slaves occurred.

There are indications that the English had no objections to slavery at this time. There was little if any opposition. As comparatively late as the middle of the seventeenth century a British attorney-general stated that, in his opinion, "negroes, *being pagans*, might justly be held in slavery, even in England itself."[1]

Once started, the flow of Africans to the West Indies gathered rapidly in volume. Men and women both, were in constant demand. Mortality, through disease, ill-treatment, and torture, was abnormally high. Breeding was at a low ebb. It was not encouraged, it being cheaper to purchase imported adult slaves than to rear them. The demand for fresh cargoes of human flesh was greater therefore than the supply.

But negroes did not constitute the sole form which these batches of human lifestock, exported from England like so many bales of cloth, took. Criminals, and in those days the most petty theft branded one as a criminal, were sent in thousands to the West Indies and the southern American states. On arrival they were sold into slavery and a "living death."

The figures relative to the slave population indicate the enormous growth of the movement. In the island of Jamaica alone, the number of slaves, in 1658, three years after its capture by the British, was 1,400. In 1670, it was 8,000. Fifty or so years later the slave population had jumped to 80,000. In 1775 it had reached 190,000. By the close of the eighteenth century it stood around 250,000. And in the year of grace 1825, the figure had reached the colossal total of 314,300. In the decade (1751-61) no fewer than 71,115 Africans were landed on the island. The average selling price was £30 a head.[2] Little wonder the trade, with all its risks and despite the heavy death-rate during transportation, attracted those who saw, or who pretended to see, nothing wrong in this traffic in human beings.

The life of a slave was one long torture. It started with his capture by the raiding parties; it ended with his death on a West Indian plantation. The conditions under which

---

[1] Horace Greeley, *The American Conflict*, Hartford, 1864.
[2] Quoted by the Rev. G. W. Bridges, *The Annals of Jamaica*, London, 1828.

the captured slaves were shipped to the islands were so
terrible that even to visualize them to-day must send a
shudder of horror through anyone with the faintest trace
of humanitarianism in his make-up. In the English ship
Brookes, engaged regularly in the West Indian slave trade,
the space allowed for a man was 6 feet by 1 foot 4 inches;
for a woman 5 feet by 1 foot 4 inches; for a boy 5 feet by
1 foot 2 inches; and for a girl 4 feet 6 inches by 1 foot.[1]
Thus were the negroes stowed between decks like bales of
wool, to be battered across the thousands of miles that
separated them from America. Little wonder that, under
such conditions, the losses during the long voyage were
prodigious. In a discussion in the House of Commons it
was mentioned that

> "Mr. Isaac Wilson had stated in his evidence that the
> ship in which he sailed, only three years ago, was of
> 370 tons; and that she carried 602 slaves, of these she
> lost 155. There were three or four other vessels in
> company with her, and which belonged to the same
> owners. One of these carried 450, and buried 200;
> another carried 466 and buried 73; another 546 and
> buried 158; and from the four together, after the landing
> of their cargoes, 220 died."[2]

Once the slaves had been landed and sold for labour
in the islands their persecutions increased in number and
extent. Before, the treatment they received, terrible as it
was, stopped short of mutilation and flogging in its more
fiendish forms, for the good and sufficient reason that a slave
who was a cripple or whose back was scarred with unheal-
able weals would not fetch as good a price as would one
sound in appearance. But when a planter had purchased a
slave he was in many cases moved by no such motives of
clemency. The probability was that he would keep the slave
until worn out with labour or until death came, and in the
meantime his object was to secure from his purchase the last
ounce of effort that torture or punishment could extract.

[1] Thomas Clarkson, *The History of the Rise, Progress and Accomplishment of the Abolition of the African Slave Trade*, London, 1808.
[2] *Ibid.*

Methods of Torture Employed

The punishment meted out to the slaves was of two kinds: that inflicted as a goad to extract the greatest amount of work possible, as a horse is goaded by its owner; and punishment given for transgressions of the laws of the islands, in particular reference to slaves on the one hand, and in reference to everybody on the other.

In the first category was the whipping regularly given to slaves of both sexes and of all ages. The overseer was never without his whip, which he used upon the slightest provocation. It almost looked as if he *wanted* the slaves to give him grounds for flogging them, and there can be no doubt at all that many slave-drivers and slave-owners secured sadistic pleasure in punishing or in witnessing the punishment of slaves.

The slightest offence was thus construed to merit the severest punishment. An instance of this was the treatment accorded Eleanor Mead, a mulatto owned by the Colchis estate, Jamaica. The incident occurred in the year 1830.

> "Her mistress, Mrs. Earnshaw, who is described by some as a lady of humanity and delicacy, having taken offence at something which this slave had said or done, in the course of a quarrel with another slave, ordered her to be stripped naked, prostrated on the ground, and in her own presence caused the male driver to inflict upon her bared body 58 lashes of the cart whip. . . . One of the persons ordered to hold her prostrate during the punishment was her own daughter Catherine. When one hip had been sufficiently lacerated in the opinion of Mrs. Earnshaw, she told the driver to go round and flog the other side."[1]

So common was the flogging of women on the plantations, in the workhouses, and in the gaols, that it was held to constitute one of the most powerful barriers to marriage. Negroes could not tolerate the agony of having their wives flogged, and, often enough, being compelled to witness the punishments. Sometimes even, such was the cruelty of the

[1] *Anti-Slavery Monthly Reporter*, 1829, p. 345.

owners, men were forced to whip their own kinsfolk. In his evidence before the House of Commons Committee, the Rev. Peter Duncan stated that:

"In the year 1823 I knew of a slave-driver having to flog his mother. In the year 1827 I knew of a married negress having been flogged in the presence of her fellow slaves, and I believe her husband too, for it was her husband and herself and other slaves who told me the circumstances. Merely because this negress would not submit to satisfy the lust of her overseer, he had flogged and confined her for several days in the stocks."[1]

There were many outstanding instances of cruelty. In the House of Commons papers for 1814, there is given the case of a planter named Huggins, who, in the public market-place of Nevis, Jamaica, submitted "twenty-one of his slaves, men and women, to upwards of 3,000 lashes of the cart-whip," one woman alone receiving no fewer than 291 strokes, and one man a total of 365. Lord Liverpool characterized Huggins' treatment of the negroes as "cruel, atrocious and even murderous."

Slave-owners of all classes and ranks appear to have taken pleasure in tormenting these human outcasts whom they owned body and soul. In the court of St. Ann's, Jamaica, in 1829, the Rev. G. W. Bridges was charged with maltreating a female quadroon. The account given was that the reverend gentleman was expecting a guest for dinner, and had ordered the girl to prepare a turkey. The guest did not turn up, and when her master found the servant girl had killed the turkey, he flew into a violent rage, stripped her to the buff, tied her up by the hands to a hook in the ceiling so that her toes barely touched the ground, and, with a bamboo rod, flogged her from the shoulders to the calves of the legs until she was a "mass of lacerated flesh and gore." Despite the girl's story and the tell-tale condition of her body, the clergyman was acquitted.

In a letter published in the *Morning Chronicle* (October 8, 1829) from a correspondent residing in Savanah la Mar, Jamaica, is an account of a flogging administered to a female

---

[1] *Anti-Slavery Monthly Reporter,* 1829.

slave for causing some clothes to be burnt as a result of putting them too near the fire.

"It was only the day before yesterday, when writing, I heard the noise of that disgraceful instrument which so often grates on my ear, proceed from a back-yard. . . . What an appalling sight did I behold! a wretched woman extended on the ground, with her clothes tied up to her waist—a powerful negro man, upwards of six feet high, lacerating her flesh; and this disgusting and abominable sight directed and superintended by a mother and her daughter."

Some of the slave-owners not only inflicted punishments on every imaginable pretext, but were so loath to be balked of their "amusement" that they practised flagellation upon the slaves until death or manumission released the victims. There was the case of the slave Ben Moss, who managed to purchase his freedom. The day before the deed of manumission made the negro a free man, his owner inflicted the maximum punishment of 39 lashes upon the poor, tottering and almost worn-out carcase.

In the course of his evidence before the Select Committee on Slavery, the Rev. William Knibb affirmed that a negro slave named Catherine Williams crawled to his house, her back covered with blood. She stated that she had been " confined in a dungeon for three months, and that she had been flogged, and that the reason was that the overseer wanted her to live with him in fornication, and that she would not do it."[1] The same witness alleged that a negro slave called Sam Swiney was punished " for the act of praying," and further that some slaves " were flogged to death."[2]

Not only did the owners flog their own slaves, they flogged those belonging to others when the opportunity presented itself, apparently taking the view that a negro, in this respect, was common property to be punished by any white man who cared to take on the job. J. B. Wild-

---

[1] *Parliamentary Papers: Report of Select Committee on the Extinction of Slavery Throughout the British Dominions*, 1832, p. 266.
[2] *Ibid.*, p. 259.

man stated in evidence that, in accordance with the system in vogue in Jamaica, severe punishment could be inflicted upon a slave without the knowledge of the owner.[1] He instanced the case of Eleanor James, one of his own slaves. In the November of 1829, this elderly female applied to a Mr. Macdonald, a Jamaican planter, for the money due to her in payment for a pig he had purchased from her. Instead of handing over the money, Macdonald ordered his drivers to flog James. With a whip continually dipped in water to add to its punishing powers, the woman was flogged, first by one driver and then by another, until 200 lashes had lacerated her back and buttocks.

In a complaint lodged by a slave Jenny against her mistress, Elizabeth Atkinson, the young woman alleged that she had been beaten unmercifully and repeatedly, kicked in the belly, trampled on, and locked in the stocks. Further, her child Philip was also ill-treated and never allowed to be with his mother. On examination, the child, as well as the mother, bore marks of severe floggings administered in all parts of the body.[2]

In the House of Commons, on July 1, 1830, during the course of a speech on slavery in the Colonies, Mr. Brougham mentioned an instance of cruel treatment meted out by an English gentlewoman to a slave girl. On suspicion of being concerned in a theft, the young negress was imprisoned in the stocks for seventeen days, during which period she was deprived of sleep by rubbing red pepper into her eyes, and she was flogged repeatedly. On removal from the stocks tasks were allotted her which were quite beyond her strength, and because of her failure to accomplish them she was again and again flogged unmercifully. Finally, in a weak and feverish condition, " she was sent to work in the fields, where she died."

Slaves were branded both for the purpose of claiming ownership in the case of escape, and as a method of punishment. There was no prohibition by Jamaica State law of branding *per se*. In certain circumstances, such as the application of a red hot iron to the breasts of the

[1] *Ibid.*, p. 538.
[2] For additional cases of the whipping of slaves, see Chapter XX.

female, it became an offence, and could be punished as an
act of cruelty.

Chains, weights and other heavy encumbrances were
attached to the limbs of slaves by night and often by day
as well, to prevent any attempt at escape. A favourite
instrument used for this purpose and also as a form of
punishment was the " iron collar." It was riveted around
the slave's neck, and had three long projecting rods
attached to it at equal intervals. These rods were shaped
something like pot-hooks, and for this reason the collar
was sometimes given this name. It is easy to imagine the
agony caused by the wearing of such a contrivance for
any protracted length of time. It was impossible to lie
down without suffering great inconvenience or pain, for
however the slave so "collared" might turn or twist, one
of the rods would come in contact with the ground and
prevent him getting any rest or ease, while the iron collar
itself exerted pressure upon the neck. Pinckard mentions
having seen a slave wandering about in a cotton field
"bearing a heavy iron collar upon his neck, with three long
iron spikes projecting from it, terminating in sharp points,
at a distance of nearly a foot and a half from his person;
and with his body flogged into deep ulcers, from his loins to
his hams." It is comforting to know that this abominable
encumbrance was removed from the negro's neck.

In some cases slaves were hamstrung in order to prevent them running away, the large tendon above the heel
being severed. An even more drastic method was amputation of one leg. Stedman says that during his stay at
Paramaribo " no less than nine negroes had each a leg cut
off for running away."[1]

A diabolical form of punishment employed in Surinam
consisted of chaining the culprit to a furnace used in the
distillation of " kill-devil,"[2] " there to keep in the intense
heat of a perpetual fire night and day, being blistered all
over, till he should expire by infirmity or old age."[3]

<hr />

[1] George Pinckard, *Notes on the West Indies*, London, 1806, Vol. III,
p 267.

[2] A species of rum.

[3] J. G. Stedman, *Narrative of a Five Years' Expedition Against the
Revolted Negroes of Surinam in Guinea on the Coast of South America
from the Year 1772-1777*, London, 1796, Vol. I, p. 96.

A bizarre form of torment is described by Clarkson, as having been devised by a West Indian colonist as an " auxiliary " form of punishment. It consisted of an iron box, in size and shape like a coffin, with holes punctured in the sides, bottom and lid. After being flogged, the victim was enclosed in the coffin, which was then drawn "sufficiently near a fire to occasion extreme pain, and consequently shrieks and groans, until the revenge of the master was satiated."[1]

" Field stocks " were much used as a means of inflicting minor punishments on female offenders when the Trinidad order (the "Model Order" as it was termed) substituting this form of punishment in place of female flogging came into force. These stocks resembled somewhat the English pillory. The hands were inserted in grooves which could be raised to any height above the head, while the feet were placed in other grooves at the bottom of the stocks. Only the toes could touch the ground. The whole weight of the body, which was suspended in mid-air as it were, rested upon the wrists and toes. In Trinidad, to increase the suffering, leaden or iron weights were tied to the wrists. It is doubtful if this form of torture was any less severe than that which it substituted. It was applicable to women of all ages and in all conditions. Not even pregnancy excused its infliction.

As age crept on, as feebleness or disease manifested itself, the slave, male or female, dragged along day after day in eternal misery. His life was one long chronicle of terror and despair. He dare not, until flesh and tissue would stand no more, betray the slightest sign that he was no longer worth his keep to his master. For well he knew the fate, once that fact was realized, which would befall him. The old, the feeble, the diseased, one and all, the moment they reached an unworkable stage, or a state in which when sent to market they were rejected as worthless, were doomed. " It was given in evidence," says Edwards, " as a fact too notorious to be controverted, that they were frequently, if not generally, put to death."

---

[1] Thomas Clarkson, *An Essay on the Slavery and Commerce of the Human Species*, London, 1786, p. 146.

Torture Will Who Torture Can

It is true that the slaves themselves, when opportunity offered, were as cruel and merciless as were their masters. The liking for and the ability to inflict torture is, as I have attempted to show in this work, restricted neither to race nor class: it is universal and timeless. During the terrible civil war that raged in St. Domingo in 1791, whites and mulattoes vied with each other in their efforts to invent and practise the most fiendish forms of torture.

" Every refinement in cruelty that the most depraved imagination could suggest was practised by the whites on the persons of these wretched men. One of the mulatto leaders was unhappily among the number: him the victors placed on an elevated seat in a cart, and secured him in it by driving large spiked nails through his feet into the boards. In this condition he was led a miserable spectacle through the city. His bones were afterwards broken, and he was then thrown alive into the flames.

" The mulattoes scorned to be outdone in deeds of vengeance and atrocities shameful to humanity. In the neighbourhood of Jeremie a body of them attacked the house of M. Sejourné and secured the persons both of him and his wife. This unfortunate woman was far advanced in pregnancy. The monsters, whose prisoner she was, having first murdered her husband in her presence, ripped her up alive, and threw the infant to the hogs."[1]

The Horrors of Mauritius

In 1810, Mauritius was captured by the British and Sir Robert Farquhar was appointed its governor. At that time it was notorious as a slave colony. The English, when they took possession of what was virtually a disgrace to anything resembling civilization, did not abolish slavery. To the contrary, they continued to allow it to be practised. They pursued this policy for all of twenty years.

[1] Bryan Edwards, *The History of the British Colonies in the West Indies*, London, 1793, Vol. III, p. 118.

It transpired that, ten years after the British occupancy, the state of the slaves on the island was deplorable. They were badly and scantily fed, often being reduced to eating carrion and offal; they were forced to labour in the terrific heat sixteen to nineteen hours a day; they were whipped brutally while at work; they were whipped in addition for the slightest offences.

There was the case of Auguste, a Creole slave, which came into the court. Auguste was owned by M. Jean Louis Diott. On the 26th day of March, 1817, he was sent to fetch a supply of water. Whether the man dallied on the way or not is by no means clear, but Diott said that he did, and forthwith ordered a driver to flog him. The slave was whipped from his naked shoulders to his buttocks. This punishment, fearful though it was, did not satisfy the sadistic Diott. He instructed the driver to remove seven of the slave's teeth. This was done, three in the lower and four in the upper jaw being wrenched out or broken with a pair of pincers. And the court, in pursuance of its task of administering justice, ordered Diott to *sell the slave!*

About the same time another case came before the court. The offence in this instance was absconding on account, so the slave, Le Cotte, affirmed, of ill-treatment. He was captured, and his master, Noel Bastil, it was alleged, gave him between 200 and 300 lashes, and then cut off his right ear, which he forced Le Cotte to eat and swallow. Bastil admitted everything but forcing the slave to eat the ear. Despite this admission, the court did not punish the owner; it merely ordered the confiscation of the slave by the government.

Even more horrible was the torture of a negro, in 1822, by a slave-owner named Peter Cotry, living near Grant Port. The slave was stripped and suspended, with a noose running around the body under the arms, so that his feet were raised slightly from the ground. Cotry then took a stick and beat the negro's body in every available part. He next smeared fat over the calves of the man's legs and set dogs to bite them. The tortured negro asked for water. He was given urine. Finally, his private parts were cut away, and mercifully, under this operation, he died. The case was too grave and the evidence too clear and abundant for the court to let

Cotry go absolutely free. They sent him to prison, from where soon after he was allowed to escape.

Nor were the women into whose power fate cast these hapless negroes any more merciful than their menfolk. There was the remarkable case of Madame Nayle of Flaco in 1823. This woman committed with her own hands some fearful mutilations upon the body of a female slave she owned. She cut off the negress's nose and her ears, she tore out several of her teeth, and finally attempted to amputate the breasts. The slave expired before the last act was accomplished. This case presented a feature which a prejudiced court seized upon to defeat justice. There was no *white* evidence available as to Madame Nayle's guilt, although the slave evidence was incontrovertible and abundant. In accordance with an ordinance of 1723 the court could, at its discretion, avail itself of slave evidence in the event of white evidence being unavailable. The court did *not,* in this instance, avail itself of such evidence. It permitted Madame Nayle to go free.

Torture of American Slaves

It was perhaps inevitable that the importation of negro slaves for work on the sugar plantations of the West Indian islands should be followed by their importation for labour in the cotton fields of the southern states of America. In 1620, a small batch of slaves, numbering a score, was landed at Jamestown from a Dutch vessel. This represented the first importation into Virginia. Once a start was made, developments were rapid. According to the United States census of 1790, there were at that time 40,370 slaves in the northern states, and 657,527 in the southern states. A colossal total.

At the beginning of 1808 the African slave trade came to a termination. This did not mean that slavery was abolished. Far from it. It merely meant that the sources of supply for *new alien* slaves had dried up. It was at this juncture that American slave-owners began to pay serious attention to the *breeding* of slaves. At this time able-bodied male slaves were fetching as much as 1,500 dollars apiece in the New Orleans market, and a young negress was worth around 1,000 dollars. Women who had proved their fertility were specifically advertised as prolific breeders. They were in great demand and fetched good prices.

In the American States, as in the British West Indies, the law was so constituted that slave-owners had the right to do to the negroes pretty nearly anything in the way of ill-treatment, cruelty and punishment short of causing mutilation or actual death. It was expressly stated in the Civil Code of the State of Louisiana that " the slave is entirely subject to the will of the master, who may correct and chastise him, though not with unusual vigour, nor so as to maim or mutilate him to the danger of loss of life, or to cause his death." An Act of Legislature of 1740 read:

> " In case any person shall wilfully cut out the tongue, put out an eye, or cruelly scald, burn, or deprive any slave of any limb or member, or shall inflict any cruel punishment other than by whipping, or beating with a horse-whip, cowskin, switch, or small-stick, or by putting irons on, or confining or imprisoning such slave, every such person shall for every such offence, forfeit the sum of one hundred pounds current money."

The existence of these laws has, on many occasions, been mentioned as evidence that the slaves were looked after by a beneficent government and that their lot was by no means so dreadful as the opponents of slavery stated. After making every allowance for exaggeration on both sides, it is obvious that these laws in themselves did something to encourage the maltreatment of the negroes. They allowed the owner a good deal of latitude in the matter of punishment. Like all laws made by one section of society for imposition upon another subservient section having neither the right to take a hand in the making of them nor the power to resist them when made, these laws were unilateral, unjust and noxious. They were deliberately made to aid the exploitation of one party by the other.

It must be remembered, too, that so far as the courts were concerned, the evidence of a slave was "tainted" to start with; and, further, that relatively few slaves would dare to make any official complaint, as the odds were either the charge would fail, in which case the negro's lot would

be infinitely worse than before, or in the event of it succeed-
ing, his next master, on the general principle of planters
and drivers " sticking up for one another," would take it
out of him.   There are, too, indications that the use of other
modes of punishment against which there were no specific
laws, or extensions and variations in the way in which the
flogging was administered, enabled the drivers and owners
to torture cruelly the slaves, and yet run little risk of prosecution.   For instance, there was the use of the " paddle,"
which left no denotative marks, to which reference has been
made in another place (cf. page 196).

In addition, the interpretation of these laws and the
manner in which they were carried out, largely washed
away any element of justice that was in them.   In relation to
the laws governing slavery in Mauritius, we have seen that
the courts interpreted them in favour of the whites, that even
in cases where white planters had been guilty of mayhem
and murder, the courts contrived, by subterfuge, evasion,
collusion, suppression of evidence and every other conceivable means, even to the extent of conniving at the escape of
the prisoner after conviction, to enable the guilty parties to
avoid punishment.   The courts, in short, dispensed what
amounted to a mere travesty of justice.   Much the same
happened in America, as indeed it did in every part of the
world where slavery existed.

Not all the slaves were badly treated.   Luck entered into
the matter a great deal.   Some negroes had the good fortune
to be bought by men or women who treated them decently
and humanly.   But these cases represented the exceptions
rather than the rule.

In most cases the slaves were flogged or manhandled for
the most trivial offences.   In many instances professional
floggers were called in to perform the task.   In the course
of his examination in the " Rescue Trials " at Boston, in
1851, a policeman named John Caphart admitted that he
had been engaged to flog " coloured persons " for a fee of
50 cents a head.   His answers to the questions put to him
were revealing :

> Q. "Do you not flog slaves at the request of their
> masters? "

A. " Sometimes I do. Certainly, when I am called upon."

Q. " In these cases of private flogging, do you inquire into the circumstances, to see what the fault has been, or if there is any? "

A. " That's none of my business. I do as I am requested The master is responsible."

Q. " Mr. Caphart, how long have you been engaged in this business? "

A. " Ever since 1836."

Q. " How many negroes do you suppose you have flogged, in all, women and children included? "

A. (looking calmly round the room). " I don't know how many niggers you have got here in Massachusetts, but I should think I have flogged as many as you've got in the State."[1]

Well, indeed, might John P. Hale, a counsel in the case, in a burst of forensic eloquence, say, of this slave-flogger: " Why, gentlemen, *he sells agony!* Torture is his stock-intrade! He is a walking scourge! He hawks, peddles, retails, groans and tears about the streets of Norfolk! "

[1] Quoted by Harriet Beecher Stowe in *A Key to Uncle Tom's Cabin*, London, 1853, pp. 7-8.

CHAPTER XV

THE WAR UPON TORTURE

The Growth of Opposition

SINCE the earliest days of civilization there has been opposition to the practice of torture. This opposition, however, has been in most cases a partial opposition only, since it merely concerned itself with judicial torture and not torture *in toto*. The use of forms of punishment or of execution which involved or were preceded by torture often enough received no denunciation from the bitterest opponents of the *quæstion*. Thus Seneca recognized the injustice of torture and its futility as a means of arriving at the truth. So did Cicero. So did St. Augustine. So did Ulpian, the famous Roman lawyer. So did Tertullian.

The history of torture shows a curious diversity between theory and practice. There has always been a very profound and definite *expressed* opposition to judicial torture at any rate, but at the same time there appears to have been little effort made to put the view expressed into practical effect. No better example of this has appeared than the English prohibition of torture in principle and the use of it in practice. The provisions of Magna Charta were interpreted as representing torture to be abhorrent to the principle of English freedom. The Bill of Rights provided that torture was a cruel and an unusual form of punishment which in no circumstances should be inflicted. Time and time again did the leading legal authorities and judges proclaim that the use of torture was contrary to English common law and could not be tolerated. But for 400 years at least judicial torture was employed, and from the time of the Anglo-Saxons onwards it has been inflicted as a form of punishment.

All through the Middle Ages, in continental Europe, torture proceeded merrily. The voices of any opponents were drowned in the chorus of approval from the multitude. Among the first to protest against its use were the famous Spanish savant, Juan Luis Vives, and Johann Graefe, who, in 1624, presented the case against torture in his *Tribunal Reformation*. Montaigne, in condemning the practice of preceding execution with torture, said:

> "For my part, even in justice itself, all that exceeds a simple death, appears to me perfect cruelty; especially in us who ought to have regard to their souls, to dismiss them in a good and calm condition: which cannot be, when we have discompos'd them by insufferable torments. . . . I could hardly persuade myself, before I saw it with my eyes, that there could be found out souls so cruell, who for the sole pleasure of murder would commit, hack, and lop off the limbs of others; sharpen their wits to invent unusual torments, and new kinds of deaths without hatred, without profit, and for no other end, but only to enjoy the pleasant spectacle of the gestures and motions, the lamentable groans and cries of a man in anguish. For this is the utmost point to which cruelty can arrive."[1]

In 1740, Frederick the Great abolished torture in Prussia, and about this time Voltaire lent his powerful pen to the cause of abolition. He interceded without success in the prosecution of the Chevalier de la Barre; and again to better effect in the case of Marc-Antoine Calas.

And now another opponent came upon the scene, to wit, Cesare Bonesana Beccaria. His famous work, *An Essay on Crimes and Punishments,* published in Milan in 1764, caused a sensation. In a masterly passage, he says:

> "No man can be judged a criminal until he be found guilty; nor can society take from him the public protection, until it have been proved that he has violated the conditions on which it was granted. What right then, but that of power, can authorize the punishment of a citizen, so long as there remains any doubt of his guilt? This dilemma is frequent. Either he is guilty,

---

[1] *Essays* (Cotton's translation), Book II, Ch. 11.

or not guilty. If guilty, he should only suffer the punishment ordained by the laws, and torture becomes useless, as his confession is unnecessary. If he be not guilty, you torture the innocent; for in the eyes of the law, every man is innocent, whose crime has not been proved. Besides, it is confounding all relations, to expect that a man should be both the accuser and the accused; and that pain should be the test of truth, as if truth resided in the muscles and fibres of a wretch in torture. By this method, the robust will escape, and the feeble be condemned. These are the inconveniences of this pretended test of truth, worthy only of a cannibal; and which the Romans, in many respects barbarous, and whose savage virture has been too much admired, reserved for the slaves alone."

The Decline of Torture

The efforts of Beccaria in Italy, leading to the abolition of torture in 1786, and of Voltaire in France, which gave to the rack and flogging their death-blows in 1789, had their repercussions in other countries. In Russia torture came to an end in 1801, in Spain in 1812.

Judicial torture in England had ended in 1640, and in 1708 it was abolished in Scotland by Act of Parliament. But punishments which were tortures in all but name still flourished in all countries. Thus, in England, burning at the stake continued until 1789, branding was not abolished until 1834, and the pillory remained in use until 1837. In France the torture of boiling oil was not discontinued until 1791, and the branding iron was kept busy until 1832; while in Russia convicts were branded until as recently as 1863.

In the early years of the nineteenth century an outcry arose at the brutal floggings inflicted in the British Army and Navy.[1] Major-General Charles J. Napier, Sir Francis Burdett, Lord Hutchinson and Sir Samuel Romilly were

[1] In each of the seven years from 1825 to 1832, the number of soldiers flogged averaged 2,000, each soldier receiving from 200 to 500 lashes. In 1831, immediately after a public outcry against flogging had been made, 1,477 soldiers were given the " cat."

among the leading and most powerful opponents of these sanguinary flogging sentences that were being given for trivial offences. Although every effort to get the use of the " cat" abolished met with failure, considerable reductions were effected in the severity of the sentences which could be given and the conditions of punishment. But it was not until 1881 that the passing of the Army Act restricted flogging to offenders in military prisons.

Penal flagellation, being one of the earliest forms of torture, continued to hold out stubbornly after many other torments had been abolished. In Great Britain, the whipping of women was the form of penal flagellation which was first abolished. The last recorded instance was in Scotland in 1817, when a woman was flogged through the streets of Inverness for drunkenness and misbehaviour. In 1820, the Whipping of Female Offenders Abolition Act became law. It prohibited the flogging of females for any crime and in any circumstances. The next step in the march towards humanitarianism was the abolition of the flogging of males in public. In 1822, the last recorded case of whipping at the cart's tail occurred, when, on May 8th, a rioter was flogged by the hangman through the streets of Glasgow.

The public were thus cheated of yet another form of amusement! But flogging went on. The " cat " was kept almost as busy within the walls of the gaols as previously it had been without. On July 7, 1823, in the course of a discussion in the House of Lords, Mr. Grey Bennet stated that during the last seven years there were no fewer than 6,959 floggings administered in the prisons of England. The governor of any gaol was empowered to order a prisoner to be whipped whenever he thought such punishment necessary for the maintenance of discipline. The government inquiry into the conditions in Birmingham Borough prison, in 1849, revealed that boys and men were flogged for trivial offences, day after day, with a severity and brutal continuity that it is probable would not have been possible had the floggings been given publicly.

The past century has seen penal flogging hotly discussed in this country, one school of thought maintaining that it is useless as a means of achieving the diminution of crime, and another school maintaining just as strongly and sincerely that it constitutes the best possible method of accomplishing this same objective. The course of the battle royal has been punctuated by many sporadic exhibitions of what may perhaps best be described as "flogging mania," on the part of the masses, resulting in panic legislation, every few decades, undoing the work of the abolitionists. The "floggers" in the past always won the battle.

In 1937, the Home Office appointed a Committee to consider the whole question of corporal punishment, and last year, this Committee, in its published report, recommended that the birching of juveniles, in all circumstances, should be discontinued, and that the use of the "cat" should be restricted to the punishment of certain grave prison offences.[1]

The War Upon Animal Torture

It took Christianity a long time to realize that animals had rights, that they were entitled to legal protection against torture, persecution and wanton destruction. In fact, cruelty to animals seems to have come in for little in the way of denunciation until the seventeenth and eighteenth centuries, when Locke, Wesley, Butler, Bentham, John Lawrence, Wilberforce, Sheridan and others championed the cause of animals. Hogarth's "Four Stages of Cruelty" did much to open the eyes of thinking people to the brutality that was in those days inherent in the treatment of animals.

When cruelty forms part of the amusement of society, the path of the reformer is a difficult one. This is the lesson of history. A telling example of the truth of this statement is provided in the futility of early attempts to get Parliament to pass a Bill to abolish bull-baiting. The first Bill of this nature was introduced in 1800 by Sir W. Pulteney. William Windham and George Canning opposed it and their opposi-

[1] At the moment of writing the Criminal Justice Bill, providing for the abolition of corporal punishment for all except certain prison offences, is going through the House of Commons. The proposal to abolish the "cat" is meeting with strong opposition from many quarters, including some sections of the popular Press.

tion was successful. A second attempt, two years later, failed too. Lord Erskine was the next to try to get such a Bill passed. And once again failure was the result. The fight waged by a handful of humanitarians against the government and the people lasted for twenty years. It was not until 1822 that an Act for the protection of animals, introduced by Richard Martin, became law.

Two years later an event occurred of the greatest importance in the history of the fight for the rights of animals: the Royal Society for the Prevention of Cruelty to Animals was formed. " During its first year," we read, " the Society successfully prosecuted in 149 cases of cruelty to animals."[1]

From the start, the movement met with many difficulties. Martin's Act of 1822, admirable as it was in its way, only touched the fringe of the subject, being restricted in its application to cattle. Many forms of animal torture and cruelty were so much a part of the ordinary everyday life of the people that it was almost impossible to get anyone to admit that they were not justifiable. Thus the use of dogs as draught-animals, which for generations was a scandal and a disgrace to Christian England. The animals were worked to death without the slightest compunction. They were compelled to pull loads far beyond their strength; they were flogged till they dropped dead or dying by the roadside. For fifteen years persistent efforts were made to have the scandal stopped. Success was achieved with a Bill which came into force on January 1, 1855.[2]

Among other notable reforms effected by the Society has been that in connexion with the slaughtering of animals for food. The invention of the R.S.P.C.A. humane cattle-killer in 1907 marked a great advance upon the old method of pole-axe[3] slaughtering, and the passing of the Slaughter of Animals Act 1933 has done much to lessen the cruelty in this particular field. The Act provides (Section I, 1) that:

---

[1] Edward G. Fairholme and Wellesley Pain, *A Century of Work for Animals*, second edition, John Murray, 1924, p. 59. For much of the information contained in this chapter concerning the fight against cruelty to animals I am indebted to this excellent work, which should be read by everyone concerned with animal welfare and the abolition of cruelty.

[2] *Ibid.*, p. 117.

[3] From January 1, 1929, the use of the pole-axe was declared to be illegal in Scotland.

"No animal to which this section applies shall be slaughtered in a slaughter-house or knacker's yard except in accordance with the following provisions, that is to say, every such animal shall be instantaneously slaughtered, or shall by stunning be instantaneously rendered insensible to pain until death supervenes, and such slaughtering or stunning shall be effected by means of a mechanically operated instrument in proper repair."[1]

Besides the R.S.P.C.A., there are several other bodies working steadfastly towards the abolition of torture in many fields. They have done much to prevent unnecessary suffering and persecution. The fight is being waged in sober earnest, and with much success.

In the United States an organization for the prevention of cruelty to animals was founded in New York City in 1866, and in this same year was passed the first law providing protection for animals. To-day practically every big American city has its own society. The American Humane Education Society, a nation-wide movement, has done and is doing great work in the campaign against cruelty.

Despite the gratifying and immense progress made, however, there is still much work to do. Especially is this the case in certain European countries, in Algeria, in India, in China and the East generally.

---

[1] The Act does not apply to the slaughter of pigs where no supply of electrical energy is available. It does not apply to Jewish and Mohammedan methods of killing any animals. It is left to local option whether or not the provisions of the Act apply to sheep. It is regrettable that by no means all the local councils have seen fit to prohibit the slaughter of sheep by the knife alone.

CHAPTER XVI

SOME NOTORIOUS TORTURERS

The Ancient Tyrants

HEROD THE FIRST (surnamed the Great) was one of the earliest of the tyrants respecting which we have any authentic records. During the years when he was King of Judea he pursued a course of unmitigated cruelty. He ordered all the children in Bethlehem to be slaughtered. He killed his own wife. Then there was Antiochus Epiphanes, conqueror of Jerusalem, who tortured the Jews physically by subjecting them to every possible form of painful death; and mentally, by prohibiting circumcision, and using swine for the purpose of sacrifice. It was Epiphanes who ordered Ulpianus to be scourged and then fastened up along with a dog and a venomous snake in a sack of ox-hide and thrown into the sea.

The Roman emperors were notorious for their cruelty and barbarity. In particular, the Cæsars ruled their subjects with the aid of torture, with blood, and with the fear ever before them of impending and sudden death. Each emperor apparently made efforts to invent novel methods of torture and punishment, and to discover new offences on which to exercise them.

For twenty-odd years Tiberius, a veritable monster of cruelty, punctuated his rule with such tortures that the guilty, in many instances, awaited not their trial but committed suicide the moment their transgressions were discovered. For offences which were the merest peccadilloes, men and women both were dragged with iron hooks through the streets of Rome. Because it was the law that virgins could not be strangled (at that time strangling was the authorized method of putting females to death) Tiberius ordered that first they should be defiled by the executioner. The emperor, not content with the miscellany of tortures in vogue, which, in truth, were fiendish enough in all con-

science, invented additional ones. One such, asserts Suetonius, was to compel

> "the poor wretches to drink a great quantity of wine,
> and presently to tie their members with a lute-string, that
> he might rack them at once with the girting of the string,
> and with the pressure of urine."[1]

The tyrannous Caligula went even further than his
grandfather Tiberius. Into the three years and ten months
of his reign he managed to crowd enough atrocities and
barbarities to satisfy the appetite of the most insatiable of
sadists. He did not confine his sentences of death to
criminals; he had innocent people openly tortured and
executed. Many he ordered to be thrown to the wild beasts,
which he purposely kept hungry in their den attached to his
palace. The sight of these animals devouring the living
humans was one of his favourite amusements. Young men
were executed in the presence of their parents. Quickly
tiring of all ordinary methods, Caligula was continually
inventing, and demanding that his favourites should invent,
fresh tortures or ways of tormenting. In his own dining-
room he had criminals tortured while he ate, stating that
witnessing their sufferings acted as an appetizer. For those
crimes which he deemed not sufficiently severe to merit
execution, he adopted a miscellany of torments, of which the
most common was branding with a hot iron or confinement
in an iron cage so narrow and so low that the prisoner had
to adopt a quadrupedal position. Mutilation was another
favourite punishment. It is said that in one instance where
a slave was guilty of theft, Caligula ordered the executioner
to cut off the man's hands and hang them about his neck so
that they dangled upon his breast. For certain crimes a slow
death was ordained, small and repeated stabs being given, so
that, in the tyrant's own words, the condemned man could
"feel himself die." Suetonius tells us he had men sawn in
two; that a poet, for an ambiguous and unappreciated jest,
was burnt in the middle of the theatre; and

> "the master of his gladiators and wild beasts, he caus'd

[1] C. Suetonius Tranquillus, *The Lives of the XII Cæsars*, 1717, p. 228.

to be cramp'd with irons, and beaten for two days together before his eyes, and did not kill him outright till his brain was putrify'd, and offended him with the stench.''[1]

Another equally notorious tyrant was Nero, who, for nearly fourteen years, pursued a course of unexampled debauchery and cruelty. A pervert, a murderer and a poisoner, he stopped at nothing. He even set fire to the capital city, singing while men, women and children were burnt alive or crushed by the falling buildings. The garden of his palace was his favourite execution ground. Here prisoners, sewn up in wolves' skins, were torn to bits by savage dogs. Others were crucified, dying slowly under the tyrant's eyes. Yet others were daubed over with inflammable materials, and set alight to act as torches in the night. Epickaris, accused of conspiracy, he ordered to be tortured until she disclosed the identity of her accomplices. In an interval in the process she strangled herself.[2]

Trajanus persecuted everyone who refused to obey his command to sacrifice to the heathen idols. Despite the intercession of Pliny, he tortured Christians and Jews alike. He had Ignatius, Bishop of Antioch, thrown to the lions in the amphitheatre at Rome. Polycarpus he ordered to be buried alive.

The emperor Maximinus lived and died a tyrant. Perhaps his greatest act of tyranny was to have 400 persons done to death in every cruel way imaginable on the pretext that they were concerned in a conspiracy against his life. Some were crucified, some were thrown to wild beasts, others were sewn up in the skins of slaughtered animals and left to die slowly of starvation.

Diocletianus, however, surpassed all his predecessors in the extent and severity of his persecutions. By his express orders, 20,000 Christians were burnt in the Church of Nicodemia. He boasted that he would eradicate Christianity, and to this end he tortured and executed its devotees throughout the Empire. In Egypt, according to Sulpicius Severus, the historian, he had 17,000 massacred in a single month.

[1] *Ibid.*, p. 274.
[2] Tacitus, *Annals*, Book XV, p. 52.

Other notorious tyrants were Severus, Gallus, Decius and Valerianus. They tortured everyone who did not sacrifice to the imperial gods and who refused to blaspheme the Christ Jesus. The Christians, and others accused or suspected of heresy, were tormented incessantly and by every thinkable method. They were tied by the heels to the tails of horses and dragged through the streets; they were whipped with the terrible *flagellum* till they dropped dead in their tracks; they were thrown headlong from the highest buildings in Rome; they were stoned till they fell dead or dying; they were flung to wild beasts; they were literally scraped to death. Those who escaped with their lives were often grievously mutilated; their noses, ears, hands and feet being amputated; their tongues or eyes cut out; their bodies scalded with melted lead or boiling oil; their teeth beaten out with hammers.

The tyrannous Urbanus, Governor of Palestine, handed virgin girls over to the brothels and had young men castrated for use as pathics. Governor Firmillianus tortured criminals and suspected heretics without mercy. Because the girl Valentina refused to offer sacrifices at his behest, says Eusebius, she was "tortured with the combs, without any mercy, so that no one man was ever torn to such a degree."

The Lacedaemonian tyrant Nabis, who reigned some two hundred years before Christ, persecuted and oppressed his people with the most extreme rigour. His demands for money and gifts from his subjects were continuous and insatiable. Failure to comply with his requests was punished by torture. Of his own devising, there was in his palace a most ingenious instrument, of which the following description is one of the best available.

"This machine, if it may be called indeed by such a name, was an image of a woman, magnificently dressed, and formed in a most exact resemblance of his wife. And when his intention was to draw money from any of the citizens, he invited them to his house, and at first with such civility represented to them the danger with which their country was threatened from the Achæans; the number of mercenaries which he was forced to retain, etc. But if all his solicitations were without effect, he

From Moore's *Martyrology*, 1809.

DRAGGING AT THE HORSE'S TAIL AND CRUCIFIXION

then used to say: I want, it seems, the power of persuasion; but Apega, I believe, will be able to persuade you. Apega was the name of his wife. Upon these words, the image of the woman that has been mentioned immediately appeared. Nabis then, taking her by the hand, raised her from her seat; and folding afterwards his arms round the person whom he had been soliciting, brought him near by degrees to the body of the image, whose breasts, hands, and arms were stuck full with points of iron, concealed under her clothes; and then, pressing the back of the pretended woman with his hands, by the means of some secret springs he fixed the man close to her breast, and soon forced him to promise all that he desired. But there were some also who perished in this torture, when they refused to comply with his demands."[1]

Torturers of the Middle Ages

In the twelfth century, Pope Innocent III began his campaign of persecution against the Albigenses, a sect whose only crime was that of dissenting from the doctrines of the Church of Rome. In the war of extermination which raged for thirty years, the heretics, as these Albigenses were described by the Pope, were subjected to every form of cruel treatment and torture conceivable. Many of them collapsed and became converted. Raymond, Earl of Toulouse, in a frenzy of fear, offered to be reconciled to the Church. The manner of his reconciliation is described by Bzovius.

"The Earl swore allegiance to the holy Roman Church. When he had thus bound himself by an oath, the legate ordered one of the sacred vestments to be thrown over his neck, and drawing him thereby, brought him into the church, and having scourged him with a whip, absolved him. He was so grievously torn by the stripes that he could not go out by the same place through which he entered, but was forced to pass quite naked through the lower gate of the church. He was also served

[1] Hampton, *The General History of Polybius*, 1772, Vol. II, p. 291.

in the same manner at the sepulchre of St. Peter the martyr at New Castres, whom he had caused to be slain."

When, in 1211, the castle of Cabaret fell, its defenders were burned at the stake or destroyed in other painful ways. The lady of the castle was pitched alive into a pit, which was then filled up with stones. When Marmaude capitulated, five thousand men, women and children were massacred. Other so-called heretical sects met with a similar fate to the Albigenses. One such was the Apostolicals, who dressed in white, with bare heads, after the manner of the apostles. Gerhard Sagarellus of Parma, founder of the sect, was burned at the stake in the year 1300. Seven years later, his successor, Dulcino of Novara, and this man's wife, Margaretha, were publicly torn to pieces with hooks and other implements, and their remains thrown into a fire.

The fifteenth century saw the trial and execution of one of the most notorious and cold-blooded torturers of all time, to wit, Gilles de Rais, Marshal of France, a plutocrat of his day and an extensive landowner, compatriot and accomplice of Joan of Arc. In secret, the man was a sadist, a murderer, and a practitioner of Black Magic. He sacrificed children to the devil after putting them to unspeakable tortures. Acting under the Marshal's instructions, his servants kidnapped children of all ages and both sexes. For years nothing was suspected. In fact, it was not until de Rais crossed the path of the Church authorities that rumour got busy, and inquiries were made, culminating in his arrest in the October of 1440. Various allegations have been made as to the number of his victims, and no doubt there has been a good deal of exaggeration, but the Marshal, under threat of torture, admitted that he had murdered 140 children. He was hanged on October 26, 1440.

It is not to be wondered at that Russia, the land where torture was an everyday affair, should have provided a monster capable of equalling the blackest deeds of Nero. Such was Ivan IV, better known as Ivan the Terrible. His case belonged to the realm of psychopathology, and the man should have been shut up in an asylum. As it was, he ruled a vast country with a rod of iron. He had a giant's power and he wielded it in the manner of a tyrant. Like a sadistic god he gloated over the sufferings of humanity. The terrible *knut* cut the flesh of men and women to ribbons before they died under his eyes. He witnessed the rack perform its deadly work. He saw his subjects burnt alive, or torn to pieces by the wild animals kept for this especial purpose. By his orders, over 20,000 of the inhabitants of Novgorod were tortured or murdered. Even his own family were not free from persecution and danger: his son was beaten to death, and the murderer who wielded the club that finally bashed out the lad's brains was Ivan himself. A sigh of relief arose to high heaven when, in 1584, the monster went to his Maker.

England had its demons of cruelty too. In the seventeenth century lived Sir George Jeffreys, holding the position of Chief Justice of the Court of the King's Bench. The irony of the situation was in the fact that no man ever more unjustly dispensed what he was pleased to term justice. His inhuman sentences, his fiendish cruelty, earned for him the sobriquet of " Bloody Jeffreys." The court over which he presided was known as the " Bloody Assizes." He sentenced hundreds to be hanged; he had hundreds of others transported—a fate worse than death. It was Judge Jeffreys who inflicted upon Tutchin that terrible flogging sentence in which the prisoner was to be whipped through every market town in Dorsetshire every year for seven years.[1] It was Judge Jeffreys who sentenced Lady Alice Lisle to be burned alive, a sentence so monstrously inhuman, in view of her crime, that the clergy intervened and managed to get it altered to beheading.

In Scotland, James II authorized the use of the boots, the rack, the thumbscrews, and various other instruments of torture. As Duke of York, he was compelled to witness the torturing of prisoners, and it was alleged that while most members of the Council were overwhelmed with horror and loathing at the sights they witnessed and would escape the duty whenever possible, the Duke enjoyed the spectacle and never let pass an opportunity of being present when a victim was to be tormented.

[1] This brutal sentence was never inflicted.

Some Eighteenth and Nineteenth Century Torturers

The trial of Warren Hastings, in which he was charged with violation of the trust reposed in him as Governor of India, accepting bribes, and conniving at many forms of corruption, including the administration of torture, revealed the atrocities performed by one of Hastings' minions. Devi Sing collected taxes and rents from the natives, and, said Mr. Edmund Burke, in his address to the High Court of Parliament during the trial of Hastings, ranked as one of the most shocking monsters in history. But let us hear Mr. Burke's allegations in his own words:

"Those who could not raise the money, were most cruelly tortured: cords were drawn tight round their fingers, till the flesh of the four on each hand was actually incorporated, and became one solid mass: the fingers were then separated again by wedges of iron and wood driven in between them. Others were tied two and two by the feet, and thrown across a wooden bar, upon which they hung, with their feet uppermost; they were then beat on the soles of the feet, till their toe-nails dropped off. They were afterwards beat about the head till the blood gushed out at the mouth, nose and ears; they were also flogged upon the naked body with bamboo canes, and prickly bushes, and, above all, with some poisonous weeds, which were of a most caustic nature, and burnt at every touch. The cruelty of the monster who had ordered all this, had contrived how to tear the mind as well as the body; he frequently had a father and son tied naked to one another by the feet and arms, and then flogged till the skin was torn from the flesh; and he had the devilish satisfaction to know that every blow must hurt; for if one escaped the son, his sensibility was wounded by the knowledge he had that the blow had fallen upon his father: the same torture was felt by the father, when he knew that every blow that missed him had fallen upon his son.

"The treatment of the females could not be described: dragged forth from the inmost recesses of their houses, which the religion of the country had made so many sanctuaries, they were exposed naked to public view; the virgins were carried to the Court of Justice, where they might naturally have looked for protection, but now they looked for it in vain; for in the face of the Ministers of Justice, in the face of the spectators, in the face of the sun, those tender and modest virgins were brutally violated. The only difference between their treatment and that of their mothers was, that the former were dishonoured in the face of day, the latter in the gloomy recesses of their dungeons. Other females had the nipples of their breasts put in a cleft bamboo, and torn off. What modesty in all nations most carefully conceals, this monster revealed to view, and consumed by slow fires; nay, some of the monstrous tools of this monster Devi Sing had, horrid to tell, carried their unnatural brutality so far as to drink in the source of generation and life."[1]

On February 24, 1806, Sir Thomas Picton, late Governor of Trinidad, was convicted of torturing a native girl named Louisa Calderon, to extort confession. And this is the tale, gory, gruesome and cold-bloodedly inhuman, which was evolved bit by bit, during the course of the trial. In the December of 1801, the girl Calderon, then aged eleven years, was living with Pedro Ruiz as his mistress. The girl, it appears, was not faithful to Ruiz. She was carrying on an intrigue with one Carlos Gonzalez, who, as a friend of Ruiz, frequented his house. Gonzalez, not content with robbing Ruiz of his lover, took some money as well. He was arrested, and the girl Calderon, suspected of being an accomplice, was arrested with him. She denied complicity, and Sir Thomas Picton thereupon gave orders for her to be tortured.

The torture itself took a somewhat unusual form. According to the depositions of Louisa Calderon herself, she was carried to the room where the torture was prepared. Here she was suspended by the left wrist from the ceiling, her right hand and foot were tied together behind her back, while the extremity of her left foot rested on a wooden spike fixed in the floor. In this painful position she re-

[1] *The History of the Trial of Warren Hastings*, London, 1796.

mained for three quarters of an hour.   The next day the torture was repeated.   On both occasions she swooned away before she was taken down.   Failing to extract a confession, her inquisitors put her in irons, of the type called " grillos." These were long pieces of iron with two rings for the feet, fastened to the wall.   Pinioned in this way, she remained for eight months in a cell like a garret, with sloping sides. The girl stated that " the ' grillos ' were so placed that, owing to the lowness of the room, she could by no means raise herself up, during the eight months of her confinement."[1]

In the British West Indies, one-time home of torture, on May 8, 1811, the Honourable Arthur William Hodge was executed behind the gaol of Tortola for the murder of his slave Prosper.   This Prosper was but one of a number of victims.   A brief abstract of the paper laid before the House of Commons in connexion with the case tells a revolting story.   On the principle of set a thief to catch a thief, Hodge employed a slave to pursue and capture runaway negroes. This slave-hunter was named Welcome, and he did not always succeed in his mission.   In the January of 1806 he made three unsuccessful expeditions.   Each time, on his return with his tale of failure, Hodge had him cart-whipped. The wounds from one flogging were still unhealed when the next whipping was administered.   But the third time was the last.   Flesh and blood gave out.   The slave died. Shortly after this occurrence two female slaves attached to the Hodge establishment, as cook and washerwoman, died. They had been hounded to death by the planter's cruelty. On an accusation of attempting to poison his wife and children, Hodge poured boiling water down their throats, had them cart-whipped, and sent them, naked as the day they were born, to work in the fields.   During the two following years, 1807 and 1808, the persecutions continued. The cart-whip was seldom idle.   Slave after slave was whipped to death for trifling offences or for no offences at all.   There was, according to the evidence, case after case where one flogging followed another without any adequate intervals for the wounds to heal.   One slave, named Gift, was literally whipped to death on his feet; another youngster,

[1] G. T. Wilkinson, *The Newgate Calendar*, 1820.

Cuffy by name, " was cut to pieces, and had hardly any black skin remaining." On March 23, 1807, a new slave was so severely flogged that he died a couple of days later, " his body," according to the testimony of witnesses, " when carried out for burial being in a shockingly lacerated state "; and Tom Boiler, flogged for an hour without intermission, succumbed within the week. One witness testified that " it was scarcely possible to remain in the sick house, on account of the offensive smell from the corrupted wounds of cart-whipped slaves." He stated further that in the three years he had been with Hodge, at least sixty negroes had been buried and only one out of the lot had died a natural death.

For stealing candles, Violet was flogged to death; her son, for the crime of " running away," shared her fate. Frequently, Hodge adopted other methods of torture in addition to whipping. Burning the inside of the mouth with a red-hot iron was one of them. Nor were the children born to the negro slaves safe from his attentions. His favourite punishment was to have them taken by the heels, head downwards, and dipped into a tub of water until near the point of suffocation. They were lifted out, allowed to recover their breath, and then re-dipped. Or they were suspended by the hands from the branch of a tree and cart-whipped. Finally there was the whipping to death of Prosper.

PART THREE

THE TECHNIQUE OF TORTURE

CHAPTER XVII

IMPALING METHODS

Crucifixion

ONE of the oldest methods of torture was crucifixion. Its antiquity is indicated in its wide use by the Phœnicians. It was employed also by the Scythians, the Greeks, the Romans, the Persians and the Carthagenians. The use of the cross was probably, in most races, antedated by impalement upon a tree-trunk.

The wooden cross took various forms in different races and at different periods in history. The form which has been immortalized by the crucifixion of Jesus was probably the most widely employed at that time. It was really a most primitive affair, consisting of one short piece of timber attached horizontally to a longer upright stake. This stake was firmly fastened in the ground before the time of execution. It was not usually so fixed for each individual case, but was a permanent affair.

It was the usual custom for the criminal, after being scourged, to carry the cross beam to the place of execution.[1] The popular notion that Jesus carried the whole cross, that is, both the upright stake and the cross-piece, is probably erroneous, since such a procedure was at variance with contemporary usage. When the place of execution was reached, the victim was stripped naked and forced to stretch himself upon the ground on his back, with his head resting upon the cross-beam and his arms stretched outwards along its length.

---

[1] In some cases the scourging was applied *after* the victim had been nailed to the cross, instead of or in addition to flogging before crucifixion.

In some cases rope was used to bind the arms to the beam; in others this procedure was dispensed with, the sole fastenings being the long nails, one of which was driven through the palm of each hand into the beam. The cross-beam, with its human burden, was then lifted to its position on the upright stake, to which it was either nailed or bound with ropes. In order that the whole weight of the criminal might not rest upon the hands, involving the risk of the flesh giving way, the body was supported by a large peg fixed in the upright stake. The feet, which were at some little distance from the ground, were nailed to the upright, and in some cases the legs were bound to it with rope. In the case of each foot, the nail, which was large and long, was driven through the instep and sole.

Death was slow and unutterably agonizing. It represented a form of torture continuing for days on end, which was sometimes prolonged by giving the criminal food and drink. The suffering was capable of being increased and intensified in a hundred ways, according to the vindictive or malignant nature of the persecutors or the executioners. The legs were sometimes broken by heavy blows; the face and breasts torn by hooked implements; the body prodded with pointed rods or stakes. Sometimes sticks were forcibly pushed into the anal orifice or the urethral passage and then redrawn. Another variation consisted of smearing the face with honey to attract insects.

The Romans and many other races left the body on the cross, letting it rot until nothing but the bare bones were left. The Jews took the corpse down immediately death came and buried it in accordance with the instructions of Moses, thus: " His body shall not remain all night upon the tree, but thou shalt in any wise bury him that day."

Crucifixion, although not often practised, emerged through the centuries. One of the last cases of which there is any record was in France, in 1127, when Bertholde, the murderer of Charles the Righteous, was crucified by the order of Louis.

The " Dice "

In this torture, which ranked as one of the minor forms employed by the Inquisition, the prisoner was forced to

VARIOUS FORMS OF CRUCIFIXION

From the 1688 (Antwerp) Edition of Gallonio's
De SS. Martyrum Cruciatibus.

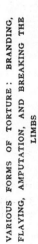

VARIOUS FORMS OF TORTURE: BRANDING,
FLAYING, AMPUTATION, AND BREAKING THE
LIMBS

From the 1688 (Antwerp) Edition of Gallonio's
De SS. Martyrum Cruciatibus.

extend himself on the floor. He was bound or held in this position. Two pieces of iron or other metal, shaped like a die, but concave on one side, were placed upon the heel of the right foot, where they were bound firmly and tightly in place with a rope. By means of a screw, pressure was applied, forcing the metal into the flesh.

" Peine forte et dure " or Pressing to Death

The uses to which this particular torture were put have already been indicated (cf. page 87). The manner of its execution is described by Stow (*Survey of London*, 1720) as follows:

> "The criminal is sent back to the prison whence he came, and there laid in some low dark room, upon the bare ground on his back, all naked, except his privy parts, his arms and legs drawn with cords fastened to several parts of the room; and then there is laid on his body, iron, stone, or lead, so much as he can bear; the next day he shall have three morsels of barley bread, without drink; and the third day shall have to drink some of the kennel water with bread. And this method is in strictness to be observed until he is dead."

According to Pike, it was customary, in England, in order to hasten death, to place a sharp piece of timber under the back of the sufferer.[1] When Major Strangeways, in 1658, was condemned to the torture of *peine forte et dure*, this procedure was not adopted. In its place a heavy piece of iron was fixed " anglewise over his heart " and the attendants increased the pressure by throwing the weight of their own bodies upon it. The major was dead in eight or ten minutes. In many cases the prisoner agreed to plead. Thus the murderer Burnworth, at Kingston, in 1726, after bearing the pressure of a mass weighing nearly four hundredweights, for one hour and three-quarters, begged for mercy. He was tried, found guilty, and hanged.[2]

It would appear that this terrible punishment was some-

[1] Luke Owen Pike, *A History of Crime in England*, 1873.
[2] *Ibid*.

times inflicted upon those who were mute from necessity. Thus, at Nottingham assizes, in 1735, an alleged murderer, deaf and dumb from birth, for failing to plead, was pressed to death. Evidently the statements of witnesses as to the authenticity of their afflictions availed these deaf and dumb suspects nothing, the judges being afraid they might be hoodwinked. That such a fear was not altogether fanciful is proved in a case occurring in Ireland. In 1740, Mathew Ryan was tried for highway robbery at the Kilkenny assizes. He could not be induced to plead, being apparently dumb, but the jury decided the affliction was simulated.

" The judges on this desired the prisoner to plead; but he still pretended to be insensible to all that was said to him. The law now called for the *peine forte et dure*; but the judges compassionately deferred awarding it until a future day, in the hope that he might in the meantime acquire a juster sense of his situation. When again brought up, however, the criminal persisted in his refusal to plead: and the court at last pronounced the dreadful sentence, that he should be pressed to death. The sentence was accordingly executed upon him two days after, in the public market-place of Kilkenny. As the weights were heaping on the wretched man, he earnestly supplicated to be hanged; but it being beyond the power of the sheriff to deviate from the mode of punishment prescribed in the sentence, even this was an indulgence which could no longer be granted to him."[1]

This peculiar form of torture seems to have been little known or used in America. The only case of which there is any record is that of Giles Cory, charged with witchcraft in 1692. He steadfastly refused to plead, and was pressed to death.[2]

[1] *The Percy Anecdotes*, 1823, Vol. VIII, p. 39.
[2] Cobbett's *State Trials*, Vol. VI, p. 679.

CHAPTER XVIII

BURNING AT THE STAKE, BRANDING, BOILING TO DEATH, THE FIRE-PAN AND THE BRAZEN BULL[1]

Burning Alive

THERE is evidence of the antiquity of this form of execution for the finding in the Bible. "If a man abide not in me, he is cast forth as a branch, and is withered; and men gather them, and cast them into the fire, and they are burned." The Babylonians, as well as the Hebrews, used it as a mode of execution for certain crimes. It is also referred to by Eusebius in his account of the death of Apphianus, a victim of Maximinus's terrible cruelty. The man's feet were wrapped in cotton that had been well soaked in oil, and then set on fire.

"The martyr was hung up at a great height, in order that, by this dreadful spectacle, he might strike terror into all those who were looking on, while at the same time they tore his sides and ribs with combs, till he became one mass of swelling all over, and the appearance of his countenance was completely changed. And for a long time his feet were burning in a sharp fire, so that the flesh of his feet, as it was consumed, dropped like melted wax, and the fire burst into his very bones like dry reeds."[1]

There would appear to be few, if any, countries where, in the early days of civilization, as well as in savagery, burning at the stake was not practised in some form.

Many savage races were accustomed to burning their captives in this way. Generally speaking, it was looked upon as a suitable method of execution for enemies, those belonging to inferior classes, or those guilty of infamous or

---

[1] Eusebius, *History of the Martyrs in Palestine*, 1861, p. 15.

repulsive crimes. Thus Yahveh used this form of punishment for incest and prostitution: "And if a man take a wife and her mother; it is wickedness; they shall be burnt with fire, both he and they; that there be no wickedness among you." Again: "And the daughter of any priest, if she profane herself by playing the whore, she profaneth her father: she shall be burnt with fire." Constantine ordered that a slave who had intercourse with a free woman should be burned alive.

It was a favourite sentence in the case of those found guilty of heresy. The Inquisition condemned thousands to the flames. It was no less a favourite method throughout all the countries of Europe, Protestant as well as Catholic, for dealing with sorcerers and witches. Thus the burning of Gilles de Rais and of Joan of Arc. In the year 1415, Dr. John Huss, rector of the University of Prague, and Jerome of that same city, a disciple of the doctor, were both burnt alive for heresy.

In Britain, for centuries, burning was recognized as a mode of execution for certain crimes, notably, as in continental Europe, for heresy. In the fifteenth and sixteenth centuries, according to the various chronicles of martyrdom compiled by Fox[1] and others, there were many such executions. The manner in which the burning was carried out is well illustrated in the following account of the execution, for heresy, in 1555, at Gloucester, in the presence of some 7,000 spectators, of Dr. John Hooper, Lord Bishop of Gloucester.

"The place of execution was near a great elm tree, over against the college of priests, where he was used to preach; the spot round about and the boughs of the tree were filled with spectators. Bishop Hooper then knelt down and prayed. Having closed his devotional exercises the Bishop prepared himself for the stake. He took off his gown, and delivered it to the sheriff; he then took off his doublet, hose, and waistcoat. Being now in his shirt, he trussed it between his legs, where he had a

---

[1] Although Fox is not always to be relied upon, the number of heretics who were burnt alive probably exceeded by far the cases he gives, or other existent records.

pound of gunpowder in a bladder, and under each arm
the same quantity. He now went up to the stake, where
three iron hoops were brought, one to fasten him round
the waist, another round his neck, and another round his
legs; but he refused to be bound with them, saying, 'You
have no need to trouble yourselves; I doubt not God will
give me strength sufficient to abide the extremity of
the fire without bands; notwithstanding, suspecting the
frailty and weakness of the flesh, but having assured con-
fidence in God's strength, I am content you do as you
think good.' The iron hoop was then put round his
waist, which being made too short, he shrank and put
in his belly with his hand; but when they offered to bind
his neck and legs he refused them, saying, 'I am well
assured I shall not trouble you.' Being affixed to the
stake, he lifted up his eyes and hands to heaven, and
prayed in silence. The man appointed to kindle the fire
then came to him and requested his forgiveness, of whom
he asked why he should forgive him, since he knew of
no offence he had committed against him. 'O sir (said
the man), I am appointed to make the fire.' 'Therein,'
said Bishop Hooper, 'thou dost nothing to offend me:
God forgive thee thy sins, and do thy office I pray thee.'
Then the reeds were thrown up, and he received two
bundles of them in his own hands, and put one under
each arm. Command was now given that the fire should
be kindled; but, owing to the number of green faggots,
it was some time before the flames set fire to the reeds.
The wind being adverse, and the morning very cold, the
flames blew from him, so that he was scarcely touched
by the fire. Another fire was soon kindled of a more
vehement nature: it was now the bladders of gunpowder
exploded, but they proved of no service to the suffering
prelate. He now prayed with a loud voice, 'Lord Jesus,
have mercy upon me; Lord Jesus, have mercy upon me;
Lord Jesus, receive my spirit': and these were the last
words he was heard to utter. But even when his face
was completely black with the flames, and his tongue
swelled so that he could not speak, yet his lips went till
they were shrunk to the gums; and he knocked his breast
with his hands until one of his arms fell off, and then

continued knocking with the other while the fat, water, and blood dripped out at his finger ends. At length, by renewing of the fire, his strength was gone, and his hand fastened in the iron which was put round him. Soon after, the whole lower part of his body being consumed, he fell over the iron that bound him, into the fire, amidst the horrible yells and acclamations of the bloody crew that surrounded him. This holy martyr was more than *three quarters of an hour* consuming; the inexpressible anguish of which he endured as a lamb, moving neither forwards, backwards, nor to any side: his nether parts were consumed, and his bowels fell out some time before he expired. Thus perished, in a manner the most horrible that the rage of hell itself could devise, in a manner more barbarous than that exercised by wild American Indians to their prisoners taken in war, the right reverend father in God, Dr. John Hooper, for some time Bishop of Worcester, and afterward of Gloucester."[1]

Some victims suffered much longer than others, as is indicated in the report of the burning of the Rev. George Marsh, in 1555. "The fire," we read, "being unskilfully made, and the wind contrary, he suffered extreme torture."[2]

Later it became customary to strangle the criminal and then to burn the corpse, but the plan sometimes miscarried. Strutt, writing in 1775, says:

"The letter of the law to this very day, I believe condemns a woman, who doth murder her husband, to be burnt alive, but the sentence is always mitigated, for they are first strangled. In the case of Catherine Hayes (who, for the murder of her husband, some few years ago, was adjudged to suffer death at the stake) the intention was first to strangle her; but as they used at that time to draw a rope which was fastened round the culprit's neck, and came through a staple of the stake, but at the very moment that the fire was put to

---

[1] Henry Moore, *The History of the Persecutions of the Church of Rome and Complete Protestant Martyrology*, 1809, pp. 256-7.
[2] *Ibid.*, p. 296.

the wood which was set around, the flames sometimes
reached the offenders before they were quite strangled
—just so it happened to her; for the fire taking quick
hold of the wood, and the wind being brisk, blew the
smoke and blaze so full in the faces of the executioners,
who were pulling at the rope, that they were obliged
to let go their hold before they had quite strangled
her; so that, as I have been informed by some there
present, she suffered much torment before she died.

Ann Williams, convicted of poisoning her husband,
burnt at the stake at Gloucester, April 13, 1753

But now they are first hanged at the stake until they
are quite dead, and then the fire is kindled round, and
the body burnt to ashes."[1]

Execution by burning at the stake was never considered by the inquisitors of Spain or by the English courts
to be a form of torture. There was, however, a " torture

[1] Joseph Strutt, *Manners and Customs of the Inhabitants of England,*
1775, Vol. III, pp. 47-8.

by fire," which constituted one of the three favourite torments employed by the Inquisitions of Italy and Spain, also, more rarely, by those in other countries, to force their prisoners to confess. The accusèd person (the torture was applied to males and females alike) was fixed in the stocks. The legs and feet were bared, and the soles well-greased with lard. A fire was lighted and the feet literally fried by the heat to which they were exposed. When the prisoner began to cry out in agony at the intolerable heat, a screen of wood or metal was placed in front of the fire and a de-

Richard Turpin torturing a woman by fire to extract information

mand for confession made. If this was refused, the screen was removed and the prisoner again subjected to the frying process. This was continued until either a confession was extracted or the victim fainted. Torture by fire was usually adopted when the pulley and the rack had failed; or where, for any reason, these tortures were inapplicable or inadvisable.

The white races in their tortures of the savages which fell into their power practised analogous methods to those used by the aborigines themselves. Bartholomew De Las Casas says:

" I once beheld four or five principal Indians roasted
alive at a slow fire, and as the miserable victims poured
forth dreadful screams, which disturbed the commanding officer in his afternoon slumbers, he sent word that
they should be strangled, but the officer on guard (I
know his name, and I know his relations in Seville)
would not suffer it; but causing their mouths to be
gagged, that their cries might not be heard, he stirred
up the fire with his own hands, and roasted them deliberately till they all expired—I saw it myself."[1]

Torture by fire was employed by thieves and others for
the purpose of extracting information. Richard Turpin,[2]
the eighteenth-century highway robber, by forcing a
woman to sit on the fire in her own house, and holding
her there by main force, induced her to disclose the hiding
place of her money.

Branding

This punishment was at one time widely practised in
England. The irons employed bore marks or letters of
various kinds, for use according to the nature of the offence.
The inside of the left hand was usually chosen as the place
upon which to apply the hot iron. Rogues and vagabonds
were branded with the letter R; thieves with the letter T;
and those guilty of manslaughter with M. The objects of
branding were twofold. There was the punishment
effected by the red-hot metal being impinged, none too
gently, on the skin; and the marking of the criminal so
that if he again be apprehended for some offence or other,
the court would be aware of his previous misdemeanour.
In some cases the branding was inflicted on other more
sensitive spots than the hand. Thus, for shop-lifting, the
penalty was burning on the cheek under the eye. For
blasphemy, the tongue was bored through with a red-hot

[1] Quoted by Bryan Edwards, *The History of the British Colonies in the
West Indies*, 1793, Vol. I, Book I, Ch. III, p. 88.
[2] The hero of a hundred apocryphal adventures, whose " ride to York "
is known to every schoolboy. Turpin was executed at York on April 10,
1739.

skewer; in a case of perjury part of the penalty was branding on the forehead with the letter P.

In France, for all kinds of minor offences, the punishment was branding with the *fleur-de-lis*. In Russia this
form of punishment was widely practised in the fifteenth,
sixteenth, seventeenth and eighteenth centuries. In addition, slaves, as a matter of routine, were branded on the
forehead and cheeks.

Boiling and Frying

Boiling to death is a very old form of execution. We
find it repeatedly referred to in ancient literature. The
modus operandi was simple. A huge cauldron or other
receptacle containing water, oil or tallow was heated until
it reached boiling-point, and into this the victim was
pitched, as often as not head first. Or, if the executioners
wished to prolong the agony of their victim, the contents
of the cauldron were brought gradually to boiling-point,
while the individual, bound hand and foot, was covered,
except for the head, with the fluid. The frying-pan method
varied little from boiling, except that, in this case, the victim was placed in a large shallow receptacle or dish containing oil, tallow or pitch and fried alive. A variation of
this procedure was where a gridiron or metal platform
was used, under which a fire was lighted.

The account of the torturing of the Maccabees, from the
pen of Josephus, is perhaps the most celebrated description
of these various tortures that is available in literature. It
relates the torments and execution of a mother and her seven
sons, at the command of that pitiless monster, Antiochus.

" The tyrant caused them to be beaten with bulls-
pizzles; first commanding Maccabeus the eldest to be
stripped and stretched out upon a rack, and his hands to
be bound, and so to be most cruelly beaten, who so
wearied his tormentors by suffering, that they rather
desired to give over than he requested it. Then was he
put upon a wheel, and a weight hanged at his feet, and
so stretched round about it, that his sinews and entrails
brake; yet all this while he called upon God. A fire was

From Clark's *Martyrologia*, 1677.

TORTURES OF THE MACCABEES

(See Text, page 164.)

kindled and he was racked on the wheel, was thrown
into it, and by flames was so burned that his bowels
appeared, yet was his mind unmoved. Then was he
taken from the fire; and slain alive, his tongue being
pulled out of his head, and he put into a frying-pan, and
so he departed out of this life, to the admiration of his
enemies, and the joy of his mother, and brethren.

" Then was the second brother, called Aber, haled by
the soldiers; and the tyrant showed him all those instruments of torment, and asked him if he would eat of the
sacrifice; which he, denying to do, his hands were bound
with iron chains, and being hanged up thereby, the skin
of his body was slain from the crown of his head to his
knees, so that the entrails in his breast were seen : then
was he cast to a cruel Libard (leopard), greedily thirsting
after blood, but the beast, smelling at him, forgat his
cruelty and went from him, without doing him any
harm. This increased the tyrant's rage, and Aber by his
torments grew more constant. Shortly after he yielded
up his soul to God.

" Then Machir the third son was brought. The
tyrant devised new torments, commanding a globe to be
brought, he caused him to be tied about it in such sort
that all his bones were put out of joint, hanging one from
another in a most pitiful manner; then the skin of his
head and face was pulled off and then was he put upon
the wheel, but he could be wracked no worse, for all his
bones were dislocated before, the blood issuing from him
abundantly—then his tongue was cut out, and he being
put into a fiery frying-pan, resigned his spirit unto God."

Josephus continues his terrible and harrowing description. He tells us how Judas, the fourth brother, was bound
to a stake and beaten, had his tongue ripped out and suffered
other mutilation before ending his life on the wheel; how
Achus, the fifth brother, was thrown into the brazen pot;
how Areth, the sixth, after being tied to a pillar, head downwards, and near enough to a hot fire to be roasted but not
burned to death, was pricked with sharp-pointed instruments
in very nearly every part of his body, had his tongue pulled
out with red-hot pincers, and was finally thrown into the

frying-pan; how Jacob, the youngest of the lot, had his hands amputated and his tongue pulled out before being cooked in the frying-pan. Then Antiochus turned to deal with the mother, who had already suffered mental agony, in witnessing these sanguinary and appalling tortures, sufficient to drive any less Spartan-like woman demented. He " caused her to be stripped, hanged up by the hands and cruelly whipped. Then were her dugs and paps pulled off, and herself put into the red-hot frying-pan."

An instance of boiling to death in England was the execution at Smithfield, in 1530, of a cook named John Roose, for poisoning seventeen persons of the Bishop of Rochester's household, two of whom died. " By a retrospective law," we read in *The Percy Anecdotes*, " Roose was sentenced to be boiled to death; a judgment, horrible as it was, which was carried into execution." And in 1541, at the same place, Margaret Dawe was boiled to death for a similar crime.

The Brazen Bull

According to Lucian, the " brazen bull " which stood in the temple of the first Phalaris, was the invention of a man named Perilaus. It ranked as one of the most ingenious and diabolical instruments of torture ever conceived in the mind of man. This apparatus, which was made of metal, was fashioned to the exact size and shape of a bull. The interior formed a hollow chamber, and there was a trap-door in the back of the bull for ingress and egress. The inventor, knowing the reputation for cruelty of the tyrant Phalaris, brought the bull to him for inspection and proceeded to explain the ingenuity of the torture it was designed to produce. The culprit, explained Perilaus, was to be shut up inside the bull and a fire kindled underneath. The agonies of the imprisoned offender would be so great that he would yell and scream with pain and fear, and these roars and screams, by means of a most ingenious arrangement of flutes in the bull's nostrils, would be transformed into a melodious lowing. Phalaris, it appears, was " filled with abhorrence for both the artificer and his work," and determined to punish him in an ironically fitting manner. But let the tyrant tell the remainder of the tale in his own words :

TORTURE OF THE WHEEL

From the 1688 (Antwerp) Edition of Gallonio's
De SS. Martyrum Cruciatibus.

TORTURE OF THE BRAZEN BULL, THE FRYING
PAN, AND THE GRIDIRON

From the 1688 (Antwerp) Edition of Gallonio's
De SS. Martyrum Cruciatibus.

" ' Well, now, Perilaus,' I said, ' if you are so sure of your contrivance, give us a proof of it on the spot : mount up and get in and imitate the cries of a man tortured in it, that we may hear whether such charming music will proceed from it, as you would make us believe.' Perilaus obeyed, and no sooner was he in the belly of the bull, than I shut the aperture, and put fire beneath it. ' Take that,' said I, ' as the only recompense such a piece of art is worth, and chant us the first specimen of the charming notes of which you are the inventor ! ' And so the barbarous wretch suffered what he had well merited by such an infamous application of his mechanical talent. However, that the noble work should not be contaminated by his dying there, I ordered him to be drawn out while still alive, and thrown down from the summit of the rock, where his body was left unburied."[1]

Ovid refers to the brazen bull of Perilaus in the well-known lines :

"Perilaus, roasted in the bull he made,
    Gave the first proof of his own cruel trade."

[1] Lucian, *Works*.

CHAPTER XIX

SQUASSATION, THE RACK, THE WHEEL, THE BOOT AND THE SCAVENGER'S DAUGHTER

Squassation or the Torture of the Pulley

THE torture of the pulley was known as the first torture of the Inquisition. With this method the victim was, as usual in most torments of the Inquisition, stripped to his drawers, his ankles shackled, and his wrists tied securely behind his back. A stout rope was then fastened to his wrists and carried over a pulley fixed to the roof of the torture chamber. The executioners drew him up with this rope until he was suspended about six feet from the floor. In this position, heavy iron weights, usually amounting to about 100 pounds, were attached to the irons on his feet. At this juncture he was asked once more to reveal the truth. Refusal meant the infliction of a number of stripes with a whip upon his naked back. The questions were repeated. Failure to confess was the signal for the torture to start in real earnest. The executioners pulled on the rope, raising the victim almost to the ceiling. Suddenly allowing the rope to slack for several feet, they then brought this rapid descent to an abrupt termination before the weights reached the floor. The shock to the body, of this suddenly terminated fall, was sufficient to jar every bone, joint and nerve in the system. In most cases it entailed dislocation. The process was repeated again and again until the culprit confessed or became unconscious.

According to the anonymous author of *The History of the Inquisition* (1828) there were various degrees of severity with which this form of torture was applied, the precise degree depending upon the nature of the crime with which the prisoner was accused and upon the will of the judge. These degrees of torture were indicated when pronouncing sentence. Thus if the judge said, " Let the prisoner be interrogated by torture," he was merely hoisted upon the rope.

If the judge said: "Let him be tortured," this meant the undergoing of squassation once only. If the judge said: "Let him be well tortured," the indication was two squassations; while the words "severely tortured" meant three squassations; and "very severely tortured" meant three squassations with "twistings and additional weights suspended from the feet."

Torture of the Rack or Wooden Horse

The second mode of torture employed by the Inquisition was the rack.[1] This apparatus varied somewhat in its construction in different countries, though its principle was the same in all. The rack stood about three feet from the ground and consisted of a stout wooden framework with sticks across it after the manner of a ladder. The victim was stretched upon this frame, his wrists and ankles being attached with strong cords to two rollers, one at each end of the rack. These rollers were operated by levers which moved in opposite directions to each other. When the victim was securely fastened on the rack, the questions to which answers were desired were put to him. Failure to reply satisfactorily was the signal for the two executioners to commence operating the levers. The result was the stretching of the victim's limbs and body. If persisted in, this was bound to cause dislocation of the joints or to drag off the members. In some cases the limbs were stretched in much the same manner as on the rack but by means of ropes and pulleys attached to rings or staples in the walls.

Occasionally the tortures of the rack were varied or increased by the use of cords in addition to the stretching mechanism. The arms and legs were bound to the sides of the rack with thin but strong cords. These cords were wound around each limb three times, and a stick was inserted in each. When all was ready for the torture to commence, the executioners twisted these sticks, thus gradually tightening the cords and causing them to cut into the flesh until the bones were reached, inflicting terrible wounds.

[1] Termed by the French, the *chevalet*, by the Spaniards, the *escalero*. It was generally referred to as the " wooden horse."

For some idea respecting the nature of the torture of the rack we are indebted to the accounts of those, and they were comparatively few, who managed to escape the clutches of the Inquisition after undergoing the terrible ordeal. One such revealing instance was that of John Coustos, who, accused of the crime of freemasonry, was, in 1743, imprisoned by the Inquisition of Lisbon. Refusing to divulge the secrets of his order, Coustos was conveyed to the torture chamber. Stripped of everything but his drawers, he was fixed on his back on the rack, his neck enclosed in an iron collar, and his feet attached to two rings. Two ropes the size of a man's little finger were wound around each arm and leg and passed through holes made for the purpose in the rack. The ropes were drawn tight by the executioners, cutting through the flesh to the bone, and causing the blood to gush out from the wounds made. The executioners bent their strength to the task four different times, and at the fourth their victim fainted through loss of blood and excruciating pain. After six weeks, which were allowed for recuperation, Coustos was again brought to the torture chamber. This time the procedure was somewhat different. He was made to stretch out his arms with the palms of his hands turned outwards. His wrists were tied, and then a machine gradually drew his hands together behind him until the backs of them touched. A second and yet a third time was the operation repeated. His shoulders were dislocated in the process; the blood gushed from his mouth. Back to his dungeon was Coustos taken, where his bones were set by surgeons. Two months passed, and then for the third time was he carried to that chamber of horrors. On this occasion, his tormenters passed a thick iron chain twice around his body, crossing it over his stomach. The chain terminated in rings which were fastened to his wrists. He was then placed against a thick wooden partition, at each end of which was a pulley. Ropes were fastened to the rings on his wrists and run through the pulleys, the other ends being fixed to a roller. This roller, being set in motion, the ropes gradually tightened, pulling the chain tighter and tighter across the stomach until not only did it bite into the naked flesh, but it pulled his wrists out of joint and dislocated the shoulders. The surgeons got to work again, and after the bones were set and the wounds

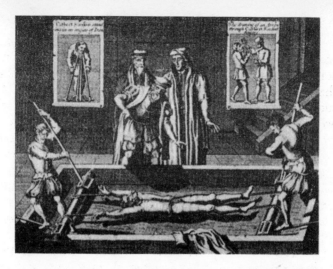

CUTHBERT SIMSON RACKED IN THE TOWER OF LONDON, 1557
(See Text, page 171.)

THE TORTURING OF JOHN COUSTOS BY THE INQUISITION OF LISBON
(See Text, page 170.)

healed, the torture was repeated. Through all this Coustos maintained a stony silence. Finding their efforts of no avail, the inquisitors sentenced him to four years' service as a galley-slave, after which he was banished from the country.

Very similar to the rack used in the Inquisition was the type employed in the Tower of London. According to his own statement, Cuthbert Simson, in December 1557, was sent to the Tower, charged with heresy, and tortured "in a rack of iron " for the space of some three hours.

"On the Sunday after," continues Simson, "I was brought to the same place again before the Lieutenant and the Recorder of London, and they examined me. As before I had said, I answered. Then did they bind my two forefingers together, and put a small arrow betwixt them, and drew it through so fast that blood followed, and the arrow broke. Then they racked me twice."[1]

The Torture of Water

Often in combination with the rack was applied the " torture of water."[2] This was generally adopted when racking, in itself, proved ineffectual. The victim, while pinioned on the rack, was compelled to swallow water, which was dropped slowly on a piece of silk or fine linen placed in his mouth. This material, under pressure of the water, gradually glided down the throat, producing the sensation experienced by a person who is drowning. A variation of the water torture was to cover the face with a piece of thin linen, upon which the water was poured slowly, running into the mouth and nostrils and hindering or preventing breathing almost to the point of suffocation. In another variation, the nose was stopped up, either by means of plugs placed in the nostrils, or by pressure of the fingers, and water was dropped slowly and continuously into the open mouth. The victim, in his desperate efforts to breathe, often burst a blood-vessel. Generally speaking, the larger the quantity of water forced into the victim the more severe was the torture.

[1] *Book of Martyrs*, 1732.
[2] Sometimes referred to as *tormento de toca*.

Of these torments employed in combination, there is
for the finding in all literature no better, more terrible
and more heartrending a description of the sufferings induced than that recounted by William Lithgow, a Scots-
man, who, in 1620, was mistaken for a spy, arrested at
Malaga, thrown into the dungeons of the Inquisition and
tortured to the very limits of human endurance. The
marvel of it all was that the man ever lived to tell his tale.
I reproduce it here in his own words.

"I was by the executioner stripped to the skin,
brought to the rack, and then mounted by him on the
top of it, where soon after I was hung by the bare
shoulders with two small cords, which went under both
my arms, running on two rings of iron that were fixed
in the wall above my head. Thus being hoisted to the
appointed height, the tormenter descended below, and
drawing down my legs, through the two sides of the
three-planked rack, he tied a cord about each of my
ankles and then ascending upon the rack he drew the
cords upward, and bending forward with main force
my two knees against the two planks, the sinews of my
hams burst asunder, and the lids of my knees being
crushed, and the cords made fast, I hung so demained
for a large hour.

"At last the encarouador, informing the Governor
that I had the mark of Jerusalem on my right arme,
joined with the name and crown of King James, and
done upon the Holy Grave, the corredigor came out
of his adjoining stance and gave direction to teare
asunder the name and crown (as he said) of that Heretic
King, an arch-enemy of the Holy Catholic Church.
Then the tormenter, laying the right arme above the
left, and the crown upmost, did cast a cord over both
arms seven distant times: and then lying down upon
his back, and setting both his feet on my hollow
pinched belly, he charged and drew violently with his
hands, making my womb suffer the force of his feet,
till the seven several cords combined in one place of
my arme (and cutting the crown, sinews, and flesh to
the bare bones) did pull in my fingers close to the palm

of my hands; the left hand of which is lame so still and
will be for ever.

"Now mine eyes began to startle, my mouth to
foam and froth, and my teeth to chatter like to the
doubling of drummer's sticks. O strange inhumanity
of men, monster manglers! I surpassing the limits of
their natural law; three score tortures being the trial of
treason, which I had, and was to endure: yet thus to inflict a seven-fold surplussage of more intolerable cruelties: and notwithstanding of my shivering lips, in this
fiery passion, my vehement groaning, and blood spring-
ing forth from arms, broke sinews, hams and knees;
yea and my depending weight on flesh-cutting cords,
yet they struck me on the face with cudgels, to abate
and cease the thundering noise of my wrestling
voice.

"At last being loosed from these pinnacles of pain,
I was hand-fast set on the floor, with this their in-
cessant imploration: Confess, confess, confess in time,
for thine inevitable torments ensue; where finding
nothing from me, but still innocent, O, I am innocent,
O Jesus! the lamb of God have mercy upon me, and
strengthen then me with patience to undergo this barbarous murder.

"Then by command of the Justice, was my trembling body laid above, and along, upon the face of the
rack, with my head downward, inclosed within a
circled hole; my belly upmost, and my heels upward
toward the top of the rack, my legs and arms being
drawn asunder, were fastened with pins and cords to
both sides of the outward planks; for now was I to receive my main torments. Now what a *Pottaro* or rack
is (for it stood by the wall of timber, the upmost end
whereof is larger than a full stride, the lower end
being narrow, and the three planks joining together are
made conformable to a man's shoulders; in the down-
most end of the middle plank there was a hole, wherein my head was laid; in length it is longer than a man
being interlaced with small cords from plank to plank
which divided my supported thighs from the middle
plank; through the sides of which exterior planks there

were three distant holes in every one of them; the use whereof you shall presently hear).[1]

"Now the Alcaide giving commission, the executioner laid first a cord over the calf of my leg, then another on the middle of my thigh, and the third cord over the great of my arm; which was severally done on both sides of my body receiving the ends of the cords, from these six several places through the holes made in the outward planks, which were fastened to pins, and the pins made fast with a device: for he was to charge on the outside of the planks, with as many pins as there were holes and cords; the cords being first laid next to my skin. And in every one of these six parts of my body, I was to receive seven several tortures: each torture consisting of three winding throws of every pin, which amounted to twenty-one throws in every one of these six parts.

"Then the tormenter having charged the first passage above my body (making fast by a device each torture as they were multiplied), he went to an earthen jar standing full of water, a little beneath my head: from whence carrying a pot full of water, in the bottom whereof there was an incised hole, which being stopped by his thumb, till it came to my mouth, he did pour it in my belly; the measure being a Spanish *sombre* which is an English pottle; the first and second devices I gladly received, such was the scorching drought of my tormenting pain, and likewise I had drunk none for three days before. But afterward, at the third charge perceiving these measures of water to be inflicted upon me as tortures, O strangling tortures! I closed my lips again-standing that eager crudelity. Whereat the Alcaide enraged, set my teeth asunder with a pair of iron cadges, detaining them there, at every several turn, both mainly and manually; whereupon my hunger-clunged belly waxing great, grew drum-like imbolstred, for it being a suffocating pain, in regard of my head hanging downward, and the water

---

[1] From this description, and the accompanying illustration, it is evident that the type of rack used in this instance differed from that employed in most of the Inquisitions and in the Tower of London.

WILLIAM LITHGOW TORTURED ON THE RACK
(See Text, page 172.)

WHIPPING AT THE CART'S TAIL AND OTHER TORTURES
From an Engraving in *Theatrum Crudelitatum Haereicorum*, 1592.

reingorging itself, in my throat, with a struggling force, it strangled and swallowed up my breath from yowling and groaning.

"And now to prevent my renewing grief (for presently my heart faileth and forsaketh me) I will only briefly avouch, that between each one of these seven circular charges, I was aye re-examined, each examination continuing half an hour, each half-hour a hell of internal pain, and between each torment, a long distance of life-quelling time.

"Thus lay I six hours upon the rack, between four a clock afternoon, and ten a clock at night, having had inflicted upon me sixty several torments. Nevertheless they continued me a large half-hour (after all my torments) at the full bending, where my body being all begored with blood, and cut through in every part, to the crushed and bruised bones, I pitifully remained, still roaring, howling, foaming, bellowing, and gnashing my teeth, with insupportable cries, before the pins were undone, and my body loosed. True it is, it passeth the capacity of man, either sensibly to conceive, or I patiently to express the intolerable anxiety of mind, and affliction of body, in that dreadful time I sustained.

"At last my head being by their arms advanced, and my body taken from the rack, the water regushed abundantly from my mouth; then they recloathed my broken, bloody, and cold trembling body being all this time stark naked; I fell twice in a sounding trance, which they again refreshed with a little wine, and two warm eggs, not for charity done, but that I should be reserved to further punishment.

"And now at last they charged my broken legs with my former eye-frightening irons, and carried me to the coach, being after brought secretly to my former dungeon, without any knowledge of the town, save to my lawless and merciless tormenters. I was laid, with my head and heels alike high, on my former stones. The latter end of this woeful night, poor mourning Hazier, the Turk, was sent to keep me; and on the morrow the Governor entered my room, threatening me with still more tortures, to confess; and so he caused every morning to make me believe I was going to be racked again, to make me confess an untruth; and thus they continued every day of five days to Christmas.

"Upon Christmas-day, Marina, the ladies' gentlewoman, got permission to visit me, and with her licence she brought abundance of tears, presenting me also with a dish of honey, sugar, some confections, and raisins in great plenty, to my no small comfort, besides using many sweet speeches for consolation's sake. The twelfth day of Christmas expired, they began to threaten me on still with more tortures, even till Candlemas. In all which comfortless time I was miserably afflicted with the beastly plague of gnawing vermin which lay crawling in lumps, within, without, and about my body; yea hanging in clusters about my beard, my lips, my nostrils, and my eyebrows, almost inclosing my sight. And for the greater satisfaction to their merciless minds, the Governor called Areta, his silver plate keeper, to gather and sweep the vermin upon me twice in eight days, which tormented me almost to death being a perpetual punishment; yet the poor infidel, some few times, and when opportunity served, would steal the keys from Areta, and about midnight would enter my room, with sticks and burning oil, and sweeping them together in heaps, would burn the greatest part, to my great release, or, doubtless, I had been miserably eaten up and devoured by them."[1]

The "water torture" was by no means confined to the Inquisition. In a miscellany of ways and in combination with various other tortures, it was used in most countries until comparatively recent times. Surreptitiously it is probably used in some form or other even to-day.

One of the most horrible instances of its employment

---

[1] William Lithgow, *The Totall Discourse of the Rare Adventures and painefull peregrinations of long nineteene yeares Travailes from Scotland, to the most famous Kingdomes in Europe, Asia, and Affrica*, 1640, pp. 469-474.

was in connexion with the torture of a number of Englishmen by the Dutch authorities at Amboyna in 1622. Amboyna is an island in the East Indies, where, in the seventeenth century, both Dutch and English trading stations were in operation. In the February of 1622 the English residents were accused by the Dutch of conspiring to capture the castle of Amboyna (the Dutch headquarters). Abel Price, an English surgeon, was imprisoned in the castle and tortured until he confessed that the surprise and capture of the castle was contemplated by his compatriots. On the 15th of the month Captain Towerson and all the other English in the town were made prisoners by the Dutch Governor. Under the threat or the actual application of torture, several confessed whatever was put into their mouths by their tormentors. Others resisted every effort to extort confessions. Their toes were split, their breasts cut, gunpowder was placed in incised wounds and exploded; water and fire were used in succession. The torture of John Clarke was typical:

> "First they hoisted him up by the hands with a cord on a large dore, where they made him fast upon two staples of iron; fixt on both sides at the top of the dore posts, haling his hands one from the other as wide as they could stretch. Being thus made fast, his feete hung some two foote from the ground; which also they stretcht asunder as far as they would retch, and so made them fast beneath unto the dore-trees on each side. Then they bound a cloth about his necke and face so close that little or no water could go by. That done, they poured the water softly upon his head untill the cloth was full, up to the mouth and nostrills, and somewhat higher; so that he could not draw breath, but he must withall suck-in the water: which being still continued to be poured in softly, forced all his inward parts, came out of his nose, eares, and eyes, and often as it were stifling and choaking him, at length took away his breath, and brought him to a swounce or fainting. Then they tooke him quickly downe, and made him vomit up the water. Being a little recovered, they triced him up againe, poured in the water as before, eftsoones taking him downe as he seemed to be

stifled. In this manner they handled him three or four severall times with water, till his body was swolne twice or thrice as bigge as before, his cheekes like great bladders, and his eyes staring and strutting out beyond his forehead: yet all this he bare, without confessing anie thing; insomuch as the Fiscall and tormenters reviled him, saying that he was a Divill, and no man, or surely was a witch, at least had some charme about him, or was enchanted, that he could beare so much. Wherefore they cut off his haire verie short, as supposing he had some witchcraft hidden therein. Afterwards they hoisted him up againe as before, and then burnt him with lighted candles in the bottome of his feete, untill the fat dropt out the candles; yet then applied they fresh lights unto them. They burnt him also under the elbowes, and in the palmes of the hands; likewise under the arme-pitts, until his inwards might evidently be seene. At last, when they saw he could of himself make no handsome confession, then they ledde him along with questions of particular circumstances, by themselves framed. Being thus wearied and overcome by the torment; hee answered yea to whatsoever they asked: whereby they drew from him a bodie of a confession to this effect; to wit, that Captaine Towerson had upon New-yeares day last before, sworne all the English at Amboyna to bee secret and assistant to a plot that he had projected, with the helpe of the Iaponers, to surprise the castle, and to put the Governor and the rest of the Dutch to death. Having thus martyred this poor man, they sent him out by foure Blacks; who carried him between them to a dungeon, where he lay five or six days without a Chirurgion to dresse him, until (his flesh being putrefied) great Maggots dropt and crept from him in a most loathsome and noysome maner."[1]

Yet another variation of the torture, involving the use of cords, was adopted in the case of Isaac Orobio, a physician, who was tormented in order to induce him to confess that he was a Jew, an allegation which he most persistently

[1] *A True Relation of the Most Cruell and Barbarous Proceedings Against the English at Amboyna*, London, 1624, pp. 11-12.

denied. The actual tortures were preceded by three years' confinement in the dungeons of the Inquisition. On taking Orobio to the torture chamber, the first method adopted was to envelop him in a garment which was tightened about his body to such an extent as to make breathing almost impossible. This they continually constricted until he was at the point of dying: then they suddenly slackened the garment, a procedure causing severe pain. Again and again they repeated this process, but without extracting a confession. In the next torture, Orobio's thumbs were tied tightly with fine cord so that the compression caused the extremities to swell and blood to spurt from under the nails. He was then made to stand on a bench with his back to the wall: ropes were passed around his body, his arms, and his legs, and thence over fixed iron pulleys. The executioners gripped the ropes and pulled upon them with all their strength, resulting in his body being drawn forcibly against the wall, causing the most terrible pain and the sensation of "dissolving in flames." And then, suddenly, the bench was jerked from under him, causing him to be hung by the cords alone, with the result that the weight of his body drew the knots tighter. Finally, a ladder-like arrangement, in which the five cross-pieces or rungs, instead of being rounded or flat, had sharp edges, was struck against his body with a violent rapid motion, causing such intolerable agony that he fainted. Even this did not exhaust Orobio's terrific ordeal. On regaining consciousness, and still refusing to admit his guilt, the prisoner was put to the final torture. A rope was tied to each of his wrists. These ropes were passed around the back of the executioner, who had donned a leather jacket especially for the purpose. Bending backwards, and bracing his feet against the wall, the executioner put every ounce of his weight and strength into the effort, causing the ropes to tighten and cut into Orobio's flesh to the very bones. Again and yet again was the process repeated, each time the ropes being moved a couple of inches farther up the arms before pressure was applied. At the second application, one of the ropes slipped from its new position into the first wound, resulting in an effusion so great that it was feared the victim would die there and then. However, the surgeon, being summoned, stated that Orobio had strength to endure further torture, and the third act was performed. Bleeding like a stricken pig and unconscious, the prisoner was conveyed to his cell. His wounds were barely healed in the two months which elapsed before the Inquisition, despairing of securing his confession, condemned him, on suspicion of being a Jew, to wear for two years the "infamous habit called Sambenito," and after that to perpetual banishment from the kingdom of Seville.

Torture of the Wheel

This method of execution involving, before death came, the most terrible and often prolonged agony, is a most ancient one, and apparently at one time had a religious significance. Through the centuries it took many forms. Josephus, Lucian, Athenaeus, and other ancient writers refer to its use, though there is some doubt as to the precise form which the torture took in those early days. Gallonio says there were many kinds of wheels. In addition to the breaking of the body on a sort of cart-wheel, which was the method usually indicated in the Middle Ages, he refers to the practice of binding the criminal upon a broad wheel resembling a cylinder, and either rolling this contrivance, with its human burden, down a hill or a mountain, or over iron spikes fixed in the ground. Sometimes, in addition, the wheel itself was furnished with spikes. At one time, and in some countries, according to Grimm, the method adopted was to drive heavy wagons over the body again and again until the bones were broken.

Breaking on the wheel was widely employed in Europe as a means of executing criminals, particularly during the eighteenth century. A more brutal and revolting manner of putting anyone to death it is difficult to imagine. The criminal was laid on his back upon an ordinary cart-wheel and bound securely to the spokes. Often in place of a cartwheel several pieces of timber nailed together to resemble a crude wheel, or a couple of beams in the form of a St. Andrew's Cross, sufficed. The executioner, armed with a sledge-hammer, an iron bar, or a heavy club, smashed the legs and arms with successive blows, finally delivering a *coup de grâce* in the stomach.

In some cases the fiendish cruelty of the judges manifested itself in prescribing the extended duration of the
sufferings which the doomed man must undergo before
death ended the torture. Thus the eighty-six-year-old John
Calas of Toulouse, who, on suspicion of having strangled or
helped to strangle his own son Anthony, was, in 1761,
sentenced to be tortured in order to induce him to name his
accomplices, and then to be " broken alive upon the wheel,
to receive the last stroke after he had lain two hours, and
then to be burnt to ashes."

Apparently there were cases where women were executed
by this method. M. de la Place mentions seeing a young
woman broken on the wheel in Brussels, for the murder of
her husband. Because of her sex, she was allowed, at her
own request, to wear a jacket and pantaloons of white satin.[1]

Bryan Edwards describes an execution of this type which
occurred under the window of his lodgings, on the 28th
September, 1791, during the course of the rebellion at St.
Domingo. Two men were broken on two pieces of timber
placed crosswise. One of them, after having each leg and
arm broken in two places, was finished off with a blow in
the stomach. The second prisoner was not so fortunate.
The executioner, after breaking his arms and legs, was about
to give the final blow, when the mob, calling out " stop,"
forced him to leave his task unfinished. They then tied the
suffering prisoner on a cart-wheel, which was hoisted from
the ground by fixing the other end of the axle-tree in the
earth, and gloating over the terrible agonies he was enduring, they left him there. How long this suffering would
have continued one can only guess at for " at the end of
forty minutes, some English seamen, who were spectators of
the tragedy, strangled him in mercy."[2]

According to Stedman, breaking alive on the wheel was
one of the methods of executing slaves practised in Surinam
at the time of his visit to Guinea towards the close of the
eighteenth century. He witnessed such an execution. In
this particular instance, the *coup de grâce* or mercy-stroke,
which constituted the characteristic termination of the torture

[1] *The Percy Anecdotes.*
[2] Bryan Edwards, *The History of the British West Indies*, 1819, Vol. III,
p. 84.

in the European technique, was not given. After the negro had been tied securely to a wooden cross, the executioner, another negro, chopped off the criminal's left hand with a hatchet. Then, grasping a heavy iron bar, with repeated blows, " he broke the bones to shivers, till the marrow, blood, and splinters flew about the field." The ropes were then unlashed. The criminal, who was not dead, " writhed himself from the cross, when he fell on the grass and damned them all."[1] He begged that his head might be chopped off, a request that was refused. For six hours he continued to live in indescribable agony, and even then death only released him from his torments as a result of an act of commiseration on the part of the guard, who knocked him on the head with the butt-end of his musket.

Stoning to Death

The antiquity of the method lies in its obviousness and convenience. Herodotus mentions its use. It was the method of execution approved by Yahveh for blasphemy, heresy, idolatry, adultery, bestiality, sodomy, *et al.*

During the seventeenth-century persecutions, at the instigation of the Pope, of the Protestants in Piedmont—which persecutions reached such a degree of horrifying barbarity that, it is said, Cromwell, no sentimentalist himself, was constrained to intercede, though in vain—a variation of this form of execution was practised. Judith Mandon, a young woman, for refusing to embrace Popery

" was fastened to a stake, and sticks thrown at her from a distance, in the very same manner as in that barbarous custom, formerly practised on Shrove Tuesday, of throwing at cocks. By this inhuman proceeding her limbs were beat and mangled in a most terrible manner, and at last one of the bludgeons dashed her brains out."[2]

---

[1] J. G. Stedman, *Narrative of a Five Years' Expedition Against the Revolted Negroes of Surinam in Guinea on the Coast of South America from the Year 1772-1777*, London, 1796.

[2] Henry Moore, *The History of the Persecutions of the Church of Rome and Complete Protestant Martyrology*, 1809, p. 642.

Torture of the Boot

The torture of the boot was considered by contemporary observers to be the "most severe and cruel pain in the world." So dreadful was the sight of a human being suffering this torment that, says Burnet, "when any are to be struck in the boot, it is done in the presence of the Council, and upon that occasion almost all offer to run away."[1] For this reason, an order had to be issued compelling a number to stay; without such an order the board would have been forsaken.

This instrument of torture was an iron container made in the shape of a boot and designed to encase the naked limb from the foot to the knee. Wedges of wood or metal were inserted between the flesh and the sides of the apparatus and driven in with a hammer. The flesh was lacerated and often the bones were crushed and splintered in a shocking and dreadful manner, the terrible punishment continuing until the victim confessed. It was rare for anyone who experienced this torture to be other than a cripple for the rest of his life.

The boot does not seem to have been generally used in the Inquisitions of Europe, though it was frequently employed in England and Scotland.[2] John Spreull, accused at Edinburgh in 1681 of being concerned in a plot to blow up the Duke of York, and steadfastly maintaining his ignorance of the affair, was put to the torture in the presence of the Duke of York and many other notabilities.

"The hangman put his foot in the instrument called the Boot, and, at every query put to him, gave five strokes or thereby upon the wedges . . . When nothing could be expiscated by this, they ordered the old boot to be brought, alleging this new one used by the hangman was not so good as the old, and accordingly it was brought, and he underwent the torture a second time, and adhered to what he had before said. General Dalziel complained at the second torture, that the hangman did not strike strongly enough upon the wedges; he said, he

[1] Bishop Burnet, *History*, 1823.
[2] Termed bootikins in Scotland.

struck with all his strength, and offered the general the mall to do it himself."[1]

In Scotland, too, an instrument named the caspicaws[2] or caschielawis was in frequent use. This was equivalent to the notorious " Spanish Boot," an iron casing for the leg and foot which had a screw attachment for compressing the calf of the leg. In some cases it was heated until red-hot, either before or after its application to the naked foot. The actual procedure varied in different countries, although the principle was the same in all. According to Pitcairn, in Scotland, the usual course was to apply the iron affair, and then heat it gradually in a movable furnace. While the iron was getting hotter, the questions were put to the prisoner. The pain was so agonizing that usually the victim was impelled to confess anything which his interrogators might wish.

There are many records of the torture having been applied. In 1596, Alesoun Balfour and Thomas Palpla were both induced to confess in this way, though not until they had suffered grievous pain, Palpla

"being keepit in the caschielawis ellewin dayis and ellewin nychtis; tuyise in the day, be the space of four-tene dayis, callit in the buitis, he beand naikit in the meane tyme, and skairgeit with towis (cords), in sic soirt, that they left nather flesch nor hyde upon him."[3]

Women were not immune from the torture of the boot. On the 1st February, 1631, the Privy Council, consisting of seventeen members, ordered

"Margaret Wod to be putt to the tortour of the bootes, the morne, at ten of the clocke, in the Laich Counsell Hous of Edinburgh; and that the whole counsell be present when the tortour is given."[4]

[1] Robert Wodrow, *History of the Sufferings of the Church of Scotland*, Glasgow, 1828, Vol. III, p. 254.
[2] According to Dr. Jamieson the term signifies " warm hose."
[3] Robert Pitcairn, *Ancient Criminal Trials*, 1833, Vol. I, p. 376.
[4] John Graham Dalyell, *The Darker Superstitions of Scotland*, 1834.

Variations of this form of torture were often adopted. At Autun, says Lacroix, high boots made of spongy leather were used. The victim, wearing these boots, was secured to a table in front of a hot fire. Boiling water was then poured into the boots, penetrating the leather and eating away the flesh.[1] In other cases, parchment stockings were used. These were put on wet, and the prisoner placed before a fire: the parchment, as it dried, shrank considerably, in the process causing insufferable agony.[2]

Yet another form of boot was known as *Brodequins*. The prisoner was seated on a strong bench, and boards of suitable width and length were placed on the inside and outside of each leg, and tightly bound in position with strong rope, the two legs in their casing being fixed together. Wedges of wood or metal were then driven with a mallet between the centre boards. Four wedges were used in " ordinary torture," and eight wedges in what was termed " extraordinary torture." The effect was that the cords bit through the victim's flesh, causing excruciating pain. In many cases the bones were splintered or broken.[3] This type of boot was used extensively in Scotland in the seventeenth century. It was described by an English visitor, says Morer (*A Short Account of Scotland*) as

" four pieces of narrow boards nailed together, of a competent length for the leg, not unlike the short cases we use to guard young trees from the rabbits, which they wedge so tightly on all sides that, not being able to bear the pain, they promise confession to get rid of it."

The Scavenger's Daughter

This diabolical apparatus was used in the Tower of London for the purpose of eliciting confession. It was used contemporaneously and alternately with the rack. The Scavenger's Daughter was strongly made of iron hoops, consisting of two parts hinged together. The prisoner was

[1] Paul Lacroix, *Manners, Customs and Dress During the Middle Ages*, 1874.
[2] *Ibid.*
[3] *Ibid.*

forced into a kneeling posture on the floor, and told to draw his body and limbs together so as to compress himself into the smallest possible space. The executioner, having passed one of the iron hoops under the prisoner's legs, knelt upon his shoulders, forcing his body downwards until it was possible to fasten the two hoops together over the small of the back. The agony which the victim of this torture suffered must have been beyond all endurance, and there is little room for wonder that in most cases a confession was obtained before the expiration of the time (one and a half hours) allotted for confinement in the apparatus. It is stated that long before this the blood was spurting from the nostrils, the mouth, and the anus, and even, on occasion, from the hands and feet. According to an entry in Rishton's *Diary*, dated December 10, 1580, two priests named Tomas Cottam and Luke Kirbye were tortured in the Scavenger's Daughter for more than an hour. Cottam, it is stated, "bled profusely from the nose."

Hurling From a Tower or Height

Doubtless this mode of execution was general among many savage and primitive races where there were precipices or rocks providing convenient means for its employment. It was also a favourite method of committing suicide.

As a prescribed legal method of execution we note its use in ancient Rome. Manlius Capitolinus met such a fate. Condemned as a rebel, he was thrown from the Tarpeian Rock. Among other notabilities to be executed in the same way was Putuanius, the mathematician, and the Emperor Zeno. Aesopus, the famous author, charged with the theft of one of the treasures of the Temple of Apollo, met this fate in the year 561 B.C. Perilaus, inventor of that diabolically ingenious instrument of torture, the brazen bull, after being nearly roasted alive in his own creation, was thrown from the rock by order of Phalaris.

There seems to be no trace of its inclusion in any penal code in later years, though it was stated that many victims of the sixteenth-century persecutions in Piedmont met their deaths in this way. A somewhat analogous method in vogue during the reign of Francis I was the *estrapade*, in which the criminal was allowed to fall from a height in such a manner as to break his limbs.

The terrible torture so often associated with this mode of execution was in the suffering which was endured before death came. The victim, with broken limbs, lay helpless until he literally starved to death. It has been stated that many such victims " actually devoured the flesh of their arms in the agonies of hunger and despair."[1] In 1655, Pietro Simond of Angrogno, with his neck and heels tied together, on being hurled from a precipice, was caught in a tree and hung there until he died of starvation.

[1] J. G. Millingen, *Curiosities of Medical Experience*, 1837, p. 100.

CHAPTER XX

WHIPPING AND BEATING

Flogging Implements and Methods of the Middle Ages

THERE is no form of punishment older than flagellation,[1] and although, in many instances, it cannot be held to rank as torture, there is always a risk where the whip is recognized as a method of inflicting judicial punishment, that it may develop into a species of torture, and that private individuals, taking the law into their own hands, may use the whip to such an extent that it is a danger to life. This may occur in many ways. It may, through the remarkable severity of the blows, the nature of the instrument used, the prolonged period of punishment, or the condition of the culprit at the time the whipping is administered, cause injury or death.

At one time or another many types of whips, rods and cudgels have been employed. Cart-whips; single-thonged whips; knotted cords; the terrible Russian *knut*; the equally terrible English cat-o'-nine-tails; whips loaded with balls of metals, hooks, etc.; birch rods; the agonizing bastinado of the Eastern nations; and, if history does not lie, metal rods brought to a white heat and used as bludgeons.

So universal was the practice of whipping, and so many are the instances of its infliction on record, that to deal with the subject with any pretensions to thoroughness would require a whole book in itself. Moreover as I have written a volume dealing exclusively and specifically with the subject,[2] I do not propose in this chapter to do more than present examples of the more characteristic forms of torture administered with the whip in different countries and for various purposes.

Flagellation was, in the early days, a method of correction

[1] For an examination of the use of the whip by the ancient Greeks and Romans see Chapter VIII.

[2] See my work *The History of Corporal Punishment: A Survey of Flagellation in its Historical, Anthropological and Sociological Aspects*, Werner Laurie, 1938.

greatly favoured by the ecclesiastical authorities. It was adopted for the most widely dissimilar offences. There was the case of the pseudo-hermaphroditic girl, who, for masquerading as a male and marrying, was handed over to the Inquisition and sentenced to 200 lashes.[1] There was Lawrence Castro, a goldsmith of Zaragoza, " condemned to be whipt through the publick streets, to be mark'd afterwards on the shoulders with a branding iron, and to be sent for ever to the gallies."[2] Occasionally the inquisitors used the whip as a means of inducing the wealthy to hand over their money and goods. Gavin tells of a Jew named Francisco Alfaro, who was incarcerated, relieved of his riches, and punished by the Inquisition of Seville. He was then allowed to recommence his trading and four years later, having accumulated " more riches," he was " put again into the Holy Office, with the loss of his goods and money."

In England, there was the scourging of Thomas Green and of John Fetty's son. The Church, when it decided to punish what it was pleased to term heresy, respected neither age nor sex.

> " The priest took the child by the hand and carried him into the bishop's house, and there amongst them they did most shamefully and without all mercy so whip and scourge, being naked, this tender child, that he was all in a gore of blood, and then in jolly bragg of their Catholick tyranny, they caused Cluny, having his coat upon his arm, to carry the child in his shirt unto his father being in prison, the blood running down his heels."[3]

In the second decade of the nineteenth century, when the Protestants living in the South of France were subjected to the persecutions of the Catholics, beating was extremely popular as a means of punishment for the females. The instrument used was not a whip but a battledore (*battoir*), and to increase the suffering of the victims, nails were driven through the wood so that their sharp points protruded from the surface, fetching blood at every blow. The skirts and

---

[1] H. C. Lea, *A History of the Inquisition of Spain*, Vol. IV, p. 188.
[2] D. Antonio Gavin, *A Master-Key to Popery*, 1725, p. 204.
[3] Fox's *Book of Martyrs*, 1732, p. 859.

petticoats of the women were turned up over their bent heads, and nail-studded *battoirs* were applied to the exposed posteriors until the "blood streamed from the women's bodies and their screams rent the air." They spared neither old nor young, they even chastised several who were pregnant. One woman, named Françoise, was stripped naked, seated backwards on a donkey, with one of her hands fastened to its tail, flogged and pelted with mud. Another, Madame Pic, was carried to a hospital in a barrow, and took two hours to recover from the injuries she had received. Many died. Many were permanently injured.

"I have seen," says M. Durand, a Catholic advocate, "the assassins in the faubourg Bourgade arm a *battoir* with sharp nails in the form of a *fleur-de-lis*; I have seen them raise the garments of females and apply with heavy blows to the bleeding body this *battoir* to which they gave a name which my pen refuses to inscribe. The cries of the sufferers—the streams of blood—the murmurs of indignation, which were suppressed by fear—nothing could move them. The surgeons who attended on those who are dead, can attest by the marks of their wounds, and the agonies which they endured, that this account, however horrible, is most strictly true."[1]

Of all the punishments which the Inquisition inflicted in the name of God, for sheer long-continued cruelty, nothing ever rivalled the treatment of the galley-slaves, who were flogged very nearly every day during the period they laboured at the oars. And these periods were sometimes five, or six, or eight years; rarely were they fewer than four. Where the Inquisitions did not impose the death penalty, they very often sentenced their prisoners to the galleys. It was a fate worse than death. For, as everyone knew, it meant a life of the most terrible hardship man could possibly endure and yet continue to live; it almost inevitably entailed death long before the sentence was completed. It meant, in the majority of instances, that the victim was *gradually whipped to death.*

[1] Mark Wilks, *History of the Persecutions Endured by the Protestants of the South of France 1814-1816,* London, 1821, Vol. I, p. 250.

Thus few ever survived the terrible ordeal. Of these few, one managed to put upon paper an account of the awful sufferings under the whip which the galley-slave was called upon to endure. This man was condemned to thirteen years' service as a galley-slave.

"Imagine," he says, "six men chained to their seats, naked as when born, sitting with one foot on a block of timber fixed to the footstool or stretcher; the other lifted up against the bench before them, holding in their hands an oar of an enormous size. Imagine them lengthening their bodies, their arms stretched out to push the oar over the backs of those before them; who are also themselves in a similar attitude. Having thus advanced their oar, they raise that end which they hold in their hands, to plunge the opposite in the sea; which done, they throw themselves back upon their benches below, which are somewhat hollowed to receive them. None, in short, but those who have seen them labour, can conceive how much they endure."[1]

This terrific labour was continued for ten, twelve and, on occasion, twenty hours at a stretch, the slaves stopping for *nothing*, not even in response to the calls of nature, not even to eat or drink, food being pushed into their mouths while they toiled at the oars. All the time, the lashing of the guards' whips continued, the bodies of the rowers streaming blood. No free man, says the writer of this horrifying account, could continue at an oar for a single hour. Under the spurs of cruelty and necessity man can perform almost superhuman tasks—for a time. And when flesh and blood could endure the strain no longer and the slave swooned in his seat (a very frequent occurrence) he was whipped mercilessly as long as his tortured body showed the faintest sign of life.

In addition to this daily flogging of the slaves at their work, the slightest insubordination or the most trivial offence was punished by whipping.

[1] *The Memoirs of a Protestant condemned to the Galleys of France for his Religion*, written by Himself. Translated by James Willington, Dublin, 1765, Vol. I, p. 59.

"The criminal is stript from the waist upward. He is extended with his face downward, his arms upon one bench and his legs upon the opposite, which are held by two slaves that stand opposite each other. The executioner, who is generally a Turkish slave, stands over him with a rope in his hand, with which he is to beat the criminal without the least mercy; for if he happens to be remiss, which is seldom the case, the *sous comite* uses him as he should have used the criminal. Thus then every stroke is laid on with the executioner's whole force, so that each blow raises a whelk as thick as one's thumb. Few that are condemned to suffer this punishment can sustain above ten or twelve blows without fainting. This, however, does not prevent the executioner from proceeding. He continues to lay on the miserable and seemingly lifeless carcase, till the number of blows ordered by the major are completed. Twenty or thirty are generally inflicted for slight offences. I have seen 50, 80, even an 100 ordered; but then those who are thus punished seldom recover. When the allotted number of stripes are given, the surgeon barber of the galley rubs the criminal's back with salt and vinegar; which, though it may prevent a gangrene, yet renews all the poignancy of his former anguish."[1]

The Jamaica Cart-whip

The whip used in Jamaica—a terrible weapon—was typical of that employed in most places where there was slave labour. It was a cart-whip, with a lash four or five yards long, tapering from a thickness of two and a half inches at the point where it was fixed to a two-foot handle, to the thinness of stout cord at its extremity. In a speech delivered to the Jamaica Assembly in 1826, Mr. Barrett said:

"I do not hesitate to declare that the cart-whip is a cruel, debasing instrument of torture, a horrible, detestable instrument, when used for the punishment of slaves. I do say that 39 lashes with this horrid instrument can be

[1] *Ibid.*, Vol. I, p. 55.

made more grievous than 500 lashes with the 'cat.' "[1]

The cart-whip was by no means the only flagellating instrument employed. There was a method of fustigation in which switches, made of the wiry, thorny branches of the ebony plant, were used. Then again it was a common practice in Jamaica to administer a sound flogging with a tamarind switch, *after* the 39 lashes with the cart-whip had been given. This practice was even *justified* on the ground that it "beat out the bruised blood." The tamarind switch, by the way, was a sort of cane or rod, thin, flexible and of the tenacity and hardness of wire. In a strong hand it made an instrument of flagellation almost equal to the ebony switch. In gaols, said Mr. J. B. Wildman, in his evidence before the Select Committee on Slavery, negroes were "bowsed" for the purpose of flogging, that is, they were roped at wrists and angles, and, in seafaring terminology, "bowsed out" with a tackle and pulleys. Even women and girls were flogged in this way in the workhouses. The following account, culled from contemporary records, tells its own story:

> "A female, apparently about 22 years of age, was then laid down, with her face downwards; her wrists were secured by cords run into nooses; her ankles were brought together and placed in another noose; the cord composing this last one, passed through a block, connected with a post. The cord was tightened, and the young woman was then stretched to her utmost length. A female then advanced, and raised her clothes towards her head, leaving the person indecently exposed. The boatswain of the workhouse, a tall athletic man, flourished his whip four or five times round his head, and

[1] According to clause 37 of an Act passed by the Jamaica legislature in the same year that Mr. Barrett made his notable indictment, it was made an offence, incurring a minimum penalty of £10, for any driver to administer more than ten lashes at one time and for any offence; or for any owner, overseer, or gaol keeper to administer more than 39 lashes in similar circumstances. How far these regulations were carried out it is impossible to say, but as the prescribed number of lashes could be given for *each* offence, it was easy for a driver or an owner with a penchant for cruelty, to trump up charges which would constitute grounds for repetitive floggings of the same slave.

proceeded with the punishment. The instrument of
punishment was a cat, formed of knotted cords. The
blood sprang from the wounds it inflicted. The poor
creature shrieked in agony. . . . Four other delinquents
were successively treated in the same way. One was a
woman, about 36 years of age, another, a girl of 15,
another, a boy of the same age, and lastly, an old woman
about 60, who really appeared scarcely to have strength
to express her agonies by cries. The boy of 15, as our
informant subsequently ascertained, was the son of the
woman of 36. She was indecently exposed, and cruelly
flogged, in the presence of her son! and then had the
additional pain to see him also exposed, and made to
writhe under the lash."[1]

The Technique in Mauritius

In the East Indian island of Mauritius two different
methods appear to have been in general use. In one method,
a triangular frame, something similar to the arrangement
common in English convict prisons, was erected, and the
offender was tied by the wrists to the point where the three
poles crossed, while the body rested against a cross-bar. In
the other method, a ladder was laid flat on the ground, and
the culprit compelled to lie prone on the ladder, to which
his hands and feet were securely tied with cords. In some
cases, where the ladder was dispensed with, he was pinioned
to the ground by main force, a slave holding each limb
firmly. But whatever the position adopted, the severity of
the flogging was the same. A driver armed with a cart-whip
or a rattan (in some cases two drivers acted as executioners,
one on each side of the culprit) flogged the bared back and
buttocks until the master considered that sufficient punishment had been inflicted. If the driver failed to do his duty
to the master's satisfaction, he was doomed to receive a taste
of the medicine he was administering.

Whips of various sizes and types were used. The one
usually employed had a wooden handle of two or three feet
in length and about two inches in diameter, attached to a
lash from two to three yards in length, tapering from its

[1] *Jamaica Christian Record*, 1830, p. 132.

thickest part, which was at the point of attachment to the handle. The rattan consisted of a cane measuring some five feet in length, which for a distance of three feet from the end was split into three parts, the solid section forming the handle. The result was a powerful three-tailed " cat," which was capable of cutting the flesh into ribbons. It was a debatable point which of these two terrible instruments of flagellation was the more punishing. Some held that the whip was the more excoriating weapon; others were in favour of the rattan. The truth is that both, in the hands of a powerful man, were capable of inflicting severe punishment, making incisions at every stroke, sending blood and shreds of flesh flying in all directions. Soldiers who witnessed these whippings stated that the military floggings in England and elsewhere, in which the " cat " was used, were nothing in comparison.

The absence of government regulations enabled the owners or managers not only to whip their slaves on any pretext or occasion, but also to continue a flogging as long as they deemed fit. Rarely were fewer than 50 lashes given. A more usual sentence was a hundred. Often more than one hundred strokes were given. The flogging over, the torture was intensified by rubbing into the bloody wounds, salt, pepper, lime-juice, or other irritating substances, on the ground that this was necessary to prevent festering.

The following account, given by an eye-witness, of the flogging of two slaves, is a typical description of what was happening every day.

" They were placed flat on their bellies, extended on a wooden beam, to which they were fastened, while two men held their hands and two their legs, and a driver, who struck alternately, was placed on each side of the sufferer. The whips employed were unusually heavy, and 120 lashes were inflicted on each. On the following Wednesday, having occasion to go to the room used as an hospital, he saw laid out the dead bodies of the same two slaves. The wounds were putrid, and sent forth a rank smell; and he afterwards saw them both carried out, tied up in mats, to the burial ground."[1]

[1] *Anti-Slavery Monthly Reporter*, 1829, p. 381.

In the United States, the cart-whip was used on most plantations. The tell-tale marks which it left, however, led to the invention of the " paddle "—a thin flat piece of wood, punctured with small holes, and attached to a long flexible handle. With this implement the most rigorous punishment could be inflicted without leaving anything in the way of evidence which could not vanish in a day or two. It was woe betide the slave that fell into the clutches of a plantation on which the " paddle " was used.

In the prisons, too, the niggers were whipped and mal-treated on the slightest pretext. Witness the revelations contained in the letter addressed by Dr. Howe to the Hon. Charles Sumner:

"If Howard or Mrs. Fry ever discovered so ill-administered a den of thieves as the New Orleans prison, they never described it. In the negroes' apartment I saw much which made me blush that I was a white man, and which for a moment stirred up an evil spirit in my animal nature. Entering a large paved courtyard, around which ran galleries filled with slaves of all ages, sexes, and colours, I heard the snap of a whip, every stroke of which sounded like the sharp crack of a pistol. I turned my head, and beheld a sight which absolutely chilled me to the marrow of my bones, and gave me, for the first time in my life, the sensation of my hair stiffening at the roots. There lay a black girl flat upon her face, on a board, her two thumbs tied, and fastened to one end, her feet tied and drawn tightly to the other end, while a strap passed over the small of her back, and, fastened around the board, compressed her closely to it. Below the strap she was entirely naked. By her side, and six feet off, stood a huge negro, with a long whip, which he applied with dreadful power and wonderful precision. Every stroke brought away a strip of skin, which clung to the lash, or fell quivering on the pavement, while the blood followed after it. The poor creature writhed and shrieked, and, in a voice which showed alike her fear of death and her dreadful agony, screamed to her master, who stood at her head, ' Oh, spare my life! don't cut my soul out! ' But still fell the horrid lash; still strip after strip peeled off from the skin; gash after gash was cut in her living flesh, until it became a livid and bloody mass of raw and quivering muscle."[1]

England's Cat-o'-nine-tails

Since flogging was authorized by the Mutiny Act of 1689, as a mode of punishment in the British Army, it was for two hundred years considered to be the best means of keeping discipline.

The cat-o'-nine-tails was the chosen flagellating instrument. It consisted of nine separate thongs of whipcord. In those early days, each thong was knotted in three places.[2] These thongs, brought down upon the naked flesh of the culprit, cut through the skin as if it were paper, the knots tearing out great lumps of flesh. The sensation which the culprit experienced, says Shipp, was " as though the talons of a hawk were tearing the flesh off the bones."[3] At the finish of the operation, the ground around the whipped individual was splashed with blood; the executioner looked for all the world as if he had just come out of a slaughter-house.

At the close of the eighteenth century a court martial had the power to order anything up to 1,000 lashes. Sentences of 500, 600 and 800 strokes were common, and were given for offences which were far from serious. Moreover, the manner in which the sentences were executed often increased the torture. Thus, in some regiments, it was customary for the flogging to be carried out in time with the tapping of a drum, the interval between each tap depending upon the instructions given to the drummer. By allowing an extended interval, it was possible to increase considerably the extent of the torture endured by the victim. Again, the weaker the individual, the more he suffered. It was usual, in any case where the victim could stand no further suffering, to finish the sentence at some other time. For instance, if the culprit succumbed at the end of 250 lashes, he was removed to his cell or to hospital until his wounds were wholly or

[1] Quoted by Harriet Beecher Stowe in *A Key to Uncle Tom's Cabin*.
[2] The " cat " used for penal floggings in England to-day has nine tails made of whipcord, but they are not knotted. The ends are " whipped " with silk thread to prevent fraying.
[3] John Shipp, *Flogging and its Substitute*, London, 1831.

partially healed, and then brought back to the triangle to receive the remainder of the sentence. Where the sentence was 800 or 1,000 lashes, it was often completed in three or four instalments. Now the greatest agony and suffering were experienced during the course of the first 200 strokes; after 300 or so, the flesh became numbed and one might as well have been lashing a dead body. Thus it was far better in every way for a culprit to have the whole of the prescribed number of lashes administered in one dose. The man with a weak constitution suffered far more than one blessed with great strength. For not only had he to suffer the intolerable agony of these first 200 lashes, on three or four separate occasions, but he had also to suffer the awful *mental torture* of knowing that the ordeal must be faced again. It was not until the early part of the nineteenth century that this barbarous practice was abandoned.

The trivial nature of the offences for which these floggings were inflicted is indicated in the following case, reported in the pages of *Tait's Edinburgh Magazine* (1833):

"A soldier of the First Regiment of Grenadier Guards, of which regiment the Duke of Wellington is Colonel, having been convicted of insubordination, intoxication on duty, and of refusal to deliver up his arms when ordered by his officer, was sentenced to receive 500 lashes. After receiving 200 lashes, the surgeon of the regiment interfered, and put a stop to the brutal punishment, in consequence of the life of the soldier being in danger. The soldier was then removed to the military hospital in a hackney coach, his back being dreadfully lacerated. As a sort of refinement in cruelty, and to increase the severity of a punishment which could not be inflicted to the full extent without depriving the unfortunate culprit of his life, a fresh hand was procured at every 20 lashes."

Often death followed these floggings. Sir Samuel Romilly mentions a soldier being flogged at Gibraltar, for being dirty on parade, with such severity that he died a few days later;[1] Sir Charles Napier tells of two soldiers flogged

_____
[1] *Memoirs*, 1840, Vol. II, p. 262.

at Corfu in 1819, both of whom died;[1] and Somerville, who himself suffered one hundred lashes for a trivial offence, gives the case of Frederick White, of the 7th Hussars, who, in 1846, according to the findings of a coroner's jury, died from the effects of corporal punishment.[2]   His crime, deemed to merit such severe treatment, was " being drunk."[3]

In the Navy, corporal punishment was administered for similar trivial offences, and with the same freeness, but the method was a different one.   The "cat" in use was not made of whipcord.   It was fashioned out of a piece of rope, some five feet in length all told.   The rope was the thickness of a man's wrist, and for three feet of its length was solid, while the remaining two feet was ravelled, each section being twisted to make a hard thong, and knotted at various points along its length.   In some cases a wooden handle was affixed, in others the solid part of the rope served this purpose.

" But," says a contemporary writer, " whether of rope or wood, upon the length of this handle depends the severity of the stroke.   In the Army, too," further observes this authority, " the drummer who flogs stands on one spot, and delivers the lash without moving his position, his arm alone giving force to the blow; but in the Navy, the boatswain's mate, who has this duty to perform, stands full two strides from the delinquent; he ' combs out the cat,' as it is termed, by running his fingers through the strands, and separating them from each other, after every lash; then waving it over his head, he makes a step forward, and, with an inflexion of his body that gives his whole strength to the operation, delivers the stroke at the full sweep of his arm.   'Tis a severe punishment thus; and I do not think any man could stand nine dozen as I have seen it ' laid in.'   An un-

---

[1] *Remarks on Military Law*, 1837, p. 151.
[2] *Autobiography of a Working Man*, 1848, p. 299.
[3] The opposition of Sir Charles Napier, Sir Francis Burdett, Lord Hutchinson and others, though it did not result in the abolition of the " cat," led to a reduction in the severity of the sentences.   But flogging still remained a species of torture.   At the time when Lord Roberts joined the service, the number of lashes which could be inflicted had been reduced to fifty, but " even under this restriction, the sight was," he states, " a horrible one to witness." (*Fifty-one Years in India*, London, 1898, Vol. I, p. 25.)

hallowed torture it is—bad as the rack of bygone times; and to the man that deserved such a punishment, hanging would be a more merciful dispensation."[1]

The sentences, considering the nature of the offences for which they were imposed, were often frightful in their intensity. For instance, in the account of a sea-voyage, we learn that on August 13, 1787, a private in the marines, Cornelius Connell, was punished with 100 lashes for improper intercourse with a female convict; and on August 31st James Baker, also a private marine, was given 200 lashes for "endeavouring to get passed, on shore, by means of one of the seamen, a spurious dollar, knowing it to be so."[2]

Cart's Tail and Other Penal Floggings

Flogging as a punishment for offences against society was prescribed in the laws of Moses, the maximum penalty being forty strokes. It was used through the centuries in practically every country, though the Romans and Greeks, as we have seen, looked upon punitive flagellation as a disgrace and restricted it to slaves.

In China and Japan the bastinado, in Russia the terrible *knut*,[3] and later the three-tailed *plet*, were in regular use. In England, in the reign of Henry VIII, a specific Act prescribed whipping at the cart's tail till the culprit is bloody, as the punishment for vagrancy and other offences. Not always, however, were the criminals whipped at the cart's tail. For less serious offences, such as drinking on a Sunday, drunkenness, suffering from smallpox, giving birth to illegitimate children, etc., the punishment was inflicted at a whipping-post. These whipping-posts were erected all up and down the country. Stow says there was one in Cheapside, "called the Post of Reformation, near the Standard there. In the year 1556, here was a man whipt, for selling of false rings."[4] The same authority says that since Edward III, for theft, the criminal was

---

[1] *Frazer's Magazine*, May 1836, p. 542.
[2] John White, *Journal of a Voyage to New South Wales*, 1790, p. 50.
[3] The use of the *knut* was discontinued in 1845.
[4] John Stow, *A Survey of London*, 1720.

TORTURE OF THE ENGLISH PRISONERS AT AMBOYNA, IN 1622

From a Seventeenth century tract.   (See Text, page 177.)

TORTURE BY FLAGELLATION

From an Engraving in *Theatrum Crudelitatum Haereticorum*, 1592.

" tied by the hands to the tail of a cart, stripped naked to the waist, whether man or woman, and lashed with a whip of four, five or six cords knotted."

Among outstanding instances of penal flogging was the case of Titus Oates, who, in 1685, was sentenced to be pilloried and afterwards whipped from Aldgate to Newgate, and in two days' time from Newgate to Tyburn, which, as the judges well knew, was equivalent to sentencing the man to be flogged to death. That Oates survived the frightful torture was due to his enormous physical strength and iron constitution, and not to the clemency of the court or the mercy of the executioner. The following description is from the pen of Macaulay:

" On the day on which Oates was pilloried in Palace-yard, he was mercilessly pelted and ran some risk of being pulled to pieces. But in the City his partisans mustered in great force, raised a riot and upset the pillory. They were, however, unable to rescue their favourite. . . . On the following morning he was brought forth to undergo his first flogging. At an early hour an innumerable multitude filled all the streets from Aldgate to the Old Bailey. The hangman laid on the lash with such unusual severity as showed that he had received special instructions. The blood ran down in rivulets. For a time the criminal showed a strange constancy: but at last his stubborn fortitude gave way. His bellowings were frightful to hear. He swooned several times, but the scourge continued to descend. When he was unbound, it seemed that he had borne as much as the human frame can bear without dissolution. James was entreated to remit his second flogging. His answer was short and clear: ' He shall go through with it, if he has breath in his body.' An attempt was made to obtain the Queen's intercession; but she indignantly refused to say a word in favour of such a wretch. After an interval of 48 hours, Oates was again brought out of his dungeon. He was unable to stand, and it was necessary to drag him to Tyburn on a sledge. He seemed quite insensible; and the Tories reported that he had stupefied himself with strong drink. A person who counted the stripes on the second day said that there were 1,700."[1]

The terrible nature of such a flogging is indicated by the fact that when a similar sentence was inflicted upon Dangerfield, the victim had to be carried to Newgate in a dying condition.

In the early part of the nineteenth century, the scenes of the most heartless floggings, so far as the British Empire was concerned, shifted from the prisons and bridewells of England, to the penal settlements of Australia. The exhibitions of cruelty in the Barrack Square of Sydney were frightful in their intensity. And on Norfolk Island, the most notorious spot of all, convicts were lashed into unconsciousness for the most trifling of offences. Sentences of 100 and 200 lashes were everyday occurrences.

"I was once present," says Therry, "in the police-office in Sydney when a convict was sentenced to 50 lashes for not taking off his hat to a magistrate as he met him on the road."[2]

In the report presented to the House of Commons concerning the infliction of punishment upon the convicts of New South Wales, the following revealing extracts, from the books of the Parramatta gaol, are given. The various orders signify the comparative triviality of the offences in relation to the severity of the sentences.

"March 31, 1823. Henry Bayne, attached to the Domain party, sentenced to receive 25 lashes every morning, until he tells where the money and property is, stolen from the house of William Jaynes, at Parramatta, by him."

"April 26, 1823. Richard Johnson, attached to the government dairy, sentenced to receive 25 lashes every morning, until he tells where he got a pair of blue

---

[1] Macaulay, *History of England*.
[2] R. Therry, *Reminiscences of Thirty Years' Residence in New South Wales and Victoria*, London, 1863, p. 43.

trousers from, being part of a robbery committed at the garden house, on the government domain, Parramatta."

In consequence of this punishment, Johnson accused another convict named John Wright of the robbery, and Wright was given the same punishment. Evidently the authorities were determined to flog the thief, whoever he was. Then, on April 5th, we find that John M'Clutchy was sentenced to 25 lashes every morning "until he tells who has harboured him during the fourteen days he has been absent from the gang"; that Charles Watson, for stealing three shirts, got 25 lashes, with a promise of another 50 lashes if he did not give information leading to the recovery of the stolen property. On April 24, 1822, for gambling, James Blackburn was sentenced to 25 lashes every morning until he disclosed the identity of his co-gamblers; on July 1st, John Downes and Hugh Carroll were sentenced to 25 lashes every second day till they told where they had hidden the money they were accused of stealing; and on October 4th, for theft, Thomas Smith was "to receive 25 lashes every second morning until he produced the property" and if after 100 lashes he failed to do this he was to be sent to Port M'Quarie to finish his sentence.

Let us shift the scene to the convict prisons of the United States. Al Jennings, train-robber and gunman, incarcerated in the Ohio State Penitentiary in the latter half of the nineteenth century, tells of prisoners being "whipped into bleeding insensibility" with razor-edged "paddles." In the North Carolina convict camps, says W. D. Saunders, writing in *Survey* (May 15, 1915), the prisoners were "whipped with a leather strap" to such an extent that they would carry the marks on their backs for the rest of their lives.[1] There were several deaths due to the severity of these floggings. As recently as 1925 "a prisoner died under the blows of the guard who was beating him."[2] In Georgia, according to the testimony of witnesses at an official investigation, a sixteen

[1] Quoted in *Prison Reform*, New York, 1917, p. 232.
[2] Jesse F. Steiner and Roy M. Brown, *The North Carolina Chain Gang*, University of North Carolina Press, Chapel Hill, 1927, p. 89.

year old white boy named " Abe " Winn, for the crime of
spilling hot coffee on the backs of pigs owned by one of the
guards, was licked with a "sanded" leather thong to such
a degree that he died in the hospital.[1]

Whipping is not now a prescribed punishment in the
United States at common law.[2] There are indications that
it is used surreptitiously, bulking largely in "third degree"
methods, a piece of rubber hose often being the instrument
employed.

Private and Sadistic Floggings

There can be little doubt that from the earliest days
there has always been a considerable amount of flagellation
administered privately and unconnected in any way with
official, authoritative or penal activities. It is quite impossible to arrive at the foggiest estimate of the extent of such
practices. The slaves in all countries and at all times were
privately flogged to an extent far greater than they were
flogged with the knowledge and authority of the courts.
Prisoners in all countries and in all ages have doubtless been
flogged on many occasions that have never been divulged in
the prison reports. And even more so, private individuals,
when opportunity has offered, have flogged children and
servants in their employ, and enemies who have fallen into
their power. The motive may have been an attempt to
extort information, vengeance, sheer cruelty, or sadism.

An example of the first of these motives was the whipping to death of Richard Hawkins by John Mills and his
gang. They charged Hawkins with being concerned in a
robbery, and demanded to know what he had done with the
stolen goods, threatening to whip him to death if he did not
confess. As Hawkins continued to deny having had anything to do with the affair, they compelled him to strip to

---

[1] Quoted in *Prison Reform*, from an article by A. C. Newell in *World's
Work*, October 1908.

[2] Some few States still retain whipping as a punishment for certain
offences, but cases where the law is put into operation are few. In Dela-
ware, at the model workhouse of Wilmington, as recently as 1938, three
paupers were flogged with a cat-o'-nine-tails for theft (see *Daily Mirror*,
January 10, 1938); and in Baltimore the offence of wife-beating is still
punished by flogging.

the waist and then began to lash him over the back, face and
arms. He begged them to spare his life, but ignoring his
every entreaty, they continued the terrible torture, whipping
him over the legs and belly, and even on the private parts.
At length Mills and Curtis went to fetch Hawkins's father
and brother, who, they thought, from some remarks made
by their victim, knew something about the whereabouts of
the stolen tea. Hawkins, who had been left in charge of a
man named Robb, expired before they returned. Mills
was eventually charged with the murder and executed on
August 12, 1749.

For sheer lust of cruelty few cases in history can equal or
excel the long series of tortures instigated by Elizabeth
Brownrigg, culminating in her execution at Tyburn on
September 14, 1767. The female monster who, before her
marriage to James Brownrigg, a London plumber, was a
domestic servant, was herself the mother of sixteen children.
She began practising as a professional midwife, running a
sort of private hospital for pregnant women, in connexion
with which she employed a succession of orphan girls as
servants. There soon, however, began to gather queer
rumours in connexion with Mrs. Brownrigg and her lying-
in hospital, and there were whispers that the young girls she
employed were treated in a manner which, even for those
days, was shocking and revolting. It was in consequence of
the death of one of these girls at St. Bartholomew's Hospital
that a coroner's jury returned a verdict of wilful murder
against James and Elizabeth Brownrigg and their son John.
According to the evidence given by girls in the service of
Mrs. Brownrigg, it was a common practice for her to lay
down upon the kitchen floor a couple of chairs so that one
supported the other, and then, aided by her husband, she
fastened her victim, previously stripped naked, upon the
backs of these chairs, and whipped her from the shoulders
to the buttocks until, from sheer exhaustion, she was compelled to desist. On other occasions, Brownrigg fastened the
girl's hands together, attached a rope to them which she
slung over a strong hook in the ceiling, and then hoisted her
victim, naked as the day of her birth, so that she swung at
the end of the rope. In this position, sometimes with a horse-
whip, sometimes with a cane, and sometimes with a broom,

she lashed or beat at the naked body until the blood gushed from the wounds. The apothecary who attended to Mary Clifford's lacerated body stated that the tears were of such severity that they appeared "as if cut with a knife; that scarce any part of her body was free from them, that her head and face were badly injured; and further that, through lack of proper attention and dressing, mortification had set in."

Jane Buttersworth beaten to death

On May 3, 1740, Mrs. Elizabeth Branch and her daughter Mary, were executed for the murder of Jane Buttersworth. According to the evidence given at Taunton Assizes, where the case was tried, the woman Branch, after accusing her servant Buttersworth of telling lies, knocked her down. Mother and daughter then beat the girl with broomsticks until she was senseless. She died soon afterwards.

Sadistic flogging occupies its own special niche in the history of flagellation. Every sexologist knows of cases where sexual excitation or satisfaction is secured by whipping human beings and animals. In the continental, South American, and Eastern brothels, special facilities are provided for wealthy perverts of this type. There are, too, those who secure sexual exhilaration or gratification from the mere sight of a person being flogged.

"The minions of Henri III of France, and other princes," says Millingen, "were decked in white robes, then stripped, and whipped in procession for the gratification of their royal masters."[1] The privileged visitors to the bridewells, when boys and girls were birched on the bare buttocks, secured, we are told, ecstasy from the sight.

"A public flogging," said Bernard Shaw, "will always draw a crowd; and there will be in that crowd plenty of manifestations of a horrible passional ecstasy in the spectacle of laceration and suffering from which even the most self-restrained and secretive person who can prevail on himself to be present will not be wholly free."[2]

[1] J. G. Millingen, *Curiosities of Medical Experience,* 1837.
[2] *The Saturday Review,* August 28, 1897, p. 224.

CHAPTER XXI

MUTILATION, DRAWING AND QUARTERING, DECAPITATION, ETC.

Mutilation

WHERE the death penalty was not inflicted, mutilation in some form or other, and in nearly all countries, at one time was a favourite method of punishment. Among savage races it took a variety of forms, notably cutting out the tongue, the eyes, and perhaps most frequent of all, castration.

The incidence of castration is, however, partly explainable in the fact that races which rarely or never practised mutilation for penal purposes, castrated criminals and prisoners, in some cases as a religious ceremony analogous to the Jewish rite of circumcision, and in other instances for sociological and sexual purposes. Thus the cutting away of the genitals was considered to constitute a sacrifice of the first rank. Eunuchs could be sold as guards for harems, or for service in brothels specializing in sexual perversion. Slaves and criminals were castrated in huge quantities to supply the demand.

The torture associated with castration is of two kinds. In the first place, there is the intense agony and great danger to life[1] which are inseparable from the operation performed in the crude manner customary among savage and primitive tribes (often involving complete ablation of the exterior genitals), where aseptic surgery is unknown and anæsthetics are not employed. In the second place there is the psychological torture which cannot ever be effaced in the case of any man who is castrated against his will; so that where he succeeds in overcoming the physical dangers and suffering,

---

[1] According to Remondino (*History of Circumcision*, Philadelphia, 1891), to provide the 3,800 eunuchs which at one time formed the annual quota of Soudan, at least 35,000 Africans were operated upon.

TORTURE BY CASTRATION
From an Illustration in Hughes's *Histoire de la Navigation*, Amsterdam, 1610.

BURYING ALIVE, DISEMBOWELLING, ETC.
From an Engraving in *Theatrum Crudelitatum Haereticorum*, 159?.

he continues to suffer mentally as long as life lasts.[1]

In Egypt, says Alexander:

" The chastity of virgins was protected by a law of the severest nature; he who committed a rape on a free woman, had his privities cut off, that it might be out of his power ever to perpetrate the like crime, and that others might be terrified by so dreadful a punishment."[2]

As the centuries went by, in civilized countries, castration was rarely employed officially or openly as a form of punishment, or as judicial torture. It has often been employed surreptitiously, by mobs taking the law into their own hands (especially in relation to sexual offences), and by individuals for the purpose of exacting private vengeance. It is occasionally employed for this purpose even to-day.

But if castration has been rare, other forms of mutilation have, at one time or another, loomed large in the penal code of every European State. The technique adopted was very nearly as crude as the surgical operations performed by the savages; a fact which added to the suffering of and risk run by the victims.

Of the Turks in the sixteenth century we read in Grafton's *Chronicles* (1809), that, on entering Austria, they

" committed such crueltie and tyranny, as never hath bene heard nor written, for of some they put out the eyes, of others they cut off the noses and eares, of others they cut off the privie members, of women they cut off the pappes, and ravished virgins, and of women great with childe, they cut their bellies and burnt the children."

For many offences it was an English custom to consign the culprit to the pillory, and inflict upon him some form of mutilation. The methods adopted were of the crudest, and calculated to entail the maximum amount of suffering.

[1] The operation of castration, which involves the amputation of the penis or the testicles (in the ancient days and among many races both penis and testicles were removed *en bloc*) must be clearly distinguished from the modern operation of vasectomy, which involves neither danger nor suffering.

[2] W. Alexander, *The History of Women*, 1779, Vol. I, p. 111.

"In the year 1560 a maid was set on the Pillory for giving her mistress and her household poison. Besides the shame of the Pillory, one of her ears were cut, and she was burnt on the Brow. And two days after she was set again on the Pillory, and her other ear cut. And but some few days after, another maid was set on the Pillory for the same crime; and her ear cut, and burnt on the brow."[1]

On June 30, 1637, John Bastwick, Henry Burton and William Prynn, convicted by the Star Chamber of libel, were sentenced to the pillory in the Palace-yard, Westminster, to be branded and have their ears cut off. The executioner, it is recorded, performed his task "with extraordinary cruelty." In the case of Prynn "he heated his iron twice to burn one cheek, and cut one of his ears so close that he cut off a piece of his cheek." The prisoner Burton,

"when the executioner had cut off one ear, which he had cut deep and close to the head in an extraordinary cruel manner, never once moved and stirred for it. The other ear being cut no less deep, he then was freed from the pillory, and came down, where the surgeon waiting for him presently applied a remedy for stopping the blood after the large effusion thereof."[2]

For perjury, in addition to branding, as mentioned in another place, an offender was sometimes put in the pillory and his ears cut off. Similarly for forgery, libel, giving short weight, and thefts not exceeding twelve pence, the punishment was the loss of one ear or of both ears according to the gravity of the offence. For sheep-stealing, the hands were cut off at the wrists.

For writing *An Appeal to Parliament; or, Zion's Plea Against Prelacy*, Dr. Leighton was condemned by the Star Chamber to be whipped and put in the pillory, and while there to have both ears cut off, his nose slit open on both sides, and to be branded on both cheeks with the letters S.S.

In France we read in the *Memoirs of the Sansons* that

---

[1] John Stow, *A Survey of London*, 1720, Book I, p. 258.
[2] *A Collection of the Most Remarkable Trials*, 1734, Vol. IV, p. 528.

one of the Huguenots "burnt alive on January 21, 1535, in the presence of the king, was a man named Antoine Poile, whose tongue was pierced and attached to his cheek with an iron pin." In 1766, the Chevalier de la Barre, a young officer of seventeen years, was accused of mutilating the figure on a wooden crucifix on the bridge of Abbeville. Although there was no evidence worth the name, other than that the youth was proved to have a penchant for the singing of bawdy songs and reading the heretical works of Voltaire, he was condemned to be put to the torture, and to have his tongue cut out.[1] Removal of the tongue was also a common punishment in France for blasphemy. For theft, the amputation of one ear or both ears, according to the amount involved, was prescribed. To induce Jews to hand over their money, their teeth were extracted; in cases of murder or arson, previous to execution, it was customary to amputate one hand.

Scalping

This peculiar method of mutilating the living (and the dead), adopted by the North American Indians, entailed the most agonizing torture. When applied to the living captive or the wounded, owing to the rough-and-ready methods adopted, it usually caused death. But there were exceptions. The idea that the practice was confined to the Redskins is a fallacy. Herodotus refers to scalping by the Scythians:

"Every Scythian drinks the blood of the first Prisoner he takes, and presents the King with the heads of the enemies he has killed in Fight. For if he brings a head, he is intit'led to a share of the Booty, otherwise not. They slew these Heads by cutting a circle round the neck close under the ears, and stripping off the skin, as they would do that of an ox."[2]

It was practised in many parts of Europe during the early centuries of civilization. The ancient German *decalvare* was a form of scalping.

The origin of the practice seems to have been connected

[1] Frederic Shoberl, *Persecutions of Popery*, 1844, Vol. II, p. 341.
[2] *History*, Book IV.

with the belief that by securing the scalp one also obtained the powers which were exhibited by its original owner. For this reason the scalps of brave or powerful warriors were held in high esteem.

Among the North American Indians the method of scalping was to grasp the hair on the crown of the head with the left hand, pass the knife around it and under the skin, at the same time tearing off the skin with the hair, the piece removed being about the size of the palm of the hand.[1]

All the scalping that was done in the pioneer days of America was by no means restricted to the Indians. The whites hunted for scalps, too. They did not collect them as trophies, or because of any reputed magical properties, but for the bounties which were offered at one time and another. This practice of offering a bounty for every Indian scalp brought in, seems to have been inaugurated by Governor Kieft, in 1641. In the next one hundred and fifty years or so many other governors pursued the same policy. The French offered bounties for British scalps, and the British offered bounties for French scalps, resulting in a state of affairs where no person's head-covering could be considered safe.

Drawing and Quartering

The ancient methods of execution in which the limbs and bodies were literally pulled apart by main force, or cut up into sections by an executioner, lived long in European civilization.

Quartering would appear to be a development of disembowelling, as the practice of cutting open the abdomen and removing the bowels, before the body was divided into sections, persisted for a long time. An analogous method of execution, prescribed for the punishment of traitors, was to remove the heart in addition to or instead of the bowels, before quartering.

According to Lacroix and other writers, this method of execution, involving, as it did, a form of torture of the most revolting nature, was not usually, in itself, enough to satisfy the demands of justice. Before execution in this way, it was

---

[1] Geo. Catlin, *Letters and Notes on the Manners, Customs and Conditions of the North American Indians*, 1841.

customary for torture of another nature to be applied to the doomed criminal. Thus a hand would be cut off, or the arms, thighs and breasts lacerated, and molten lead or boiling pitch poured into the wounds.[1]

These preliminary tactics over, the manner of carrying out the execution, says the same authority, was to attach a stout rope to each limb of the criminal, binding the arm with the rope from the wrist to the elbow and the leg from the foot to the knee. Each rope was secured to a strong bar of wood or metal, which was then harnessed to a horse. The four horses were induced to give short jerks, causing the victim, in his intolerable agony, to scream for mercy. When the executioners were satisfied with these proceedings, they whipped all four horses simultaneously in different directions, dragging the criminal's limbs from their sockets. Sometimes the tortured body still held together, in which case the executioners chopped and cut with hatchets at each joint, as a butcher chops at the carcase of a beast, until the limbs were drawn away from the still living trunk. The whole procedure often dragged on for hours.

Perhaps the most sensational and terrible case on record, and incidentally the last that took place in France, was the execution of Robert François Damiens, in 1757, for the attempted assassination of Louis XV. The court found Damiens guilty of *lèse-majesté* and parricide, and ordered

> " that he be taken to the Grève and, on a scaffold erected for the purpose, that his chest, arms, thighs, and calves be burnt with pincers; his right hand, holding the knife with which he committed the said parricide, burnt in sulphur; that boiling oil, melted lead, and resin, and wax mixed with sulphur, be poured in his wounds; and after that his body be pulled and dismembered by four horses, and the members and body consumed by fire, and the ashes scattered to the winds. The court orders that his property be confiscated to the King's profit; that before the said execution, Damiens be subjected to *question ordinaire et extraordinaire*, to make him confess the names of his accomplices."

[1] Paul Lacroix, *Manners, Customs and Dress During the Middle Ages*, 1874.

For over two solid hours was Damiens tortured with the boot, but in the face of agony so frightful that it drew forth shrieks of anguish, and time and again brought him to the point of fainting, he refused to speak. At length, when his limbs were crushed and broken, the surgeons said he could stand no more. On the scaffold, before the end came, Damiens was to endure greater torture. In the process of burning his arm, the executioners stated that "when the blue flame touched Damiens's skin, he uttered a frightful shriek, and tried to break his bonds. But when the first pang had shot through him, he raised his head and looked at his burning hand without manifesting his feelings otherwise than by grinding his teeth."[1] And so the awful tortures, one after another, were inflicted—the deliberate tearing of his chest and limbs with pincers, the pouring of boiling oil, lead, etc., into these wounds—until finally, the four horses were urged by the executioners to drag the limbs from his body. So tough were the sinews, however, that for hours the straining and pulling continued: at last, in desperation, the still living body was quartered with the knife. Casanova tells us that he and his companions "had the courage to watch the dreadful sight for four hours," and says that "I was several times obliged to turn away my face and to stop my ears as I heard his piercing shrieks, half his body having been torn from him, but the *Lambertini* and the fat aunt did not budge an inch."[2]

The method appears to have been unknown in England. There was, however, in vogue at one time a form of execution for those guilty of treason which, although not comparable, for sheer barbaric cruelty, with drawing and quartering, involved a species of torture the very thought of which is enough to make one shudder in disgust. The procedure is described by Stow:

"That the traitor is to be taken from the prison, and laid upon a sledge, or hurdle, and drawn to the gallows, or place of execution, and there hanged by the neck until he be half dead, and then cut down; his entrails to be

---

[1] *Memoirs of the Sansons*, edited by Harry Sanson, London, 1876.
[2] *The Memoirs of Giacomo Casanova di Seingalt*, translated by Arthur Machen, London, 1922, Vol. V, p. 22.

cut out of his body, and burnt by the executioner; then his hand is to be cut off, his body to be divided into quarters; and afterwards his head and quarters are to be set up in some open places directed; which usually are on the City Gates, on London Bridge, or upon Westminster Hall. And to render the crime more terrible to the spectators, the hangman, when he takes out the heart, shews it the people, and says, here is the heart of a traitor."[1]

According to Holinshed,[2] after hanging until half dead, the criminal was " taken down and *quartered alive* " before the bowels were cut from the body; an opinion which is born out by Strutt, who says:

" Traytors were drawn upon hurdles to the gallows, then hanged up for a little space, and let down and quartered: and their quarters were set up in the most conspicuous parts of the towns, and cities; but if the malefactor was a nobleman, he was beheaded instead of being hanged. Some were dragged by the heels, at the horse's tail, to the place of execution."[3]

It seems highly probable that the procedure varied somewhat at different times and in different circumstances. At any rate, according to official records, on October 19, 1685, for the crime of high treason, John Fernley, William Ring and Henry Cornish, were given the following sentence:

" You must, every one of you, be had back to the place from whence you came, from thence you must be drawn to the place of execution, and there you must severally be hanged by the necks, every one of you by the neck till you are almost dead; and then you must be cut down, your Entrails must be taken out and burnt before your faces, your several heads to be cut off, and your bodies divided into four parts, and these to be disposed of at the pleasure of the King; and the Lord have mercy on your souls."

[1] John Stow, *A Survey of London*, 1720.
[2] *Chronicles*, 1807.
[3] Joseph Strutt, *Manners and Customs of the Inhabitants of England*, 1775, Vol. II, p. 72.

This particular mode of execution did not apparently apply to women, for at the same trial, and for the same crime, Elizabeth Gaunt was found equally guilty. She was sentenced " to be burnt to death."

Decapitation

This method of execution is not considered to involve any form of torture in its actual technique, the head being severed from the body and death being instantaneous. While this is true with regard to such automatic appliances as the guillotine, and, even earlier, the Halifax gibbet, it was by no means so when the executioner used an axe. Only one possessed of the skill that comes with long practice, combined with great strength and a keen-bladed axe, could expect to sever the head from the body with a single blow. Usually many blows were required, and the victim suffered intense agony before the end came. It is recorded that when De Thou was executed in Paris, it was not until the eleventh blow that the head was separated from the trunk.[1]

Flaying Alive

This old method of condemning the criminal to as lingering and painful a death as one can well conceive was popular among many primitive races. It was used in China and other Eastern countries. It was a favourite method of torture of Asdrubal, founder of the new Carthage, in the second century before Christ.

Flaying was not unknown in Europe, although there are not many records of its adoption. One notable instance was the execution of the Chamberlain of the Count de Rouci, in 1366.[2] During the persecutions of the Waldenses in 1655, Jacopo Perrin and his brother, David, had the skin stripped off their arms and legs, " in long slices till the flesh was quite bare ";[3] while Paolo Garnier of Roras was first castrated and then stripped of his entire skin while still alive.

In Turkey, this particular form of torture was much used, especially for piracy and other serious crimes.

[1] *Memoirs of the Sansons.*
[2] *Ibid.*
[3] Samuel Morland, *The History of the Evangelical Churches*, 1658.

CHAPTER XXII

BURYING ALIVE, HANGING ALIVE IN CHAINS, STARVATION, THE "VIRGIN MARY," ETC.

Burying Alive

APART from savage races, burying alive as a specific method of execution seems to have been but infrequently practised. According to Plutarch, the loss of her virginity by a maid was punished in this way. There are indications of its employment in France. The Duc de Soissons, it is alleged, caused to be buried alive, a male and female serf, for the offence of marrying without his consent. Women were also condemned to be buried alive for certain offences. According to Lacroix, in 1460, a woman named Perette, accused of theft, was condemned by the Provost of Paris to be "buried alive before the gallows."[1]

In the thirteenth century, during the war of extermination against the Albigenses, the sister of Aymeric, Governor of Le Voeur, was placed alive in a pit, which was then filled up with stones.

Allied to burying alive was the method of execution sometimes adopted in the Middle Ages, in which the culprit was placed in a cavity or cellar and "walled in." It was used in Germany and Switzerland. In many cases, however, where skeletons have been discovered in the walls of ancient buildings, these are not necessarily indications of executions or murders having been committed in any true sense. On the contrary, they provided evidence of the commission of religious sacrifices or rites. It was a custom to "build in" a living person, usually a child, as a means of propitiating the gods or demons and preserving the building from destruction. (Cf. page 26.)

[1] Paul Lacroix, *Manners, Customs and Dress During the Middle Ages*, 1874.

Hanging Alive in Chains

In many civilized countries hanging alive seems to have been far more widely practised than burying alive, possibly the reason being that the torture was thereby greatly prolonged. It appears to have been a favourite method of execution in Jamaica and other West Indian islands. Edwards says that two of the men concerned in the murders committed in Ballard's Valley were hung up alive in irons in Kingston and left there until they died of starvation, and that a number of people surrounded the gibbet and talked with the murderers.[1] Stephen refers to the same miscreants, stating that they were indulged, at their own request, with a hearty meal, immediately before they were suspended; and that one survived nine and the other seven days.[2] He says also that in Dominica, a man named Balla, leader of an insurrection which took place there about 1788, was gibbeted alive, and was a week in dying.[3] In 1759, at St. Eustatia, a negro convicted of murder was placed in irons and hung upon a gibbet alive, in the broiling sun. For thirteen days he suffered terrible agony, shrieking continuously. His most urgent plea was " Water, water ! "[4]

In Surinam, slaves were sometimes executed by suspension alive from a gallows. The method was as peculiar as it was diabolical. After an incision had been made in the criminal's side, between the ribs, an iron hook was inserted into the wound, and the body, with head and feet hanging downwards, suspended by means of a chain. The torture occasioned by this method must have been indescribable in its severity, and sometimes, it was averred, three or more days elapsed before death came.

According to the writer of an article in *Once a Week* (May 26, 1866) there is, or was, on exhibition in the Museum of the Society of Arts in Kingston, Jamaica, an iron cage which was used for imprisoning criminals who were sentenced to be hanged alive. The criminal was stripped naked

---

[1] Bryan Edwards, *The History of the British Colonies in the West Indies*, 1793, Vol. II, Book IV, Ch. III, p. 66.
[2] James Stephen, *The Slavery of the British West India Colonies Delineated*, 1830.
[3] *Ibid.*
[4] *Gentleman's Magazine*, Vol. XXIX, 1729, p. 93.

BREAKING ON THE " WHEEL " OR CROSS

From *Once a Week*, 1866.

IRON CAGE USED IN JAMAICA FOR HANGING CRIMINALS ALIVE

(See Text, page 219.)

before being confined in the cage. When the cage was discovered it contained the skeleton of a woman, and this
skeleton was removed to the Museum along with the
apparatus itself. The criminal, once imprisoned in the cage,
which was suspended from the branch of a tree, was left to
die of starvation, thirst and exposure. As this instrument of
torture must surely be one of the most remarkable of its kind,
I reproduce the picture of the cage, which was apparently
built around its human occupant, and the description of it,
both culled from the pages of *Once a Week*.

   " Round the knees, hips, and waist, under the arms
and around the neck, iron hoops were riveted close about
the different parts of the body. Iron braces crossed these
again, from the hips right over the centre of the head.
Iron bars and plates encircled and supported the legs, and
at the lower extremities were fixed plates of iron like
old-fashioned stirrups, in which the feet might have
found rest, had not a finish to the torture, compared to
which crucifixion itself must have been mild, been contrived by fixing in each stirrup three sharp-pointed spikes
to pierce the soles of the victim's feet. The only support
the body could receive, while strength remained or life
endured, was given by a narrow hoop passing from one
end of the waist bar in front between the legs to the bar
at the back. Attached to the circular band under the
arms, stood out a pair of handcuffs, which prevented the
slightest motion in the hands; and on the crossing of the
hoops over the head was a strong hook, by which the
whole fabric, with the sufferer enclosed, was suspended."

Now although the evidence that gibbeting alive was
practised in the British West Indies is incontrovertible,
there is a remarkable dearth of evidence as regards its
practice in England itself. There are many authorities
who stoutly deny that it was ever practised at all. Certainly official records seem to make no mention of any
such sentences,[1] even if they were given. There are, how-

---

[1] There was a statute which allowed the judge, at his discretion, to
order the *corpse* to be hung in chains or dissected. As late as the eighteenth
century, there appear to have been many cases of criminals being hung in
chains after execution. Apparently the public derived satisfaction and
pleasure from the spectacle, for in *Notes and Queries* (January 10, 1874)

ever, several references to the practice in historical and sociological works. Of these the most important is that of Holinshed, a reliable historian, who says:

> " But if he be convicted of wilful murther, doone either upon pretended malice, or in anie notable robberie, he is either hanged alive in chains nere the place where the fact was committed (or else upon compassion taken first strangled with a rope) and so continueth till his bones consume to nothing."[1]

A correspondent in *Notes and Queries* (Fourth series, Vol. XII, p. 298) quotes Chettle's statement that " whereas before time there was extraordinary torture, as hanging wilful murderers alive in chaines "; and another correspondent in the same journal (Fourth series, Vol. XI, p. 83) says that the notorious highwayman, John Whitfield, was gibbeted alive on Barrock, a hill outside Carlisle, about the year 1777. " It is said," writes this contributor, " he hung for several days, till his cries were heartrending, and a mail-coachman who was passing that way, put him out of his misery by shooting him." In the *Scottish Historical Review* (April, 1905, p. 226) a case occurring in Scotland is given, that of " John Davidson, who was for piracy condemned on 6th May, 1551, to be ' hanged in irons,' at a stake within flood mark of the shore, at Leith, until he died."

In 1383 there occurred a remarkable case involving torture by hanging alive. The man who was executed in this strange way, was an Irish friar who had presented himself to King Richard II and accused the Duke of Lancaster of treason. The manner of his torture was this:

> " Lord Holland, and sir Henrie Greene, Knight, came to this friar, and putting a cord about his necke, tied the other end about his privie members, and after

a correspondent stated that he remembered seeing " several pirates suspended on the side of the Thames opposite Blackwall." Visitors to taverns commanding a view of this spot were provided with " spy glasses," and this correspondent further remarks that when these corpses were removed " some of the papers of the day complained of the people of London being deprived of their amusements, in not being able to enjoy the view of these pirates."

[1] *Chronicles*, 1807, Vol. I, p. 311.

hanging him up from the ground, laid a stone upon
his bellie, with the weight whereof, and peise of his
bodie withall, he was strangled and tormented, so as
his verie backe bone burst in sunder therewith, besides
the straining of his privie members; thus with three
kinds of tormentings he ended his wretched life. On
the morrow after, they caused his dead corps to be
drawne about the towne, to the end it might appeare
he had suffered worthilie for his great falsehood and
treason."[1]

Apparently hanging alive was not unknown in Germany. It seems, from Moryson's account, to have taken a
peculiarly fiendish shape.

" Near Lindau I did see a malefactor hanging in
iron chains in the gallowes, with a massive dogge hanging on each side by the heels, as being nearly starved,
they might eat the flesh of the malefactor before himself died by famine; and at Frankforde I did see the like
punishment of a Jew."

The Black Hole of Calcutta

The year 1756 saw the death by suffocation, in a
prison cell, after hours of excruciating torture, of 123 persons. The place was Calcutta, the night was close and
sultry, and the only available air in a cell measuring some
eighteen feet square came through two small barred windows. Tormented by intolerable thirst, lack of fresh air,
and the urinous odour of the cell, the prisoners struggled
with one another to reach the windows and breathe. The
guards passed small quantities of water through the aper-
tures, and held up lights so as to be able to watch the fight
that ensued to secure the water. Many undoubtedly were
trampled to death. By half-past eleven, according to the
account given by one of the survivors, a considerable proportion of the prisoners were dead, and many more were
delirious. When the doors were opened next morning out
of the 146 who had been crowded into this apartment only
23 were alive.

[1] Holinshed's *Chronicles*, 1807, Vol. II, p. 763.

Torture by Starvation

Imprisonment without food has always been a form of punishment for minor crimes, to induce confession or secure evidence.

According to Michelet it was customary in Germany to punish a slave by putting him under a cask for three days.

The torture known as *prison forte et dure* was at one time used in both France and England. It consisted, says Pike, of " perpetual imprisonment and starvation."[1] About the reign of Henry IV it gave place to " pressing " or *peine forte et dure*.

Drowning

In many ancient races drowning was a form of human sacrifice to the demons supposed to have their habitat in the waters. Throwing animals of all kinds, as well as human beings, into the river or the sea, was supposed to appease the rage of the demons, which rage was demonstrated in the occurrence of storms.

In Rome, drowning was the mode of execution for the bigamist and the patricide. In many countries it was a method of infanticide. It is often adopted to-day by those who wish to get rid of unwanted children, mainly owing to the fact that its detection is extremely difficult.

Drowning seems to have been a favourite mode of disposing of sorcerers and witches during the persecutions of the Middle Ages. And in France, under Charles VI, sedition was punished by drowning.

Torture of the Boats

This unique and revolting form of torture is a relic of ancient days, and even then it appears to have been rarely employed. It is mentioned by Plutarch as the manner in which Mithridates was put to death by the Persian tyrant Artaxerxes. He took, says the historian, no fewer than seventeen days to die, and must have suffered unimaginable agony in the process. The elaborate manner in which

[1] Luke Owen Pike, *A History of Crime in England*, 1873.

the torture was executed may be summarized as follows.

Two small boats of exactly the same size and shape were secured. In one of them the victim was extended flat on his back, with his head, his hands and his feet all projecting over the sides. The second boat was then turned upside down and fitted over the first. In this way the culprit's body was enclosed within the two boats, while his feet, hands and head were left outside. Food was then offered, and in the event of it being refused, the victim was pricked or otherwise tormented until he complied with the request. The next step consisted of filling his mouth and smearing his face with a mixture of milk and honey. He was then exposed to the full glare of the sun. In a short time, flies and insects began to settle on his face. As the hours and then the days went by, the biting of the insects drove the prisoner to distraction. And meanwhile, within the cavity made by the two boats, nature pursuing her course, the accumulated excrement stunk to heaven and became a mass of corruption. When death came, and the upper boat was removed, the flesh was found to be devoured, and " swarms of noisome creatures preying upon and, as it were, growing to his inwards."

The Kiss of the " Virgin Mary "

The inventiveness of the torturer has at one time and another taken many and strange forms, but surely never did anyone devise a more diabolical engine of torment than the unique and formidable " Virgin," which Colonel Lehmanowsky, who claimed to have seen it at the Inquisition at Madrid, said " surpassed all other in fiendish ingenuity."

Early in the nineteenth century there were many who affirmed that the " Virgin " was purely legendary; and in support of their contention they stressed the significance of the fact that no specimen of this peculiar and sinister instrument of torture appeared to be in existence. They cast doubt upon the veracity of the statements made by Colonel Lehmanowsky and others.

There were, it is true, many rumours as to existence of these engines in German castles, and the term *Jungfernkuss* (the kiss of the " Virgin ") was well known in Germany. But nothing more tangible than these rumours and tales, which might well have been pure myths, seemed to be available.

In 1832, however, Mr. R. L. Pearsall, who was extremely interested in the subject, was informed by Dr. Mayer (Keeper of the Archives of Nuremberg) that at one time such an apparatus had undoubtedly existed in the castle of Nuremberg. Two years later, Mr. Pearsall, after diligent inquiries, made further progress. At Salzburg, he was shown a torture chamber in which it was affirmed the " Virgin " had once stood. Finally, the only specimen of the apparatus which is believed to exist, was run to earth. It formed part of the collection of antiquities owned by a Baron Diedrich, who had bought it, he told Mr. Pearsall, from someone who had secured it during the French revolution.

It is probable that this instrument of torture was invented in Spain sometime in the sixteenth century, and was imported into Germany during the time that Charles V reigned over both countries. The following description of the " Virgin Mary " was given by a French officer serving under General Lasalle, who, when the French entered the city of Toledo, examined the dungeons of the Inquisition there.

" In a recess in a subterranean vault, contiguous to the private hall for examinations, stood a wooden figure, made by the hands of monks, and representing the Virgin Mary. A gilded glory encompassed her head, and in her right hand she held a banner. It struck us all, at first sight, that, notwithstanding the silken robe, descending on each side in ample folds from her shoulders, she should wear a sort of cuirass. On closer scrutiny, it appeared that the forepart of the body was stuck full of extremely sharp narrow knife-blades, with the points of both turned towards the spectator. The arms and hands were jointed; and machinery behind the partition set the figure in motion. One of the servants of the Inquisition was compelled, by command of the General, to work the machine, as he termed it. When the figure extended her arms, as though to press someone most lovingly to her

heart, the well-filled knapsack of a Polish grenadier was
made to supply the place of a living victim. The statue
hugged it closer and closer; and, when the attendant,
agreeably to orders, made the figure unclasp her arms
and return to her former position, the knapsack was
perforated to the depth of two or three inches, and
remained hanging on the points of the nails and knife-
blades. One of the familiars, as they are called, of the
Inquisition gave us an account of the customary mode of
proceeding on using the machine. The substance of his
report was as follows :

"Persons accused of heresy, or of blaspheming God
or the Saints, and obstinately refusing to confess their
guilt, were conducted into this cellar, at the further end
of which numerous lamps, placed round a recess, threw
a variegated light on the gilded glory, and on the head
of the figure and the flag in her right hand. At a little
altar, standing opposite to her, and hung with black, the
prisoner received the sacrament; and two ecclesiastics
earnestly admonished him, in the presence of the Mother
of God, to make a confession. 'See,' said they, 'how
lovingly the blessed Virgin opens her arms to thee! on
her bosom thy hardened heart will be melted; there thou
wilt confess.' All at once, the figure began to raise
extended arms: the prisoner, overwhelmed with astonish-
ment, was led to her embrace; she drew him nearer and
nearer, pressed him almost imperceptibly closer and
closer, till the spikes and knives pierced his breast."[1]

Held thus firmly in that deadly and agonizing grasp, he
was questioned and asked again to confess his guilt. If he
refused, the arms gradually tightened their grasp, slowly but
surely squeezing the life out of the body. It depended upon
the executioners whether refusal to confess caused death, or
whether, as was usually the case, the victim was released
from the clutches of the " Virgin " and taken to his dungeon
to recover sufficiently to undergo renewed and possibly fresh
tortures.

In Germany, the engine was used in a rather different
way, according to Dr. Mayer. The figure stood at the edge

---

[1] Frederic Shoberl, *Persecutions of Popery*, 1844, pp. 132-4.

of a concealed trap-door, and when the victim was released
from the deadly embrace of the "Virgin," he fell through
this trap-door upon a sort of cradle of swords in the cellar
below. These swords were arranged so as to cut the body
into pieces. The precise manner in which the scissor-like
blades of this machine worked is not known, but it is
probable that the impact of the victim's body put some
mechanism into motion, which revolved the cutting blades.

Apparently the machine examined by Mr. Pearsall in
Germany was not used for the purpose of extorting confession. Its embrace was a death clasp, for after injuring
grievously the victim, it hurled him upon the knives below.
"The construction of the figure," says Mr. Pearsall, "was
simple enough." It was of sheet-iron on a strong framework. The front formed two folding doors. There were
thirteen quadrangular poniards fitted inside the right breast
of the figure, and eight on the inside of the left breast.
Inside the face were two more of these poniards, "clearly
intended for the eyes of the victim," which indicates that
he must have been pushed or persuaded to walk backwards
into it, "and have received in an upright position, in his
breast and head, the blades to which he was exposed."[1]

[1] *Archæologia*, Vol. XXVII, 1838.

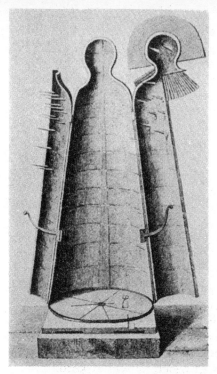

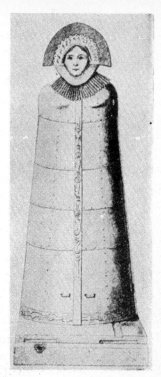

THE " VIRGIN MARY "

Interior view (showing spikes).   Front view (closed).

VIEW OF THE CUTTING APPARATUS IN THE CHAMBER BENEATH THE
" VIRGIN." THE VICTIM DROPPED UPON THESE BLADES

From *Archaelogia*, 1838.

CHAPTER XXIII

TORTURE BY ORDEAL

The Red-hot Iron Ordeal

ALL ordeals were intimately connected with religion or superstition. For centuries it was considered that the human body, under the influence of the gods, could withstand fire. For this reason a guilty person was unable to secure divine protection, while an innocent individual could go through any ordeal unscathed. The leading ecclesiastics held these beliefs most firmly, as did also many of the so-called scientists of those days. We see an indication of this trend of thought in the Biblical stories of Abraham escaping unscathed from the fiery furnace into which he was hurled by Nimrod; and of Shadrach, Meshach and Abednego, who, bound and helpless, were cast, at the command of Nebuchadnezzar, "into the midst of the burning fiery furnace," walking forth without "an hair of their heads singed," although the fire was so excessively hot that the flames "slew those men" that threw in the God-protected trio.

The "hot-iron" or analogous ordeals were used by most savage and primitive races, as well as in early and medieval European civilization. The ordeal was referred to by Sophocles. Grimm mentions that the Empress Richerda, wife of Charles the Fat, under accusation of adultery with Bishop Liutward, proved her innocence by walking unscathed through a blazing fire.

In England and in Europe generally, the ordeal consisted either of carrying in the naked hand, for a prescribed distance, a lump of iron, weighing from two to three pounds, heated until it was red-hot; or of walking, with bare feet and blindfolded, over nine red-hot ploughshares laid upon the ground at unequal distances. In some cases, and in relation to certain accusations, the subject was compelled to place the naked foot upon each ploughshare. It was by this form of trial that Queen Emma, mother of Edward the Confessor, was enabled to prove her innocence when accused of adultery with Alwyn, Bishop of Winchester. Innocence of the charge was established where the accused person successfully passed through the ordeal without sustaining any injury.

The basic grounds upon which the ordeal was held to prove the innocence or guilt of the accused being purely divine, insomuch that it was thought to constitute " a judgment of God," the performance was attended with a good deal of ceremony, and was carried out under the superintendence of a priest. Before the actual trial, the accused must live for three days on " bread, water and herbs," and attend all masses. In every case the test was preceded by prayers, the drinking of a cup of holy water by the accused; and, where the ordeal consisted of carrying the hot-iron, the sprinkling of the hand which was to be used.

The fact that so many persons proved their innocence by appealing to this form of ordeal and escaping without burns, suggests either knowledge of some method of protecting the skin from burning, as suggested by Burckhardt in relation to the analogous custom among the Bedouins of licking a red-hot spoon (cf. page 230); or collusion between the accused and the officiating priest.

The ordeal of the hatchet (*kirapo ja zoka*) practised by the Wakamba tribe, is a variation of the hot-iron ordeal; and has, too, a magical significance analogous to the religious hocus-pocus associated with the ordeal of the ploughshares by more civilized races. Thus the medicine-man who administers the oath, makes the suspected individual repeat the following formula : " If I have stolen the property of ——— (naming the person), or committed this crime, let Mulungu (Heaven) respond for me, but if I have not stolen, nor done this wickedness, may he save me."[1] The medicine-man then draws the red-hot iron blade of the hatchet four times in succession over the outstretched hand of the accused. If innocent, it is thought that he will suffer no injury, and in consequence the searing of the flesh is convincing proof of guilt.

[1] J. Lewis Krapf, *Travels, Researches and Missionary Labours During an Eighteen Years' Residence in Eastern Africa*, 1860, p. 173.

This tribe, says the same authority, has another test known as the ordeal of the needle. A long needle is made red-hot, and then drawn through the lips of the suspected person, whose guilt is established should there be an effusion of blood from the wound.

Ordeal of Boiling Water

In this form of trial, which had the same religious significance as, and in its popularity was contemporaneous with, the red-hot iron ordeal, the accused had to plunge the naked hand and arm, up to the elbow, into a vessel containing boiling water, and take out some object deposited there, usually a coin, a stone or a ring. The technique varied somewhat in different countries and sometimes in the same country for different offences. These variations were usually concerned with the weight of the object to be retrieved from the vessel of boiling water, and the time it had to be held in the hand, or, in the case of a heavy stone or weight, the distance it had to be carried. In other cases the variations were concerned with the depth of the water in the vessel. The hand was then wrapped up in a cloth or bandage, no dressing of any kind being applied, sealed by the priest, and left for three days. It was then uncovered. If the flesh was found to be uninjured the accused was discharged as innocent.

Other liquids were often used in preference to water, e.g. pitch, oil, tallow. In India boiling oil was generally used. The occasion was one of great solemnity. Forbes says:

"In general, on the day appointed for the trial, many religious ceremonies are used by the Brahmins, and the prisoner; the vessel is consecrated, and the ground on which the fire is lighted, is previously covered with cow-dung; a substance much employed in religious ceremonies by the Hindoos. When the oil is sufficiently heated, a leaf of the holy pippal (*ficus-religiosa*) is put into the vessel, and when it has evidently felt the effect of the fire, a solemn prayer is offered by the superior Brahmin; the accused is then ordered to take out the ring or coin which had been placed at the bottom of the vessel. There are some instances where the prisoner had been terribly burnt; and there are many others equally well attested, where the hand and arm received no injury."[1]

This and analogous forms of trial have persisted in India until comparatively recent years. In 1846, a merchant of Arrah, it was alleged, put some of his servants, whom he suspected of theft, to the ordeal of boiling water. In the same year, a magistrate of Tanjore reported that a man in his district, who missed some small article from his house, "proceeded, as a matter of ordinary routine, to dip the hands of his three wives into boiling cow-dung to induce them to confess if they had taken it."[2] And again, in 1867, a case was mentioned in the Bombay *Gazette*, where a camel-driver, suspected of theft, was put to the ordeal of boiling oil.[3]

In reference to the apparently miraculous phenomenon of a person being able to plunge the naked hand into boiling liquid, there may be an explanation available. According to Voltaire, at the time when the ordeals of this nature were so generally used, there were many persons in possession of a secret method of plunging the hand into boiling water with impunity. This method consisted of rubbing the skin with spirit of vitriol and alum mixed with the juice of onions.[4] Burckhardt and others, in relation to the hot-iron ordeals, have stated that if iron is heated to such a degree that it is white-hot rather than red-hot, it can be "licked" with safety. (See articles on "Ordeal" in *Encyclopædia Britannica* (eleventh edition) and Hastings' *Encyclopædia of Religion and Ethics*.)

[1] James Forbes, *Oriental Memoirs*, 1813, Vol. II, p. 390.
[2] *Once a Week* (New Series), Vol. VIII, 1871, p. 103.
[3] H. C. Lea, *Superstition and Force*, Philadelphia, 1878, p. 250.
[4] I have no knowledge of the power of the chemical preparation referred to by Voltaire, in the way of conveying impunity to the scalding effects of boiling water, and I know of no one who has had the temerity to put the method to a trial; but many years ago, in relation to a very different matter, I was assured by an old tar-boiler that it was possible, once one acquired the knack, to dip one's finger into boiling tar without suffering any ill effect.

The Cold-Water Ordeal

This peculiar and popular form of trial was based upon the belief in the magical and purifying properties of water. It was held that water, being under divine influence, would automatically reject those guilty of sin or crime.

The cold-water ordeal was much used in England immediately after the introduction of Christianity. The trial was carried out under the direction of a priest, who, immediately before operations were commenced, made the following harangue:

"I conjure you, O man! in the name of the Father, of the Son, and of the Holy Ghost; by the Christian religion which you profess; by Jesus, the only begotten son of God; by the Holy Trinity; by the Holy Gospels, and by all the holy relics of the Church, that you presume not to draw near to the altar, or to receive the communion, if you are guilty of the crime whereof you are accused; or, if you have consented to it; or, know by whom it was committed."

The priest then prayed. After these religious overtures the accused was stripped naked, securely bound hand and foot, a rope fastened around his middle, and a knot made in the rope at a distance from the body of half a yard. These preparations completed, the prisoner was thrown into the water. Sinking to such a depth that the knot in the cord was drawn under the surface was considered to be proof of innocence. Failure to sink was accepted as a sign of guilt.

This form of ordeal acquired an added popularity during the witch persecutions of the Middle Ages. It was held to be peculiarly and specifically valuable in the detection of wizards and witches, owing to the fact that those holding commerce with the devil possessed the unique characteristic of being lighter than water: they could not possibly sink. Scribonius was one of, if not the first to propound this theory; and, in later centuries, when the campaign against witchcraft reached its greatest height and intensity, the ancient belief was brought out and given much publicity.

James I maintained that the water ordeal was infallible as a test for witchcraft, and so did Matthew Hopkins, the English witch-finder supreme. Ironically enough, however, Hopkins was to regret the day he had so enthusiastically and didactically proclaimed the virtue and infallibility of this test. He was thrown into the water himself, proved to be a wizard, and duly executed as one.

In the English witch-trials by the water ordeal, a technique rather different from the one in vogue among the Anglo-Saxons was adopted. The suspected person was trussed up cross-wise; the thumb of the right hand being tied to the big toe of the left foot; and the left-hand thumb to the big toe of the right foot. A rope was tied around the middle of the body, and the accused thrown into the water, or towed across, in the case of a stream. What percentage sank and were proved innocent does not appear, but I suspect it was a precious small one; for, obviously, those carrying out the test were prejudiced against the accused to start with. By adroit manipulation of the rope they were easily able to prevent the culprit sinking.

Despite the abolition of the water ordeal, the belief in its efficacy persisted, and occasionally mobs took the law into their own hands and submitted suspected individuals to the test in defiance of official prohibition. According to Königswarter, in 1815 and 1816 there were many such trials of persons suspected of witchcraft in Belgium; and at Danzig, in 1836, an old woman, accused of sorcery, was twice plunged into the sea, and as she rose to the surface, was " pronounced guilty and was beaten to death."[1]

A particularly notorious instance in England was the murder of Ruth Osborne, at Tring, in 1751. This seventy-year-old woman, along with her husband, both accused of witchcraft, were stripped naked and submitted to the water test, the woman dying immediately afterwards. The ringleader, Colley, was tried for murder and sentenced to death, at Hertford Assizes.[2] Again, on July 22, 1760,

" at the general quarter sessions for Leicester, two persons concerned in ducking for witches all the poor old women

[1] Quoted by H. C. Lea, *Superstition and Force*, 1878.
[2] *Gentleman's Magazine*, Vol. XXI, 1751.

in Glen and Burton Overy, were sentenced to stand in the pillory twice, and to lie in jail one month."[1]

In the nineteenth century the practice persisted, a case occurring in the parish of Sible Hedingham, Essex, in which an old man, reputed to possess supernatural powers, was subjected to the water ordeal.

Torture of Ruth Osborne and her husband by the
" cold-water " ordeal

" On August 3rd last," says *The Times* (September 24, 1863), " he was barbarously hustled away in a crowd of people to the sluice of a water-mill, thrown into the stream, and so cruelly used that about a month afterwards he died, according to medical evidence, of the injuries received."

[1] *Ibid.*, Vol. XXX, 1760.

CHAPTER XXIV

MISCELLANEOUS FORMS OF TORTURE

The Pillory and the Stocks

THESE two forms of punishment represent variations of one principle: that of exposing the culprit to public degradation. Although, in many cases, confinement either on the pillory or in the stocks could not be said to involve torture, there was a possibility of the crowds inflicting severe injuries and humiliations upon anyone so imprisoned. Then, too, the psychological aspect was one not to be overlooked. In addition, imprisonment on the pillory was usually only a part of the sentence. It was often preceded or followed by flogging. In other instances it involved mutilation (cf. page 210).

Although the prisoner was confined on the pillory by the neck and hands only, it can well be imagined that to remain for hours on end with one's neck surrounded by what, to all intents and purposes, was an immense immovable wooden collar, was in itself a sufficiently severe punishment. The prisoner was not only helpless, but he was at the mercy of anyone who wished to injure or humiliate him.

This form of punishment appears to have reached its apogee in the sixteenth century. It was applied indiscriminately to men and women, and for a large number of minor offences. In 1555 we find that a woman was put on the pillory for beating her child. In 1556 there is a record of a procuress being confined on the Cheapside pillory " for the conveying of harlots to citizens, apprentices and servants," and, later in the same year, a child and her mother, the one for being a prostitute and the other " for procuring her own child and bringing her to whoredom."[1] In 1637, John Lilburn, for printing and publishing seditious literature, was sentenced in the Star Chamber, to be whipped through the

---

[1] John Stow, *A Survey of London*, 1720.

streets of Westminster and confined on the pillory. And for writing *The Shortest Way with the Dissenters*, Daniel Defoe was placed on the pillory.

The practice continued through the centuries. We find, in 1751, Egan and Salmon, for participating in highway robbery and murder, were sentenced to stand on the pillory in West Smithfield, prior to their imprisonment. This particular case is noteworthy, as it proves that the punishment of the pillory often represented a terrible and dangerous ordeal. The mob, which gathered about the exposed

John Waller pelted to death while on the pillory

prisoners, pelted them with turnips, potatoes, stones, etc., to such tune that in less than half an hour Egan was struck dead by a stone, and Salmon received injuries which later proved fatal. In 1732, John Waller, for robbery and perjury, was sentenced to exposure on the pillory at the Seven Dials, London, and died there as a result of injuries inflicted by the missiles hurled at his head by a bloodthirsty mob.

A somewhat crude form of pillory used by the Anglo-Saxons is described by Strutt. It consisted of a split piece of pliant wood which was bent round the offender and fastened at the top so as to prevent or hamper his movements. "While the prisoner was thus confined, he was whipped with a scourge of three cords each having a large knot at the end of it."[1]

The stocks confined the feet or the hands, occasionally both. The punishment was capable of causing extreme pain. In the sixteenth and seventeenth centuries, stocks were to be found in every town or village, and they were rarely without occupants. All kinds of minor offences were punished in this way.

One of the most recent cases of which there is any record was reported in the *Leeds Mercury* (April 14, 1860): at Pudsey, John Gambles, for gambling on a Sunday, was sentenced to sit in the stocks for six hours.

A special form of stocks, known as bilboes, was much used in the West Indies in the slavery days. The foot was clamped in a long iron bar. Often ten or a dozen slaves were secured in one of these bars. They were released each day in order to perform their labour, and then imprisoned again, the punishment continuing for three weeks or more.

The Thumbscrews

The application of painful pressure to the thumbs was long employed in England in order to induce a prisoner to plead or a witness to give evidence. This pressure, in its simplest form, was supplied by a piece of strong but thin string tried around the thumb. The invention of the thumbscrew enabled more pressure to be applied, even to the extent of crushing the digit to a mass of pulp. The excruciating pain induced by this particular form of torture is evidenced by the fact that few who were subjected to it failed to confess. Bishop Burnet, in his *History*, says that after the boot and the " waking " had been tried without avail, the thumbscrews, applied to Spence and Carstairs, caused them to confess all they knew :

" When the torture had its effect on Spence, they offered the same oath to Carstairs. And, upon his refusing to take it, they put his thumbs in the screws; and drew

[1] Joseph Strutt, *Manners and Customs of the Inhabitants of England*, 1775, Vol. I, p. 40.

TORTURE OF THE TREES AND OF DRIVING
SPIKES UNDER THE FINGER AND TOE NAILS

From the 1688 (Antwerp) Edition of Gallonio's
De SS. Martyrum Cruciatibus.

EGAN AND SALMON ON THE SMITHFIELD
PILLORY

(*See Text, page* 235.)

them so hard, that as they put him to extreme torture, so they could not unscrew them, till the smith that made them was brought with his tools to take them off."

When, in 1779, Howard visited the prison at Lavenham in Suffolk, " the keeper had a number of thumbscrews, sent by the magistrates, to secure the prisoners."[1]

There are indications that the thumbscrews, or thumb-kins, as they were called, were much used in Scotland, until the end of the seventeenth century. The last recorded instance of their use was in 1690, when Henry Nevil Payne, suspected of complicity in the plot to restore King James to the throne, was tortured for two days in succession with the thumbkins.

They are alleged to have been used by the slave-owner in the British colonies. Dalyell says that " if a witness regarding the slave-trade shall be credited, he saw girls at needle-work in Jamaica, with a thumbscrew on the left hand."[2]

Torture of the " Iron Gauntlets "

The " iron gauntlets " were used in the Tower of London, under authority from the Crown, the Privy Council or the Star Chamber. These gauntlets consisted of constricting irons placed around the wrists, and gradually tightened by means of a screw. The pressure of the apparatus itself was only part of the torture. The prisoner was made to stand upon blocks of wood or a stool. Chains or ropes attached to distant points on a beam were then fastened to the prisoner's wrists. When secured in this way, the support under the feet was removed, leaving the victim suspended in the air, his whole weight being thrown upon the wrists. The " gauntlets " cut deep into the flesh; the arms swelled.

" I felt," says F. Gerard, one of the sufferers, " the chief pain in my breast, belly, arms, and hands. I thought that all the blood in my body had run into my

---

[1] John Howard, *The State of the Prisons*, 1784, p. 207.
[2] John Graham Dalyell, *The Darker Superstitions of Scotland*, Edinburgh, 1834, p. 653.

arms, and began to burst out of my finger ends. This was a mistake: but the arms swelled, till the gauntlets were buried within the flesh. After being thus suspended an hour, I fainted: and when I came to myself, I found the executioners supporting me in their arms: they replaced the pieces of wood under my feet, but as soon as I was recovered, removed them again. Thus I continued hanging for the space of five hours, during which I fainted eight or nine times."[1]

Torture of the Glove

A remarkable and fiendish form of torture which, in some respects, resembled the " iron gauntlets," was used by the Inquisition of Murcia, according to the account of Don Juan Van Halen, as late as the year 1817. Van Halen was arrested on September 21st of that year, and charged with a political offence. He pleaded innocence. Owing to his steadfast denials of the accusations made against him, he was ordered to be tortured. The executioners proceeded to raise Van Halen from the floor by placing two high crutches under his arm-pits, thus suspending his body in the air. The right arm was then securely tied to the corresponding crutch, but the left arm was extended in a horizontal position with the hand open. Upon this hand a wooden glove, which extended to the wrist, was tightly fitted. Attached to the glove were two irons which extended to the shoulder and kept the whole apparatus in position. Cords were next passed around both legs and the body, and securely bound to the crutches, so that movement of any part was impossible. At this stage, the inquisitors again put their questions, and charged their prisoner with plotting the overthrow of the sovereign and of the Catholic religion. Once again Van Halen denied the charges and repeated his protestations of innocence. Then the torture began. Let Van Halen tell of his sufferings himself:

" The glove which guided my arm, and which seemed to be resting on the edge of a wheel, began now to turn, and with its movements I felt by degrees an

[1] John Lingard, *A History of England*, 1823, Vol. V, Note (U), p. 651.

acute pain, especially from the elbow to the shoulder, a general convulsion throughout my frame, and a cold sweat overspreading my face. The interrogatory continued; but Zorilla's question of ' Is it so? Is it so? ' were the only words that struck my ear amidst the excruciating pain I endured, which became so intense that I fainted away, and heard no more the voices of those cannibals."[1]

The Ducking-Stool

There is a good deal of confusion between the ducking-stool and the cucking-stool, the two terms, in later years, being used to indicate the same form of punishment. Both were widely used for the punishment of minor offences, especially in relation to strumpets and scolds.

The cucking-stool is much the older of the two. It was mentioned in the Domesday Book as being used in the city of Chester. Wright says the name means simply a " night-chair," and that in all probability the " original punishment consisted only in the disgrace of being publicly exposed, seated upon such an article, during a certain period of time."[2] There seems to be no justification whatever for any supposition that this original stool was ever used for submerging offenders in water, and it would appear, from the scanty information available, to have been a very harmless form of punishment.

The ducking-stool,[3] on the other hand, represented an ordeal to be dreaded. The manner of its use was this. A chair or stool was fixed to the end of a long pole. When the culprit was seated in the chair, the pole was lifted, either by a number of persons standing on the bank of the river or pond, or operated by some mechanical contrivance, and the chair, with its human occupant, ducked in the water. In many cases a muddy or stinking pond was selected for the purpose. It was used for the punishing of scolds and strumpets, and was popular in Scotland as well as England.

---

[1] *History of the Inquisition*, 1850, p. 405.
[2] Thomas Wright, *The Archæological Album*, 1845.
[3] Also termed the trebucket, tribuch and thewe.

According to the London *Evening Post* (April 27, 1745), one of the last instances on record of its use was at Kingston, when, for scolding, "a woman was ducked in the river Thames in the presence of two or three thousand people."[1]

An unusual instance of the use of a ducking-stool in a prison is given by Howard. The Liverpool bridewell, in 1779, was one of the few English prisons of that time to have such a thing as a bath installed. However, this bath was not used for its legitimate purpose. At one end of the bath there was a standard for a long pole, at the extremity of which was fastened a chair. Every female, on entering the prison, was placed in the chair and given a thorough ducking, thrice repeated.[2]

The ducking-stool appears to have been introduced to the United States from England. There is a record of its use in 1818, in the case of Mary Davis, found guilty of scolding and sentenced to be publicly ducked.

The Scold's Bridle

The ducking-stool was displaced to a very great extent by the scold's bridle, or branks, an ingenious and cruel method of tormenting women. This bridle was constructed of iron, something after the fashion of a helmet, except that it was merely a framework, and offered no obstruction to the sight or the movement of anything other than the tongue, which was effectually silenced by a piece of iron which projected *into the mouth*, acting as a gag; and it may be stated, an exceedingly uncomfortable and cruel gag at that. In referring to the branks, Plot says:

"They have such a peculiar artifice at Newcastle and Walsall, for correcting of scolds, which it does, too, so effectually, and so very safely, that I look upon it as much to be preferr'd to the cucking-stoole,[3] which not only endangers the health of the party, but also gives the tongue liberty 'twixt every dipp; to neither of which

---

[1] Quoted in Chambers's *Book of Days*, 1863, p. 209.
[2] John Howard, *The State of the Prisons in England and Wales*, p. 258.
[3] The writer is here obviously referring to the ducking-stool.

THE SCOLD'S BRIDLE

From an Illustration in Gardner's *England's Grievance Discovered*, 1655.

TORTURE OF THE ROPE

From an Engraving in *Theatrum Crudelitatum Haereticorum*, 1592.

(See Text, page 245.)

this is at all lyable: it being such a bridle for the tongue . . ."[1]

Not all the bridles in use were such harmless affairs. The specimens which have been preserved in many museums throughout the kingdom indicate the variety of designs that were used, some of which were undoubtedly capable of inflicting severe pain and injury, and the wearing of which, even for a short time, must have constituted a form of torture. In some cases the part which penetrated the mouth was sharply pointed, rowelled like a spur, or studded with spikes. These bridles were capable of lacerating the tongue and the sides of the mouth. Wilson mentions a peculiarly " frightful instrument " found at Forfar; and another specimen discovered in Edinburgh.[2]

The bridle was employed as a punishment for slander and defamation of character. It was also much used, as the name Witche's bridle indicates, for punishing those suspected or accused of witchcraft. The instrument was specifically indicated in all such cases, owing to the belief then current that all witches possessed the power, by means of some special devil's formula which they chanted or recited, of turning themselves into animals and transporting themselves through space, at will. In combination with the wearing of the bridle, witches were often prevented from sleeping by a relay of guards whose duty it was to see that the prisoners did not snatch so much as a moment's repose.

A curious form of bridle was used at the notorious Norfolk Island convict prison. It was made of leather and wood, and effectually covered the mouth except a small hole left for breathing purposes. " When the whole was secured with the various straps and buckles, a more complete bridle in resemblance could not well be witnessed."[3]

The iron collar, or jougs, as it was generally termed, was an apparatus peculiar to Scotland. It was fixed round the neck of the culprit. Attached to this collar was an iron chain, which, in turn, was fastened to a post or a tree. It was the equivalent of the English pillory or stocks.

[1] Robert Plot, *The Natural History of Staffordshire*, 1686, p. 389.
[2] Daniel Wilson, *Prehistoric Annals of Scotland*, 1863.
[3] John West, *The History of Tasmania*, Launceston, 1852.

Torture of the Pendulum

Nothing that those arch-fiends the inquisitors of Spain ever devised in the way of torture was more nicely calculated to cause prolonged agony of mind than what was well named the "torture of the pendulum." It was sometimes used to extract confession, the death-dealing instrument being stopped when the prisoner expressed willingness to give all the information required; often it was used as a means of execution. The victim was placed upon a table top and tied securely so that it was impossible for him to move anything but his eyes. Above him was a large heavy pendulum, the bottommost part of which had a curved cutting edge. This pendulum, when first set in motion, was near the roof of the chamber. As it swung to and fro, gradually but surely the shaft of the pendulum lengthened, and the prisoner, gazing upwards with a dread that compelled him, even against his will, to watch the movements of the hanging knife, endured the horror and agony of seeing the edge approach nearer and ever nearer to his face. Eventually the keen blade slashed the skin, continuing its remorseless cutting until life was extinct. But long before the end came, in most cases long before the pendulum blade actually drew blood, the prisoner was a raving lunatic.

No better description of this particular torture is there for the finding than that presented in Edgar Allan Poe's famous story, *The Pit and the Pendulum*, which, although a work of fiction, is a realistic description of the sufferings endured by those who, only too often, were tortured in this way.

Torture of the Bath

In the days when ancient Rome possessed its magnificent thermæ, with their hot-air apartments and sudatories, a common method of execution was to shut up the culprit in one of these baths. Where the object was to punish or to extort confession rather than to kill, the prisoner was left in the bath until on the verge of suffocation. No mortal could withstand the atmosphere of the sweating or the hot-air bath for any considerable time, the duration of the period preceding suffocation being lessened or extended at will by lowering or increasing the temperature.

There is no doubt, too, that this and analogous forms of torture have been employed in various countries through the ages. Heat and water in all their forms have always been employed by torturers, both official and private, public and surreptitious. Thus the pouring of water, drop by drop, upon the prisoner's head; or the use of the " wet cloth " in conjunction with the rack (cf. page 171).

It is not generally known, but is nevertheless a fact, that any form of torture involving the play of water continuously upon a sensitive part, is one of the most insufferable and agonizing of torments it is possible for human ingenuity to devise. An extension of the " dropping of water " torture, is the use of a watering-can without the rose. With the victim on his back, a stream of water from a height of about six feet is poured steadily upon the forehead, a procedure which, " according to experts," says Lea, " will make the stoutest criminal beg for his life in a few seconds."[1] An amplification of this method is the use of the shower bath. According to the same authority, this form of water torture has been used in America. It has even caused death. " At the New York State prison at Auburn, in December 1858, a strong healthy man, named Simon Moore, was kept in the shower-bath for a half to three-quarters of an hour, and died almost immediately after being taken out."[2]

Military Tortures

In addition to flogging, certain other painful forms of punishment were at one time used in the Army. One of the strangest of these was known as the " wooden horse."[3] This appliance was constructed of wood. Planks were nailed together so as to form an elongated sharp ridge or angle which represented the horse's back, supported by four legs, some six or seven feet high, fixed to a stand. Wheels were fitted so that the whole affair was movable at will. To

---

[1] H. C. Lea, *Superstition and Force*, p. 450n.
[2] *Ibid.*, p. 450n.
[3] It is important that the " wooden horse " used in the Army should not be confounded with the rack (cf. p. 169).

heighten the resemblance to a horse, a head and a tail were attached. The offender was mounted upon the "horse," with his hands tied behind his back, and heavy weights attached to his feet. He was compelled to remain in this position for hours at a stretch. The pain which must have been experienced is easily imaginable. The appliance was used in America as well as in England. According to Alice Morse Earle, " Garret Segersen, a Dutch soldier, for stealing chickens, rode the wooden horse for three days, from two o'clock to close of parade, with a fifty-pound weight tied to each foot, which was a severe punishment."[1] The same writer says that " at least one death is known in America, in colonial times, on Long Island, from riding the wooden horse."[2] Its dangerous consequences led to its abandonment in England. Grose says: " At length, riding the wooden horse having been found to injure the men materially, and sometimes to rupture them, it was left off."[3]

Another peculiar instrument of punishment was the whirlgig, a kind of circular cage, made of wood, and capable of revolving on a pivot at tremendous speed. The delinquent, imprisoned in the cage, became, says Grose, " extremely sick, and commonly emptied his or her body through every aperture."[4] " In the American Army," according to Alice Morse Earle, " it is said lunacy and imbecility often followed excessive punishment in the whirlgig."[5]

" Picketing,"[6] a favourite army punishment, is described by Grose :

> " A long post being driven into the ground, the delinquent was ordered to mount a stool near it, when his right hand was fastened to a hook in the post by a noose round his wrist, drawn up as high as it could be stretched;

---

[1] Alice Morse Earle, *Curious Punishments of Bygone Days*, 1896, p. 128.

[2] *Ibid.*, p. 129.

[3] Francis Grose, *Military Antiquities*, 1788, p. 200.

[4] *Ibid.*, p. 204. This remark seems to indicate that the whirlgig was employed for civil as well as military punishments, and for females as well as males, though I can find no records of the appliance being put to any use outside the Army.

[5] Alice Morse Earle, *op. cit.*, p. 133.

[6] It was a form of this torture that was used by Governor Picton in the case of the native girl, Louisa Calderon (cf. p. 149).

a stump, the height of the stool, with its end cut to a round and blunt point, was then driven into the ground near the post before mentioned, and the stool being taken away, the bare heel of the sufferer was made to rest on this stump, which though it did not break the skin, put him to great torture."[1]

Some Bizarre Tortures

One of the most revolting, and at the same time most unique methods of torture was that used at one time in Holland. The victim was stripped, and tied hand and foot, face upwards, on top of a table or bench, or secured to stakes fixed in the ground. An iron vessel, of basin-like shape, containing several large dormice or rats, was turned upside down upon the prisoner's stomach. The next step was to light a fire on top of the metal container. The animals, driven frantic by the heat, and unable to escape, burrowed their way into the prisoner's entrails.

Somewhat similar was a method which, it is alleged, was used in Germany during the seventeenth-century persecutions of the Protestants, following the death of Martin Luther. A large and fierce cat was tied or caged upon the naked abdomen of the prisoner. The animal was then pricked or otherwise tormented until, in rage and desperation, it tore with claws and teeth the flesh beneath it, gnawing into the bowels.

A peculiar form of torture used by the French Huguenots in their persecution of the Catholics, consisted of sawing the body with a rope. The victim, stripped naked, was dragged backwards and forwards, with a sawing motion, along a tightly stretched, hard-fibred or wire rope. This species of torture was of the most agonizing description, the rope cutting into the flesh to the bone.

A torture used in the Inquisition at Macerata in Italy is described by Archibald Bower, who was a member of the Council, until disgust at the persecutions inflicted caused him, in 1726, to flee the country. An instrument, resembling somewhat a smith's anvil, surmounted with an iron spike, was placed in the centre of the floor. The prisoner,

[1] Francis Grose, *op. cit.*, p. 201.

his hands and feet bound securely and fastened to ropes attached to pulleys, was hoisted to the ceiling and then " let down with his back bone exactly on the spike of iron," where his whole weight rested. He was kept there until he confessed or fainted.

Another unusual form of torture employed at the same Inquisition was specifically designed for women. Tow, pitch and cotton were wrapped around the victim's arms, and then set on fire and allowed to burn until the flesh was consumed.

The Lydians, in their tortures, says Smith, used an instrument full of sharp points. It was applied to the victim's body in the way that a card is used in combing wool. The Jews, remarks the same writer, appear to have used the harrow or thrashing-machine in much the same manner.[1]

Hippolyte de Marsillis, a fifteenth-century writer, refers to a method of torture in which goats were allowed to lick the prisoner's naked feet, which had previously been watered with brine. He states that this constituted " an indescribable torment." Other methods referred to by the same authority were putting hot eggs under the arm-pits, allowing a stream of water to fall upon the abdomen from a great height, and tying candles to the fingers.

In the thirteenth century, according to Lea, a unique form of torment was invented by Theodore Lascaris, applicable in cases of suspected sorcery. A lady of the court was accused of this crime, and to induce her to confess, the emperor " caused her to be enclosed naked in a sack with a number of cats."[2] The method, despite the severe suffering caused, failed in its object.

" Little Ease " and " Torture of the Rats "

In the Tower of London, during those days when the walls of that grim structure, could they have spoken, might have told many sorry tales of the tortures of the rack, the boots, the Scavenger's Daughter, and the " iron gauntlets," there existed a dark cell of such small dimen-

[1] W. Smith, *Dictionary of Greek and Roman Antiquities*, 1842.
[2] H. C. Lea, *Superstition and Force*.

sions that no grown man could stand upright in it, or lie at full length on the floor. Walking about was impossible. All the occupant could do during the seemingly interminable hours when he was confined in this dungeon was to adopt a squatting position. The cell was called "Little Ease," a most significant and descriptive sobriquet.

An even more terrible cell in the Tower was that known as the "dungeon amongst the rats," to which prisoners, by special warrant of the Privy Council, were sometimes condemned for the purpose of extorting confession. The floor of this dungeon was below high-water mark, and with the rise of the tide it became covered with stinking water. But this was not all. With the water came hordes of hungry rats. To sleep was to court injury or death. And so, in that dark stinking water-ridden cell, the prisoner fought the rats on the one hand and sleep on the other, until, weary and exhausted, he could fight no longer.

In the Bastille of Paris there was one dungeon, says Lacroix, "the floor of which was conical with the point downwards so that it was impossible to sit, or lie, or stand in it."[1] In the reign of Queen Anne, we are told, the debtors' prisons were in a shocking state, and because the inmates had no money to buy food they were sometimes reduced to catching rats and mice to avoid dying of starvation. Indeed many did die from sheer lack of food. Others contracted diseases, as in the case of Dr. John Hooper who, in 1555, was confined in the Fleet prison, alongside which a filthy, evil-smelling ditch ran, poisoning the atmosphere the prisoners had to breathe. Even as late as the nineteenth century the conditions of the hulks or "floating prisons" which were moored in the Thames, the Medway and in Portsmouth Harbour, housing thousands of convicts, were terrible. They were insanitary and they were full of vermin.

Thus the prisons of all countries, from the beginning of civilization until well into the nineteenth century, might well, without any exaggeration, have been described as torture chambers. The inmates were badly fed and inhumanly treated; they were given work, which, in itself, was little removed from actual torture, and punished in

[1] Paul Lacroix, *Middle Ages*, Vol. I, p. 407.

various ways for the slightest breach of an iron system of discipline.

Various Prison Tortures

A remarkable seventeenth-century pamphlet, dealing with the treatment meted out to English parliamentary prisoners, in the year 1643, by Captain William Smith, Provost-Marshal General of the King's Army, and the prison-keeper at Oxford, provides staggering revelations. There were 180 prisoners all told, and they were forced into one room of such small dimensions that they were compelled to lie upon one another. They were allowed one pennyworth of bread and a can of small beer apiece each day. They were asked to take up the Protestation and serve in the King's Army. All refused, and, says the writer, thereupon Smith " drives us all up again into the Tower, striking us with his cane, swearing deeply that he would make us take it, or he would make us to shit as small as a rat; and so kept us still to our former allowance." On February 6th some of the prisoners were removed from the Castle to the bridewell, " where we were about forty of us put down into the dungeon, about foure weeks thronged, in so little roome, that we were scarce able to stirre one by another, the place also being made very noysome, because we eased ourselves in the same, so that in some place of it, we might go over the shooes in pisse and filth." As they became weaker and weaker through ill-treatment and lack of food, the state of their cell became worse. " One eased nature as he lay, and another was troubled with vomiting." Smith, to add to their suffering, now deprived them of water. So desperate did the prisoners in the Tower become that they drank their own urine. But let us read further:

" They knock't for water. Ockdon, the Captaine's man, came and told them he could help them to none (though the river runee by the doore) they being dry knock't again. Smith came himself, and said I will give you water, caused three or four of his men to come arm'd to guard his person, and cal'd down one that was my Lord saies Miller, and layes him in irons neck and heels; and one sergeant Wallis he canes him at least fifty blowes over the head, and wounds him very sorely, that he hath lost one of his joints; and after this layes him in irons 28 pound weight, neck and heeles, and so keeps him in 48 hours in a nasty dungeon without bread or water, or any other sustenance; and caned Lieutenant Whithead, and lay'd him in irons; and to colour over his tyranny, commands his men to say, they made a mutiny."

One prisoner attempted to escape but was recaptured.

"Smith laid him in irons, hands and feet, and so keepes him about eight weeks; by reason of this cruell usage, he fell very weak and sick, and in his sicknesse he would not suffer anybody to come to helpe him in his great extremity, so that for three weeks he lay in his owne dung and pisse, and so by a long and languishing disease, being pined to nothing, in a great deale of woe ended his days."

Two more tried to escape, and failed. These Smith tortured by burning them with matches "between the fingers to the bone."[1]

Now let us skip a matter of a hundred years and take a look at the conditions prevalent in English prisons at the time when Howard published his famous revelations. At Knaresborough, in Yorkshire, the prison for town debtors, at the time of Howard's tour of inspection (1779) consisted of one room some 14 feet by 12 feet. It had an earthen floor, and was in a most offensive state, as an *uncovered* sewer from the town ran through the cell. "I was informed," writes Howard, "that an officer, confined here some years since, for a few days, took in with him a dog to defend him from vermin; but the dog was soon destroyed, and the prisoner's face much disfigured by them."[2]

In a large number of foreign prisons, according to Howard, not only were the conditions inhuman and disgust-

[1] Lord Sommers, *Tracts*, London, 1795.
[2] John Howard, *The State of the Prisons*, London, 1784, p. 410.

ing, but torture was common. In Rome he found the old inquisitorial method of torment known as "the pulley" still in use; in Madrid he inspected a torture room, the walls of which were stained with blood; in Amsterdam, he came across a prisoner whose limbs had been dislocated to such an extent that he was incapable of working; at the prison *Lá Porte de Halle* of Brussels, the gaoler told him that "he had seen a man suffering on the torture-stool for 48 hours ";[1] in Liége he discovered the guards patrolled outside the prison for the express purpose of preventing people stopping to listen to the cries of the prisoners in the torture chamber; in Ghent, at the prison *De Mamelocker*, it was admitted that "lately a man sat 24 hours on the edged stool ";[2] he was informed that in Antwerp gaol, a criminal, when he suffers the torture, "is clothed in a long shirt, has his eyes bound, and a physician or surgeon attends him : and when a confession is forced from him, and wine has been given him, he is required to sign his confession, and about 48 hours afterwards he is executed."[3] At this prison also Howard was shown a small dungeon in which it was said "that formerly prisoners were suffocated by brimstone, when their families wished to avoid the disgrace of a public execution."[4]

He saw the "black torture room" of Munich gaol; he found, in Aix-la-Chapelle prison, "an old man with irons on his hand, who was confined on suspicion, and had twice suffered the torture to force a discovery of his confederates ";[5] in Hanover he was informed that, only two days before, a confession of guilt had been extracted from a criminal by torture, the hair from his head, his breast, and other parts having been torn off by the executioner; in Zurich, in Florence, and in Osnabrug, he discovered that the torture chambers were in constant use. In Denmark he found that mutilation was still practised; in Italy prisoners who attempted to escape were punished with 100 and 200 lashes a day for three consecutive days. And all this was happening about a hundred and fifty years ago. It is a grim, a dismaying, and an unforgettable record.

[1] John Howard, *The State of the Prisons* (Appendix), 1780, p. 97.
[2] *Ibid.*, p. 99.
[3] *Ibid.*, p. 101.
[4] *Ibid.*, p. 101.
[5] *Ibid.*, p. 95.

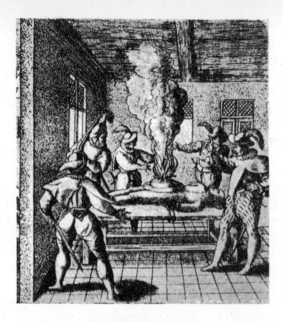

TORTURE OF THE RATS
From an Engraving in *Theatrum Crudelitatum Hæreticorum*, 1592.
(See page 245.)

THE TREAD MILL AT BRIXTON PRISON

Now let us move forward another fifty years or so and again turn our attention to the English prisons. Early in the nineteenth century, an engineer named Cubitt invented an infernal affair called the treadwheel or treadmill, for the use of prisoners condemned to hard labour.[1] It was built on the principle of the ordinary water-wheel, the treads or steps providing standing room for a row of from ten to forty prisoners. Each prisoner, who grasped a bar or rung fixed above his head, was compelled to move his legs exactly as if ascending a flight of steps, only he never altered his position, the steps passing from under his feet. The effort which each person made to avoid his legs sinking with the tread, was equal to that of ascending. At first sight, the punishment did not appear excessive, but in practice, a quarter of an hour's labour on the treadmill was enough to exhaust a fully developed man.

For twenty-five years this form of hard labour was common throughout the prisons of England. Then, in the 1840's, another diabolical engine was invented, to wit, the crank. In appearance, the machine resembled a domestic knife-cleaner as much as anything. The prisoner's task was to turn the handle. There was a little clock attachment which registered the number of revolutions made. The prisoner was required to turn that handle completely round 10,000 times a day: a stupendous task. To realize the exact nature of this task, let us glance at the findings of the Committee appointed to inquire into the condition and treatment of the prisoners confined in Birmingham Borough prison in 1852-3 when, following Governor Maconochie's retirement (October 1851), Lieut. Austin became governor and introduced new and severer disciplinary methods.

" We were assured," says the Report, " that, in order to accomplish such a task (10,000 revolutions of the crank) a boy would necessarily exert a force equal to one fourth of the ordinary work of a draught horse; the average estimate of the work of a boy, in ordinary labour out of a prison, being about one tenth of the same; and, indeed, that no human being, whether adult or juvenile, could continue to perform such an amount of labour of this

[1] The first prison to install a treadmill was Brixton, in 1817.

kind for several consecutive days, especially on prison diet, without wasting much and suffering greatly."

These 10,000 revolutions of the crank were spread over various parts of the day, true enough, but it was a rule that if a prisoner did not perform his task in the allotted time he must continue labouring at the crank, *without food*, until the required number of revolutions was completed. More and further, the prisoners were set *impossible tasks* and punished for not doing these tasks. There was introduced into the prison an instrument of torture known as the "punishment jacket," which merits a word of description. It was a sort of glorified strait-jacket, with a perfectly rigid leather collar three and a half inches deep, and rather less than a quarter of an inch thick. The prisoner was put into the strait-jacket, with his arms tied together on his chest, and strapped to the wall in a standing position. The collar was fastened so tightly round his neck "there was no room to get a finger between it and the flesh," and, stated the chaplain in the course of his evidence, Abner Wilks, a boy of fifteen years, who was punished in this way, "could not bite a piece of bread held to his mouth owing to the tightness of the collar." In this position, men and boys were often kept for four, five, or six hours, and sometimes for a whole day. Edward Andrews, aged fifteen, committed to three months' imprisonment on March 28th for the crime of stealing four pounds of beef, was given crank labour on March 30th. Failing to perform his allotted task, he was fed on bread and water only. A second failure was punished in the same way. The third time he was put on crank labour, Andrews broke the clock attached to the machine. He was then put in the "punishment jacket." This was April 17th. Two days later and he had another dose of the "jacket." Again and again was he punished in this way. On April 27th came tragedy. The night-watchman found the boy hanging by his hammock strap from one of the bars of the cell window, stone dead.

Witness after witness gave evidence of the cruel treatment meted out to prisoners within the walls of that grim Birmingham gaol during the two years immediately following Governor Maconochie's retirement. There were tales of prisoners stripped naked and drenched with cold water for the most trivial offences; there were accounts of terrible floggings; and there was unimpeachable evidence of the dark cells being in continual use. An old man of sixty-four, of poor physique and suffering from disease, was kept labouring at the crank hour after hour; prisoners who were a long way removed from manhood were worked and punished until death would have been welcomed. And indeed, death did come to three prisoners, and at that, while they were locked up in their solitary cells.

The Commissioners, after examining the witnesses, and considering the evidence, stated:

> "With respect to Captain Maconochie, we are fully satisfied that he is a gentleman of humanity and benevolence, whose sole object, in undertaking the government of the prison, was to promote the reformation of the prisoners, and the well-being of society. . . ."

On the other hand, however, they found the conduct of Lieutenant Austin, first as deputy-governor, and later, and, *in particular, as governor*, " was deserving of the most severe censure "; they spoke of the surgeon's conduct " in terms of strong condemnation "; and " the subordinate discipline officers of the gaol were in many instances guilty of wanton and very reprehensible severity."

These revelations had their effect, and initiated a reformatory campaign which revolutionized the treatment of criminals in English prisons. The full results of this campaign have been seen in this past half century. The reforms do not apply throughout the civilized world, however, and even in countries claiming to practise the most humanitarian of methods there is still much room for improvement. The Dartmoor mutiny of January, 1932, it was alleged, was primarily due to the unsatisfactory conditions then prevailing in the prison. Apart from poor food, damp and draughty cells, the treatment of convicts in many English prisons, according to Stuart Wood, is often lamentable.[1]

Towards the close of the nineteenth century, a method,

---

[1] See *Shades of the Prison House* by Stuart Wood, Williams & Norgate, 1932.

reminiscent of the inquisitorial days, for compelling suspected criminals and others to talk, was still used in France.
This method consisted of confinement in the *souricière*, a cell
about three feet square, where the prisoner could not sit, lie
down, or stretch his legs. At the Seine Assize Court, in
connexion with a murder case, says *The Times* (February 22,
1893), when a barber charged with the crime was acquitted,
it transpired that this suspect and a woman witness had been
imprisoned in the *souricière* for weeks.

The treatment of prisoners in the Onondaga County
Penitentiary, near Syracuse, New York, was the subject of
a revealing article published in *The Outlook* (August 2,
1916), in which it was stated that "added to the penalty of
chains (weighing 12 to 16 lbs.) riveted to the bodies of
prisoners who had attempted to escape, was the severe additional punishment of being obliged to wear the chains for
months at a time, 'day and night,' which means, of course,
even when sleeping and bathing."[1]

In an article in *Survey* (May 15, 1915), by W. D.
Saunders, relating to conditions at the convict camp in
Pasquotank County, North Carolina, it was stated that the
prisoners who were engaged on road construction were
"chained on their bunks and chained together by a master
chain," the ends of which were "padlocked to trees outside
the tent." They were punished by flogging: a leather strap
"two inches wide and half an inch thick" fastened to a
hickory handle being used. The convicts were not only
chained during working hours as well as at night, but to
prevent any attempt at running away, were shackled with
"iron bands on their ankles which cut into their flesh,
making running sores that never healed because the iron
bands were never removed."[2]

According to the *Spectator* (February 27, 1897) recently,
it was alleged that in Spain "salt is put in contumacious
prisoners' water, thus producing a thirst against which
human nature is incapable of standing out."

In the year 1919, the conditions of inmates of Turkish
prisons in Constantinople was the subject of an inquiry. In
the *maison d'arrêt* (house of detention), the prisoners,

---

[1] Quoted in *Prison Reform*, compiled by Corinne Bacon, H. W. Wilson
Company, New York, 1917, p. 79. [2] *Ibid.*, p. 232.

"clothed in filthy rags" and "swarming with vermin," were kept for months on end awaiting their trial. One Greek youth of eighteen years, with five other prisoners, had been first thrown into prison twelve months before. "Neither he nor they have ever been tried, and to-day he is wasted to a skeleton and his five companions dead."[1]

Generally speaking, it would appear that torture, in some form, administered either openly or surreptitiously, is a feature of the penal institutions of most countries. It would further appear to be difficult to ensure that torture does not occur, seeing that those in authority have opportunities for inflicting suffering in forms which may be described as disciplinary measures or justified as legitimate punishments: e.g., "beating up" for trivial offences, forcing prisoners to "trot" until they drop from sheer exhaustion, sometimes for no offences at all. In some countries this last-named method has been adopted in military prisons, the culprit, carrying full equipment, being compelled to do all exercises and tasks at "the double."

It is noteworthy that once a convict is adjudged guilty of an offence *inside* the prison he has little hope of being able to protest against any form of ill-treatment to which, in the name of punishment, he may be subjected.

---

[1] *Report on Conditions in Turkish Prisons*, H.M.S.O., 1919.

CHAPTER XXV

METHODS OF SELF-INFLICTED TORTURE

The Flagellants

IN the thirteenth century, to be precise, in the year 1260, appeared the first large-scale religious movement which had as its main tenet, self-flagellation. For some generations previously, the political, economic and sociological conditions prevailing in Italy had been creating in the minds of the populace, and particularly in the more blatant and fanatically religious sections of it, something akin to despair. Everywhere tyranny and anarchy manifested themselves. Then, in 1259, the great plague which swept the district brought things to a head. Raniero Fasani, known as the hermit of Umbria, preached the doctrines of self-appeasement, self-sacrifice, atonement and martyrdom as means of placating God and securing divine interference in the affairs of man. He went further. He gathered together a number of enthusiastic followers. Under the name of " *Disciplinata di Gesu Cristo,*" this fanatical band marched through northern Italy, preaching their gospel and adopting self-flagellation[1] as part of their rubric. With their bodies bared to the waist, carrying whips, sticks, twigs, and every manner of crude flagellating instrument, marching in procession, they scourged themselves and one another until, if the accounts handed down to posterity do not exaggerate, the blood ran down their bodies. As they marched, they called for recruits. And not surprisingly, to anyone acquainted with the psychology of mass emotion, they got them. Then, as is the way of epidemics, pathological and sociological, after two

---

[1] It is probable that the Adamites, as the members of a heretical sect flourishing about A.D. 200 called themselves, first practised self-flagellation, reserving the discipline as well as the practice of nudity for their private gatherings in connexion with the religion they professed. In any public processions, the shoulders only were bared, and flagellation was not practised.

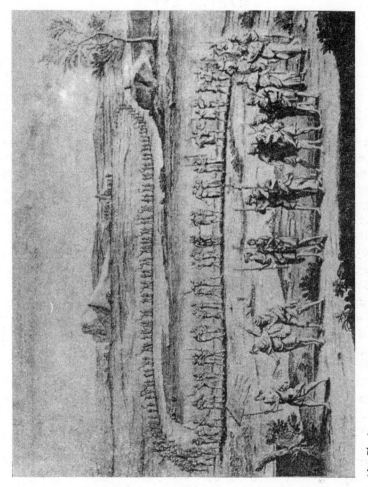

After Picart.

PROCESSION OF THE FLAGELLANTS

years or so of sensational life, the movement declined and died.

In 1347 the Black Death swept Europe like a whirlwind. Everywhere was dismay, depression, and all the familiar results that follow a major catastrophe. The Flagellants once more appeared on the scene, and with renewed vigour preached their tenets of atonement and martyrdom. Throughout continental Europe the movement flourished and spread. There were many different organizations, all motivated by the same spirit of self-sacrifice, humility and goodwill to one's fellow men. Men and women, too, of all classes and creeds joined the processions. Criminals even became fanatical flagellators.

The procedure was much the same everywhere. Marching in procession, armed with their instruments of flagellation, on arrival at a town or village, they held a crusading meeting. Often they had two or three meetings in the same place in one day. Sometimes these meetings were held in the churches; more often they took place in the market square or in some other public gathering place. The Flagellants stripped themselves to the waist, and sprawled on the ground, forming themselves roughly into a circle. According to the crimes or offences for which they desired to make atonement, they took up specific positions. Thus, the adulteress prostrated herself on her face; the murderer on his back; the perjurer lay on his side. Then, to the accompaniment of prayers, of psalm-singing, of lamentations, and pleas for divine intervention, they were flogged by the officiating priest or dignitary. Then they flagellated each other and, on occasion, themselves.

Gardner gives an interesting account, from the pen of an eye-witness, of a flagellating service performed in a church in Rome during Lent :

" Being resolved to satisfy my curiosity on this singular subject, by being present at the ceremony, I went one evening, along with several friends, to the church of the Caravita, where it is performed on the Tuesdays and Thursdays of Lent. The service commenced about an hour after sunset. The church is spacious, and the number of men present was, as nearly as we could judge, about five hundred. There were only six or eight small candles, so that from the first we could only see indistinctly. During prayers, two or three attendants entered, each having an iron hoop on which were suspended about a hundred leathern thongs, which were distributed among the congregation; but some had brought their whips along with them. We examined the thongs and found them exactly like good small English dog-whips, hard and well-knotted towards the point, but we did not succeed in obtaining one. After prayers, we had a sermon of some length, on the advantages of punishing the body for the good of the soul, and especially that sort of penance which is inflicted by means of whips. During the sermon the lights were extinguished one after another, and the concluding part of it was delivered in total darkness.

" After the sermon was concluded a bell rang, and there was a slight bustle and hustling, as if those present were removing part of their dress; a second bell rang, and the flagellation commenced. It lasted fully a quarter of an hour; hundreds were certainly flogging something, but whether their own bare backs, or the pavement of the church, we could not tell. To judge from the sounds, some used the whips, and others their hands, but the darkness was so total, we could see nothing; and besides having some little fear for our own persons we had got into a snug corner where we calculated no thongs could reach us. The groaning and crying were horrible. When the flagellation ceased, prayers were read, during which the penitents put on their clothes and composed their countenances. Lights were brought in and the congregation dismissed with the usual benediction."[1]

Other observers have expressed suspicion regarding the genuineness of many of the practices of these Flagellants, and undoubtedly the movement presented many opportunities for deception and, possibly, even for self-deception. At the same time there can be no question that many men and women, in their fanatical zeal, did undoubtedly castigate themselves, or allowed themselves to be whipped by others,

[1] James Gardner, *The Faiths of the World*, 1858, Vol. I, p. 901-2.

with unmerciful severity. The evidence is voluminous and incontestable. In this connexion De Lolme writes:

> "The cruel severities exercised upon themselves by the modern Penitents, are facts about which all writers of relations agree; all mention the great quantity of blood which these Flagellants lose, and throw to and fro with their disciplines. It is even commonly reported, I do not know with what truth, in the places where such processions are performed, that those who have been used for several years to discipline themselves in them, cannot leave it off afterwards without danger of some great disorder, unless they get themselves bled at that time of the year at which these ceremonies used to take place. Madame D'Aunoy says, that the first time she saw one of these processions, she thought she should faint away; and she concludes the account she has given of the gallant flagellating excursions that have been above mentioned, with saying, that the gentleman who has thus so handsomely trimmed himself, is often laid up in his room for several days afterwards, and so sick that he cannot go to Mass on Easter Sunday."[1]

A century ago, at least, the last remnants of any such flagellating movements in Europe vanished. The religious devotee of to-day, in civilized countries, has no taste for harsh self-disciplinary measures. But in certain primitive races, the phenomenon has persisted. There was, as comparatively recently as fifty years ago, a secret order among the Pueblo Indians, practising flagellating rites very similar to those flourishing in Europe during the Middle Ages. This order, which styled itself "The Hermanos Penitentes or Penitent Brothers," was, says a writer in the *Dublin Review* (1894), founded some three hundred years ago. Because of the strong hostility and condemnation of the Church and the State, the identity of the members of the cult had to be kept secret. To this end, during the celebrations held in Lent, those taking part had their faces covered with hoods. In addition to flagellation administered privately and publicly, there was, asserts the writer, who himself witnessed one of

---

[1] De Lolme, *The History of the Flagellants or the Advantages of Discipline*, London, 1777, p. 311.

the celebrations, " a representation of the Crucifixion, carried out with such realism that the death of a victim is by no means rare."

Self-tortures of Saints and Penitents

Self-punishment, or voluntary submission to torture, under the name of discipline, from the beginning of time, was a feature of most religious cults. It was expressly sanctioned by the Church of Rome; it was regularly practised in the monasteries and nunneries. The most popular method was flagellation, and there are grounds for supposing that, in the majority of cases, the penitents practised self-flagellation, with scourges of their own choosing and in privacy, rather than submit to fustigation at the hands of others. Thus St. Liguori, according to Cardinal Wiseman, disciplined himself with such extreme severity that his secretary was constrained to interfere lest the martyr should lash himself to death; while St. Pacificus used cords and chains upon his own flesh three times a week to such a degree that his body was covered with blood.

About the year 1000, the notorious Fulk, murderer of Conan, Duke of Brittany, made three separate pilgrimages to the Holy Land, on the last of which, to render his penance complete and in every way satisfactory to God and the Church, he caused himself to be drawn naked upon a hurdle, wearing a halter around his neck, through the streets of Jerusalem, while an attendant lashed him continuously with scourges, crying out at intervals " Lord! have mercy on the traitor and forswearer Fulk."

This voluntary submission to various kinds of torture, and to flagellation in particular, seems to have been a favourite method of atonement for murder and other serious crimes. King Henry II, for conniving at, if not actually commanding, the murder of Thomas à Becket, allowed himself to be flogged in Canterbury Cathedral. Similarly, for heresy and other crimes, real or fictitious, with which they were accused, Raymond, Count of Toulouse; William, Duke of Aquitaine; Foulques, Count of Anjou; and the Marquis of Tuscany, submitted to scourging. The women too adopted similar tactics. Thus St. Hildegarde, St. Maria, Catherine of Cordona and Queen Anne of Austria.

THE PENANCE OF KING HENRY II

From *Specimens of Ancient Sculpture and Painting,* 1780.

After Picart.

PENITENCE OF THE GERMAN JEWS IN THEIR
SYNAGOGUE

No less an authority than De Lolme, in his *History of the Flagellants*, comments on the phenomenon as follows:

" The practice of voluntary flagellation soon spread itself far and wide; and we find it to have been adopted by numbers of persons eminent on account either of their dignity, or their merit, several of whom have been mentioned by Father Gretzer. Among them were St. Andrew, Bishop of Fiesola, Laurence Justinian, Abbot Poppo, and especially St. Anthelm, Bishop of Bellay, who lived about a hundred years after Dominic the Cuirassed and Rodolph of Eugubio, and gloriously trod in the footsteps of these two holy men. ' Every day (it is said in that saint's life, which was written by one of his intimate friends), every day he scourged himself, making lashes fall thick on his back and sides, and by thus heaping stripes upon stripes, he never suffered his skin to remain whole, or free from the marks of blows."

In China much the same practices were at one time current. One famous penitent monk, belonging to the order of Bonzes, used a nail-studded chair. The slightest movement of the sitter resulted in the sharp points, which were as close together as it was possible to place them, piercing the body.[1]

The Indian " Suttee "

This ancient and tragic Hindu practice represents the limits to which self-sacrifice and incidentally self-torture can go; for it signifies nothing less than the self-destruction of .the widow, by fire, upon the funeral pile of her husband. An essential feature of the sacrifice is its purely voluntary nature. The widow is not compelled to sacrifice herself, and any attempt at coercion, either by relatives, friends or priests, is condemned and prohibited.

At the same time the Shastras promised glory and blessedness in the future life to those who practised the rite, and went so far as to state that it was " proper for a woman to cast herself upon the funeral pile of her husband." Further, the widow who neglected to sacrifice herself forfeited the respect of her people. And this was not all. Her nose and

[1] B. Picart, *Religious Ceremonies*, Vol. IV, p. 229.

ear-rings were dragged off by main force, and her hair cut away. If she wore ornaments, she was ordered to remove them, or they were pulled off. She was compelled to observe lifelong chastity.

The following description of the rite, given by a native Hindu, is authoritative:

"After ceremonies of purification had been performed upon the spot, strong stakes of bamboo were driven into the ground, enclosing an oblong space about seven feet in length and six in breadth, the stakes being about eight feet in height; within this enclosure the pile was built of straw, and boughs, and logs of wood: upon the top a small arbour was constructed of wreathed bamboos, and this was hung with flowers within and without. About an hour after the sun had risen, prayers and ablutions having been carefully and devoutly performed by all, more especially by the Brahmins and Lall Radha, who was also otherwise purified and fitted for the sacrifice, the corpse of the deceased husband was brought from the house, attended by the administering Brahmins, and surrounded by the silent and weeping friends and relations of the family. Immediately following the corpse came Lall Radha, enveloped in a scarlet veil which completely hid her beautiful person from view. When the body was placed upon the pile, the feet being towards the west, the Brahmins took the veil from Lall Radha, and, for the first time, the glaring multitude were suffered to gaze upon that lovely face and form; but the holy woman was too deeply engaged in solemn prayer and converse with Brahma to be sensible of their presence, or of the murmur of admiration which ran through the crowd. Then turning with a steady look and solemn demeanour to her relations, she took from her person, one by one, all her ornaments, and distributed them as tokens of her love. One jewel only she retained, the *tali*, or amulet placed round her neck by her deceased husband on the nuptial day; this she silently pressed to her lips, then separately embracing each of her female relations, and bestowing a farewell look upon the rest, she unbound her hair, which flowed in thick and shining ringlets almost to her feet, gave her right hand to the principal Brahmin, who led her with ceremony three times round the pile, and then stopped with her face towards it, upon the side where she was to ascend. Having mounted two or three steps, the beautiful woman stood still, and pressing her hands upon the cold feet of her lifeless husband, she raised them to her forehead, in token of cheerful submission: she then ascended and crept within the little arbour, seating herself at the head of her lord, her right hand resting upon his head. The torch was placed in my hand, and overwhelmed with commingled emotions I fired the pile. Smoke and flame in an instant enveloped the scene, and amid the deafening shouts of the multitude I sank senseless upon the earth. I was quickly restored to sense, but already the devouring element had reduced the funeral pile to a heap of charred and smouldering timber. The assembled Brahmins strewed the ashes around, and with a trembling hand I assisted my father to gather the blackened bones of my beloved uncle and aunt, when having placed them in an earthen vessel we carried them to the Ganges, and with prayer and reverence committed them to the sacred stream."[1]

The popularity of the rite is indicated by the fact that, despite the protestations and condemnation of the British government, in the decade of 1815 to 1825, a total of 5,997 widows sacrificed themselves. Lieutenant-Colonel Sleeman states that on November 24, 1829, he had to suffer "an old widow to burn herself with the remains of her husband, who had that morning died upon the banks of the Nerbudda."[2]

In 1830, the authorities succeeded in abolishing *suttee* throughout India, but there are indications that it continued to be practised surreptitiously in various parts for many years. "The last case I heard of," says Wilkins, "was about 1880."[3]

[1] Quoted by James Gardner, *The Faiths of the World*, 1858, Vol. II, p 875.

[2] Lieut.-Col. W. H. Sleeman, *Rambles and Recollections of an Indian Official*, 1844, Vol. I, p. 25.

[3] W. J. Wilkins, *Modern Hinduism*, 1887.

CHAPTER XXVI

MODERN METHODS OF TORTURE

Torture in Russia in the Nineteenth and Twentieth Centuries

BEFORE the coming of the Soviet, the peasants of Russia were treated by the aristocracy and the landowners as animals are treated in civilized countries to-day. They were badly fed, they were worked very nearly all the hours that God sends, they were severely punished for the slightest negligence, they were chained to one another, they were driven to their work as a herdsman drives his cattle, their life was a living death. Many committed suicide. Many were whipped so atrociously that they either died under the lash or expired shortly afterwards.

At the trial, in 1853, of Mme. de Svirsky, a landed proprietress, it transpired that

" she used to force her serfs to eat their excrement or rotted eggs. She used to strike them with an *arapnik*, or make them sit naked upon ice. She forced a little girl to eat a plait of hair. A wolf-bitch was kept in her courtyard, and she often set it upon the peasants. One woman was nearly killed by it; another received thirty wounds."[1]

In connexion with police activities, and especially as regards political offences, torture was frequently employed. Alexinsky refers to its use in 1906-7, by the police of Riga, in order to induce prisoners to confess their guilt and to divulge the names of their associates.[2] The methods employed were equal in their barbarity and cruelty to anything of which the inquisitors of the Middle Ages were guilty. Three revolutionaries arrested on March 14, 1906,

[1] Gregor Alexinsky, *Modern Russia*, translated by Bernard Miall, Fisher Unwin, 1913, p. 84.
[2] *Ibid.*, p. 280.

264

had " their nails and hair torn out, they were struck upon the genital organs, their bones were broken."[1] In November of that same year, a young man of twenty-two years " was transformed, in a detective police bureau, into a hairless and mutilated old man."[2]

These were not isolated instances. They are merely typical cases out of a category of tortures the very reading of which makes one shudder with horror. Alexinsky, as ex-deputy of the Duma, speaks with authority and conviction. His book should be read by all who think that torture in Europe was abolished a hundred years ago.

The Bolshevist Atrocities

Now let us turn to the atrocities committed by the Bolshevists in 1918-19. The report of the Deniken Commission established beyond any dispute that many of those who were executed by the Bolshevists were subjected to the most terrible torture before being actually killed. Mutilations and flogging were common forms of ante-mortem treatment.

An official communiqué from Vladivostock, dated January 14, 1919, reveals that " officers taken prisoners by Bolshevists here had their shoulder straps nailed into their shoulders."[3] Some were found with their eyes gouged out, and without noses. Bishop Andronick was buried alive.

Another report states that in July 1918, during the fighting in the Usuri district, Czech soldiers were found with their " private parts cut off, their faces slashed, their eyes gouged out, and their tongues cut out." These mutilations had been " inflicted before death."[4]

General Knox reported to the British War Office:

" At Blagoveschensk officers and soldiers from Torbolof's detachment were found with gramophone needles thrust under their finger nails, their eyes torn out, the marks of nails on their shoulders where shoulder straps had been worn."[5]

[1] *Ibid.*, p. 281.
[2] *Ibid.*, p. 281.
[3] *A Collection of Reports on Bolshevism in Russia*, H.M.S.O., 1919, p. 26.
[4] *Ibid.*, p. 27.
[5] *Ibid.*, p. 45.

The catalogue of horrors is as terrifying in its immensity as it is frightful in its details. Nineteen-year-old Miss Bakouyeva was found still writhing in agony after having had a bayonet slowly forced into the same spot thirteen times. The faces of two priests named Bleiwe and Bjeschanitzki, when their dead bodies were discovered, "were mutilated almost beyond recognition"; labourers were flogged and beaten with rifle-butts until they gave evidence; many victims, before being executed, were forced "to dig their own graves."[1] At Pskoff, 150 Russians, captured by the Reds, were handed over to the Mongolian soldiers, "who sawed them in pieces."[2]

For sheer fiendish ingenuity and barbarity the tortures employed by the *Che-ka* were reminiscent of those days when the Tower resounded with the screams of the victims of the rack and its analogues. Melgounov's interesting work,[3] to which I am indebted for particulars of the activities of the *Che-ka*, and to which book I would refer the reader desirous of further information, mentions several of the forms which these torments assumed. The "wreath," a leather strap with screw and nut attachment, was clasped around the forehead, and at every turn of the screw into the nut, with consequent compression, the victim suffered the most excruciating pain. The "iron glove," the exterior surface of which was covered with spikes, strapped on the torturer's hand, inflicted terrible wounds upon any part of the victim's body which was battered with it. In another method of torture, the prisoner was extended face upwards on the floor. His shoulders and head were firmly held by four men and his neck stretched "taut," while a fifth man beat it with the butt-end of a revolver or a cudgel until the "blood gushed out of the mouth and nostrils."[4] Branding on the forehead, "crowning" with barbed wire, rolling in a nail-studded barrel, scalding with boiling water, injecting powdered glass into the rectum, holding lighted candles to the genitals, were a few out of a miscellany of tortures commonly used.[5]

[1] *Ibid.*, p. 46.
[2] *Ibid.*, p. 23.
[3] Sergey Petrovich Melgounov, *The Red Terror in Russia*, Dent, 1925.
[4] *Ibid.*
[5] *Ibid.*

Torture in Abyssinia

One of the countries in which torture continued to flourish with a degree of universality and barbarity rivalling that of former days, was Abyssinia. One reason for this was, of course, the continuance of the slave-trade. The very way in which the slaves were shackled was a form of torture in itself. The manacles upon the slave's feet were fixed so closely together that it was quite impossible for him to walk. All his movements were made in short jumps, exactly as a child moves in playing leap-frog. Often, in addition to these shackles, one hand was chained to the feet in such a manner that the slave was bent double.

The conditions of the prisoners in the gaols of Abyssinia, both slaves and others, were horrible beyond description, as was revealed by Mr. Lawrence Kerans, who, along with other British residents, were imprisoned in 1863. This Englishman, in a letter to his parents, said:

" I am now a year and six months in prison, with chains of 20 lbs. weight on the legs; and lately the right hand has been attached to the feet. You cannot imagine what fearful sufferings I have to go through every day."[1]

In 1893, according to statements published in the Press, the Negus of Abyssinia condemned one of his pages, who was detected plotting against the emperor's life, to have his right hand amputated, his tongue cut out, and then to be " exposed in the desert under the glare of the sun, to be eaten by the hyenas."[2]

Torture in South-West Africa

The harsh treatment of the natives by officials and farmers in the German colonies in Africa previous to the war of 1914-18, is revealed in a grim and forbidding report presented to the Houses of Parliament in 1918.

For all kinds of trivial offences men and women were punished severely, flogging apparently being the favourite method employed. Usually the procedure was to hold

[1] Charles T. Beke, *The British Captives in Abyssinia*, 1867, p. 194.
[2] *Spectator*, December 23, 1893, p. 908.

down the culprit over a barrel and flog him on the buttocks and hips with a heavy sjambok, as many as 25 to 50 lashes being often given. Deaths often followed such floggings. Johann Noothout stated on oath :

> " I discovered bodies of native women lying between stones and devoured by birds of prey. Some bore signs of having been beaten to death. . . . The manner in which the flogging was carried out was the most cruel imaginable . . . pieces of flesh would fly from the victim's body into the air."[1]

Another witness stated that women were harnessed to carts and " made to pull like draught animals." If they failed to perform their task well they were flogged with sjamboks.

Alfred Katsimune stated on oath that : " Hardly a day passed without flogging taking place of local natives or natives sent in from the farms." On one occasion he was ordered to flog a middle-aged Berg-Damara, " whose master complained to the police that he had been impertinent." The sentence was 25 lashes. " In the course of the thrashing the sjambok curled round his thigh and injured his private parts. No medical treatment was given to him. He went back to his hut and died a few days afterwards."[2]

The Chinese Communist Atrocities

In the December of 1927 the Chinese city of Canton was seized by the Communist party. The insurrectionists were a motley crew. There were peasants and soldiers, bandits and criminals, with all the rabble that collects whenever an opportunity for looting and murdering occurs. Rightly or wrongly, Russia was blamed for the whole affair; the Nanking Government stating that the man responsible for carrying out the coup was Kovchek, a Russian, who had arrived in Canton only the week before hostilities commenced.[3]

---

[1] *Report on the Natives of South-West Africa and their Treatment by Germany.* Prepared in the Administrator's Office, Windhuk, South-West Africa, H.M.S.O., London, 1918, p. 100.

[2] *Ibid.*, p. 115.

[3] *The China Year Book*, Tientsin, 1928, p. 1401.

A REMARKABLE PHOTOGRAPH TAKEN DURING THE CHINESE COMMUNIST ATROCITIES OF 1927–28

The Reds evidently chose their time well.   On Sunday, December 11th, to the accompaniment of the rattle of machine-guns and everything else that would shoot, they swept through the city, killing all who attempted to obstruct their path.   In a matter of hours, Canton was completely in their power.   Then began a period of terrorism equalling anything history has to relate.   It was a brief period, true enough, but when torture and death are at work, arbitrary methods of reckoning time can no longer be taken into account.   One lives a whole lifetime in every single hour. For three days the Reds worked their will, and to every known anti-communist, to every citizen who did not join the mobs, cheer their antics and, often enough, participate in their atrocities, those three days represented an eternity. Not for an instant were they free from the fear and possibility of having to suffer a painful and lingering death.   Men and women both, after being put to every form of torture known to the Oriental mind, were openly butchered.

On December 13th, after fierce fighting, the city was recaptured by General Li Fu-Lin's troops.   This marked not the end, but the continuation of the reign of terror.   The "Whites," as these anti-communists were called, repaid torture with torture, massacre with massacre.   They exacted a fearful vengeance.   For every known or suspected communist Canton became as terrible a danger spot as, a few hours before, it had been for every known or suspected anti-communist.   According to *The China Year Book* (1928)

"it was reported that thirteen Russians had been arrested of whom five, including at least one Soviet Consular official, had been executed, and the remainder were being paraded through the streets previous to execution."

Some of the corpses were gathered up and buried, but in many cases they were left to rot in the streets.   In their mangled and mutilated state, these human bodies presented an awesome sight.   There are indications that both sides in the struggle, in putting their victims to death, made free use of that most frightful torture termed the "Death by the Thousand Cuts."

Driven out of Canton city, the Reds continued to pursue

their terrorist activities in various towns and villages of
South-West China.   The reports from these districts, published in the Press at the time, tell a sorry story.   " In one
case," says *The Times* (March 3, 1928), " 300 Buddhist
monks were locked in their temple, which was set on fire,
all of them perishing."   Prosperous tradesmen were tortured
until they parted with their money; " driving splinters
under the finger nails " being " a favourite device."[1]   Executions took gruesome and bizarre forms, in some cases
reminiscent of the ancient Aztec sacrifices, the victims'
hearts being torn out, cooked and eaten.[2]   Father Wong,
" it was publicly announced," was to be " executed by the
slicing process ";[3] and a similar fate was the lot of an eighty-
year-old Chinese friend of Bishop Valtorta.[4]

Torture in Modern Warfare

War and torture are bedmates.   Precisely the same
underlying motives that induce the individual to cry aloud
for vengeance against another individual induce the nation
to clamour for the blood of the inhabitants of any country
with which there exists a state of war.   The gospel of the
nation at war is hate; its objects are vengeance and retribution.

When once war breaks out, torture may be recognized
as an inevitable concomitant.   Even if the governments
concerned ostensibly denounce and prohibit torture, it
occurs nevertheless.   There is no way in which bodies of
men or individuals can be prevented from surreptitiously
practising torture upon such of their enemies as fall into
their power where licence to kill and maim has been freely
given.   The exaggeration associated with the reports of
enemy atrocities, which forms part of every combatant
State's propagandistic machinery, is probably more an
exaggeration in regard to particularized or individual cases
than in any generalized sense.   The extent of these atrocities

---

[1] *The Times*, March 10, 1928.
[2] *Ibid.*, March 10, 1928.
[3] *Ibid.*, December 29, 1927.
[4] For a description of the slicing process (" Death by the Thousand
Cuts ") see page 106.

EXECUTED COMMUNISTS, CANTON, DECEMBER, 1927
The man in the foreground is a Russian Consular Official.

VICTIM OF THE CHINESE COMMUNIST ATROCITIES IN CANTON,
DECEMBER, 1927

is never admitted or even fully known by the State directly or indirectly responsible for their committal, and for this reason neither the allegations of torture on the one hand nor their repudiation on the other can be accepted as authentic.

During the world war of 1914-18 torture in all its most extreme forms was rampant. When the Austro-Hungarian troops first invaded Serbia, they put to death by torture soldiers and civilians alike. The account which Professor Reiss gives of these atrocities is as awesome in its details as it is horrifying in its volume. Men and women were mutilated in the most shocking way before they were finally done to death. Cutting away the nose, the ears, the limbs, the breasts, and putting out the eyes, were common forms which these mutilations took. Men were castrated, women were raped, in the most brutal manner. From a long list of instances, two may be given.

" Mirosava Vasilievitch, aged 21, violated by about 40 soldiers, genital organs cut off, her hair pushed down the vagina. She was finally disembowelled, but only died immediately after this being done."[1]

" Maxim Vasitch, aged 53, was tied to a mill-wheel which was then set in motion. Whenever the wheel carried him round to the Austrians, they diverted themselves with prodding him with bayonets."[2]

For sheer brutality in their methods and the number of the atrocities they committed, however, it would appear that the Turks, in their operations against the Armenians in 1915-16, surpassed all the other combatants participating in the European war. The documents which were presented to the English Parliament in the October of 1916 exhibit a frightful record of terrorism.

According to the statement of a German eye-witness, the people living in Hartpout and Mezré were subjected to ferocious tortures. He says:

[1] R. A. Reiss, *Report Upon the Atrocities Committed by the Austro-Hungarian Army During the First Invasion of Serbia*, English translation by F. S. Copeland, Simpkin Marshall, Hamilton Kent & Co., 1916, p. 70.
[2] *Ibid.*, p. 114.

"They have had their eye-brows plucked out, their breasts cut off, their nails torn off; their torturers hew off their feet or else hammer nails into them just as they do in shoeing horses."[1]

According to other witnesses, the bastinado was frequently employed, the victims being beaten until they were unconscious. From 200 to 800 strokes were often inflicted in efforts to extract information. After one dose of the excoriating bastinado delivered upon the soles of the feet, boiling water would be poured upon the sensitive flesh,[2] and another dose of flogging inflicted.

Torture by mutilation, by burning with hot irons, and beating with clubs and hammers seems to have been commonly employed. The Turkish peasants, armed with scythes, we are told, massacred the Armenians by shearing away their ears, noses, hands, feet, etc.

Whenever and wherever there is war the same dismal story of torture seems to apply. At Nanking, during the Japanese-Chinese fighting of 1937-8, we read in that sober and terrible record compiled by Mr. H. J. Timperley of the rapes and tortures carried out by the Japanese Army.[3]

Terrorism in Ireland

Turning our eyes nearer home, we find the Anglo-Irish war of 1920-1 not free from cruelty, torture and persecution. The Irish Republicans adopted terrorist tactics; the Government forces retaliated with measures just as grim, just as brutal, and just as reprehensible. A reign of terror prevailed. Murder, arson and looting were everyday occurrences. In Dublin, on November 21, 1920, a day which was to go down in history as "Bloody Sunday," fourteen British officers and ex-officers were put to death, and several others wounded. "In two or three cases," says *The Times* (November 22, 1920), "officers' wives were pulled out of

[1] *The Treatment of Armenians in the Ottoman Empire 1915-16.* Documents presented to Viscount Grey of Fallodon by Viscount Bryce. H.M.S.O., 1916, p. 90.

[2] *Ibid.*, p. 340.

[3] See *What War Means: The Japanese Terror in China,* compiled and edited by H. J. Timperley, Gollancz, 1938.

bed and their husbands were murdered before their eyes."
In the afternoon of that same fatal day, a body of " Black-
and-Tans " went out to Croke Park, where some 15,000
persons were watching a football match, and fired into the
crowd. Nine were killed, one died of heart failure, and
fifty were wounded.

Each side accused the other of practising torture, probably with equal truth. Thus: " Men were made to crawl
along the streets, and were taken and stripped and
flogged, and sent back naked to their homes."[1] And
again, men with blackened faces fetched out the two sons
of Patrick M'Elligott in their " night attire in a downpour
of rain "—they were " cruelly beaten with the butt ends
of rifles and kicked."[2]

There were allegations of Sinn Feiners being taken to
Dublin Castle and tortured until they gave information.
The "Black-and-Tans"[3] had authority to act as they
wished, and undoubtedly they abused this authority.
Hard-boiled eggs, while still hot in their shells, were,
according to General Crozier, " placed in the armpits of
prisoners, the arms being strapped to their sides," and in
other cases, behind locked doors, victims were beaten up
by "bullies." "In Munster," says the same authority, " a
seventeen-year-old Sinn Fein boy was stripped naked and
tied to a triangle for daily flogging till such a time as he
would elect to tell the name of the murderer of a policeman which he was supposed to know."[4]

The American Lynchings

James Irwin was a negro living at Ocilla in the
southern State of Georgia. He was guilty of murder and
deserved to be punished. He paid the penalty with his
life, but first he was subjected to a series of extraordinary

[1] Michael Collins, *The Path to Freedom*, Talbot Press, Dublin, 1922,
p. 85.
[2] *Ibid.*, p. 86.
[3] The " Black-and-Tans " were mainly English, Scotch and Welsh ex-
soldiers. They were given this name because they had no complete
uniforms, usually wearing khaki trousers and black civilian coats, or black
trousers and khaki jackets.
[4] Brigadier-General F. P. Crozier, *Ireland for Ever*, Cape, 1932, p. 201.

tortures, witnessed by an enthusiastic mob of thousands of people. He was chained to a tree-trunk. One after another, and joint by joint, his toes and his fingers were cut off; his teeth were pulled out with pliers. And, "after further unmentionable mutilations," his "still living body," saturated with gasolene, was set on fire, and "hundreds of shots were fired into the dying victim."

Raymond Gunn, a negro of Maryville, Missouri, guilty of rape and murder, was executed by a batch of civilized people. And here was the manner in which he died. He was chained to the ridge-pole of the village schoolhouse, after shingles on either side of the pole had been removed. The negro's clothing was then soaked with gasolene, and quantities of the same fluid were thrown over the wall and floor of the building, which was then set alight. A crowd numbering between three and four thousand men, women and children watched, for a full ten minutes, the writhings of the chained victim.

Now these two incidents occurred, not in the days of Nero; not when the Spanish Inquisition was functioning in all its glory; not even a hundred years ago when Englishmen still enjoyed bear- and bull-baiting. They happened within the present decade, in the years 1930 and 1931 respectively. And the details which I have presented baldly, briefly and sombrely, are not taken from the pages of a work of fiction, nor even from the columns of a sensational newspaper. I am indebted for them to a soberly written and fully documented book by Dr. Arthur F. Raper, entitled *The Tragedy of Lynching,* published in 1933 by the University of North Carolina Press. It is a ratiocinative and cogitative record, well worth the careful study of every student of the social problems of the world we live in.

Even the crimes of murder and rape were not always existent as excuses for mob hysteria and premeditated torture. A band of masked men, on July 29, 1930, drove out to the home of a seventy-year-old negro farmer named Mincey, carried him off by force to a lonely spot, and there manhandled him until "his clothing was beaten into shreds and his skin and flesh torn from his back." The incident occurred soon after midnight, and the negro managed to crawl back to the road, where he was found at dawn "writhing in pain." He died two hours later of "cerebral hæmorrhage."[1]

The "Third Degree"

The term "third degree" is peculiarly of American origin, and of modern American origin at that. By the inhabitants of every country in Europe the "third degree" is supposed to be restricted in its practice to the place where the term originated. Of the truth of this I am, however, extremely dubious.

The "third degree" refers exclusively to the methods employed by the police officials in their efforts to induce a suspected or an accused person to confess his guilt or to give away the names of his partners or associates in crime. It is, in effect, equivalent to the *quæstion* of the Romans, and of the Inquisition; it is analogous to the tortures instigated by the English Star Chamber. The only point of difference is that "third degree" methods are illegal; they are not recognized or officially countenanced by American law.

This fact that the "third degree" is unofficial in its purpose and in its methods, is as significant as it is important. It means that there is no specified technique which the police may employ, and there are no restrictions or regulations as to the extent of such torture as is applied. The greatest evil associated with "third degree" methods is therefore the fact that they are uncontrolled or indefinite.

The methods employed are calculated to induce submission of the victim either by sheer brute force exemplified in various forms of physical torture, or through the gradual wearing down of will-power or resistance as a result of long-continued and reiterated questions, threats, *et al.*, which may be termed psychological torture *in excelsis*. In many cases the purely physical methods follow extended questioning.

It may be taken as axiomatic that the repetition of questions again and again in the same manner and the

---

[1] A. F. Raper, *The Tragedy of Lynching*, p. 172.

same words, and by one officer after another, will undermine the resisting powers of the majority of individuals. In particular will this method prove effective with first offenders. It will often prove effective with innocent persons, for one of the greatest sociological evils of torture in any form, is, as we have seen, its powers of causing the innocent to admit guilt. Where this " extended questioning " is accompanied with the deprivation of food, as it so very often is, its efficacy is greatly enhanced. Because of its effectiveness, and because it is almost impossible for a victim to prove that he has been submitted to this form of ordeal, it is the method more often practised than any other. Further, it is no unusual thing for the prisoner to be deprived of sleep as well as food until he " comes through." In other cases, the questioning is alternated with periods of solitary confinement in dark cells, or without sleeping equipment. There is, in particular, one instance on record, indicative of the lengths to which, on occasion, the police will go in this respect. The defendant in *Deiterle* v. *State* (1929), accused of murder, was confined in a mosquito-infested cell without any sleeping accommodation, and then, weary from want of sleep, he was questioned " throughout the next morning and part of the afternoon, with the scalp of the dead woman at his feet."[1]

Terror induced by threats is frequently tried to induce admission of guilt. A police officer may threaten to shoot the accused, and has been known to go so far as to press a revolver, loaded with blank cartridges, against the head or stomach and pull the trigger. In other cases, negroes have been told they would be handed over to the mobs waiting for an opportunity to lynch them. And there was the case of *Davis* v. *United States* (1929) where the accused was conducted to the morgue " at three in the morning and made to examine the wounds of the deceased for forty-five minutes."[2]

Of purely physical methods, which are usually adopted with known criminals, and others whom the police have a

[1] *Harvard Law Review*, February 1930.

See the article in this journal for much interesting information respecting " third degree " methods in the United States. A large number of cases in which such methods have been employed by the police are cited.

[2] *Ibid.*

shrewd idea would be impervious to questioning, attempts at terrorizing, etc., the customary procedure is that referred to as "beating up." Two or three officers manhandle the prisoner, using their fists and feet. Whipping is also common. The rubber truncheon, or a length of hose-pipe, is frequently used. The methods indeed are endless.

"I have seen a man beaten on the Adam's apple so that blood spurted from his mouth," writes Mr. Lavine, a New York newspaper man. "I have seen," continues the same authority, "another put in the dentist's chair, and held there while the dentist, who seemed to enjoy his job, ground down a sound molar with a rough burr."[1] Variations of the water torture employed in the Spanish Inquisition have been used, and Lea refers to the use of the shower-bath in American prisons many years ago (cf. page 243). Even the electric chair has been employed.

It is the proud boast of England that "third degree" methods are unknown. It is, of course, difficult, if not impossible, to prove whether this statement is strictly true. Police officers will never admit that any such methods are used, and the word of a citizen accused or suspected of crime counts for little against the statement of a policeman, even in England. While there may be few occasions when a police officer actually uses violence to an accused individual to compel him to talk, it is by no means certain that "extended questioning" is a method of which the English police are altogether innocent. The disclosures in connexion with the Savage case, for one, revealed a method of questioning which was, at any rate, most unsatisfactory and unfair.

Doubtless "third degree" methods, or some analogous forms of intimidation, are practised in most civilized countries. In India, according to Sir Cecil Walsh, "they appear to be applied impartially to anyone who seems to a corrupt police officer to offer a favourable opportunity for practising a little extortion."[2]

---

[1] Emanuel H. Lavine, *The Third Degree*, Nash & Grayson, London, 1931, p. 4.
[2] Sir Cecil Walsh, *Crime in India*, Benn, 1930, p. 279.

CHAPTER XXVII

FORMS OF TORTURE OF ANIMALS

The Criminal Prosecution of Animals

THE torture of animals would fill a huge tome in itself, and in this work, the exigencies of space alone render it impossible to do more than glance at the more salient features of the subject.

In the early days of civilization and all through the Middle Ages, animals were considered, like human beings, to be guilty of various offences, and for these offences they were tried, found guilty and duly punished. Thus, in accordance with the old concept of Plato, an animal which killed a human being was a murderer and deserved death. In particular were animals found guilty of unnatural relations with mankind put to death, as provided in the laws of Moses.

In 1457, a sow was hanged for the murder of a five-year-old child; in 1474, at Bâle, for the "unnatural crime of laying an egg" a cock was sentenced to be burned at the stake.[1] In 1565, at Montpellier, a mule, found guilty of bestiality, was sentenced to be burned alive, and as the animal was held to be vicious as well, its feet were mutilated before the execution.[2] In 1557, in France, a pig found guilty of.devouring a child was sentenced to be "buried all alive."[3]

On June 6, 1662, at Newhaven, a cow, two heifers, three sheep and two sows, were all executed, together with a man named Potter, for the crime of bestiality.[4]

The torture of animals to extract confession, their groans and cries being interpreted as admissions of guilt, was at one time widespread. An extraordinary case is related by Gavin.

---

[1] E. P. Evans, *The Criminal Prosecution and Capital Punishment of Animals*, Heinemann, 1906, p. 162.
[2] *Ibid.*, p. 146.
[3] *Ibid.*, p. 138.
[4] Cotton Mather, *Magnalia Christi Americana*, 1702, Book VI, Ch. III, p. 38.

CLEARING UP AFTER THE COMMUNIST INSURRECTION IN CANTON,
DECEMBER, 1927

See Text, page 269.)

From Ford's *Tauromachia*, 1852.

A SCENE AT A SPANISH BULL-FIGHT

At the University of Zaragosa there was a professor named Guadalaxara who was intensely disliked by the students. One night, having discovered the dead body of a horse in a field just outside the town, these students waylaid the professor, took him into the field where the horse lay, and ripping out the contents of the animal's belly, placed the professor, bound hand and foot, in the aperture, sewing the severed hide together, and allowing only the man's head to protrude underneath the horse's tail. In this plight the professor remained all night, continually crying out to scare away the dogs which came to eat the flesh of the dead horse. Next morning, labourers going to work in the fields saw the corpse and heard the cries issuing from it. They hied them to the town and, in great excitement, told a strange tale of a speaking horse. The inhabitants turned out in a body, and as they approached the field in which the corpse lay, they heard the cries and yells of Guadalaxara, who was frantically attempting to draw their attention and thus secure his release. None would go near, however. Instead, word of the queer affair was sent to the Inquisition, and immediately an order was issued that the horse be brought to the Holy Office. The inquisitors saw Guadalaxara's head protruding and they heard his tale, but, says Gavin:

> "the wise Holy Fathers trusting not to his information, gave orders to the officers to carry the speaking horse to the torture, which being done accordingly, as they began to turn the ropes through the horse's belly, at the third turning of them the skin of the belly broke, and the real body of Guadalaxara did appear in all his dimensions, and by the horse's torture, he sav'd his life."[1]

Bull-baiting and Bear-baiting

The sporting propensities of the British people have always been proverbial. It is a pity that these sports, in so many respects, have been associated with cruelty of the most infamous description. Notable among animal sports involving cruelty and torture were bull-baiting, horse-baiting and bear-baiting.

---

[1] D. Antonio Gavin, *A Master-Key to Popery*, 1725, p. 212.

Apparently the first bull-bait was held in 1209 at Stamford, Lincolnshire. There was an annual bull-bait established in 1374 at Tutbury, Staffordshire. These exhibitions became very popular, and were patronized extensively by the aristocracy as well as the common people. Sir Thomas Pope entertained Queen Mary and the Princess Elizabeth with a bear-bait. When the Danish Ambassador visited England in the reign of Elizabeth, he was received by the queen at Greenwich and "treated to the sight of bear- and bull-baiting."

"There is a grant of this Queen to Sir Saunders Duncombe, dated October 11, 1561, 'for the sole practice and profit of the fighting and combating of wild and domestic beasts within the realm of England, for the space of fourteen years,' and so much did England's maiden queen esteem the refined pleasure of bear-baiting, that there is an order of the Privy Council, dated July 1591, prohibiting any plays from being publicly exhibited on Thursdays, because on that day bear-baiting and similar pastimes had been usually practised, as it was complained that the reciting of plays was a 'great hurt and destruction of the game of bear-baiting and like pastimes, which are maintained for her majesty's pleasure.'"[1]

In some cases the animals were tortured before the bait commenced, and in preparation for it. Thus bulls had their tails docked, their ears cropped, their horns sawn off, and pepper blown up their noses. Bears were blinded. The following description of a bull-bait is from Blaine's *Encyclopædia of Rural Sports* (1840):

"The animal is fastened to a stake driven into the ground for the purpose, and about seven or eight yards of rope left loose, so as to allow him sufficient liberty for the fight. In this situation a bull-dog is slipped at him, and endeavours to seize him by the nose; if the bull be well practised at the business, he will receive the dog on his horns, throw him off, and sometimes kill him; but,

[1] *The Percy Anecdotes*, collected and edited by Rueben and Sholto Percy, London, 1820-3.

From Ford's *Tauromachia*, 1852   BULL-FIGHTING IN THE PLAZA DE TOROS, MADRID

on the contrary, if the bull is not very dexterous, the dog will not only seize him by the nose, but will cling to his hold till the bull stands still; and this is termed *pinning the bull*. What are called good game bulls are very difficult to be pinned : being constantly on their guard, and placing their noses close to the ground, they receive their antagonist on their horns; and it is astonishing to what distance they will sometimes throw them. It is not deemed fair to slip or let loose more than one dog at one and the same time."

In bear-baiting the animal was usually secured by a chain. Then five or six men, standing around in a circle, armed with heavy whips, punished him without mercy. Horse-baiting, which was common in the sixteenth and seventeenth centuries, was practised in much the same way as bull-baiting.

The Spanish Bull-fight

Bull-baiting and bear-baiting were only excelled in sheer cruelty by the bull-fights of Spain, which, to the eternal shame of twentieth-century civilization, are still in existence. Here it is not alone the bull that is tortured until death is welcomed, but the horses who engage in the sport receive terrible injuries and are treated with a callousness to suffering which is rarely equalled. A bull, in his fight for life, will often kill half a dozen horses. "It is a piteous sight," writes Ford, "to behold the mangled horses treading out their protruding and quivering entrails, and yet carrying off their riders unhurt."[1]

To add to the bull's anger and agony, the *banderillas* or barbed darts which the *toreador* throws, explode the moment they strike the animal. Neither is anything undone to goad the frightened horses to renew the conflict. If one refuses to enter or re-enter the arena, his eyes are bandaged, and he is forced to face a terror he cannot see. For the horses and bulls are there to provide entertainment for the frantically cheering crowd. Says Ford, "The riders have a more than veterinary skill in pronouncing off-hand what wounds are mortal or not. Those thrusts which are not

[1] Richard Ford, *Tauromachia, or the Bull-Fights of Spain*, 1852.

immediately fatal, are plugged up by them with tow, and then they remount the crippled steed, and carry him, like a battered battleship, again into action."[1]

Miscellaneous Forms of Modern Animal Cruelty

It is impossible ever to indicate the countless ways in which civilized people in these so-called humanistic days torture animals of all kinds, both wild and domestic. Even those who do not themselves participate in any kind of cruelty to animals, often encourage, indirectly or unconsciously, some form of torture. There are a score of ways in which this is done every day.

Perhaps the most widespread of all forms of torture is in connexion with the manner in which animals and birds, intended for food, are killed. It is true that in the past few decades great improvements have been made in the slaughtering of cattle and all large animals. In England, the passing of the Slaughter of Animals Act, 1933, has done much to eliminate needless cruelty, making "stunning" of cattle compulsory.

The Jewish method of slaughtering animals of all kinds is still practised in England and in America, involving terrible suffering in the "bleeding to death" which forms part of the *kosher* rite. To understand the reason for the Jewish method of slaughtering (*Shechita*) we must hark back to the days when animal sacrifices were offered to Yahveh, the god of Israel. The blood of the sacrificial offering was of vast importance. Being the seat of the life[2] or soul of the animal, it was of far more importance than the flesh. Whether or not the flesh was eaten by Yahveh's subjects and worshippers, the blood belonged to God Himself. It must not be drunk; it must not be consumed with the flesh. It was ordained by God Himself that blood is a means of atonement: in this lies the reason for its taboo as an article of food.[3] The commands given and repeated

---

[1] *Ibid.*

[2] Genesis ix. 4; Leviticus xvii. 11.

[3] The interpretation of the "blood taboo" is a singularly wide one, applying to all animals and birds, and even to "blood spots" in eggs. It applies, by implication, to human blood. Fish is the one exception, there being no mention of, or implication respecting, fish in the Bible. The

again and again in the Pentateuch are clear and implicit. Thus: "And whatsoever man there be of the children of Israel, or of the strangers that sojourn among you, which hunteth and catcheth any beast or fowl that may be eaten; ye shall even pour out the blood thereof, and cover it with dust."[1]

To ensure that the blood of the animal is drained from the body as thoroughly as possible the Jews elaborated their specific method of slaughtering, respecting which Dr. Heiss, Abattoir Director of Straubing, Bavaria, says, "We consider the *Shechita* one of the most barbarous methods of slaughter and one which it is our duty to contend against with every means in our power."[2]

What then is the *Shechita*, or the method of slaughtering all animals destined to become *kosher*? Dr. Rowley, in his excellent pamphlet, *Slaughter-House Reform*, described the ritual thus:

"First the animal is thrown to the floor by having its feet jerked out from under it (the fall has not infrequently broken its horns, or otherwise injured it); then its body is partly hoisted by a chain fastened about a hind ankle, then an appliance is gripped about its muzzle and its head is twisted over until its face is flat against the floor and its neck upturned; then the long knife cuts deep across the throat, and for a space, often running into several minutes, it kicks and plunges in its wild attempts to rise, threshing about the bloody and slimy floor in its dying agony—a sight as pitiable and heartrending as one can well endure. That's the Jewish method, described without exaggeration, as I have seen it more than a score of times."[3]

Then there are the "tortures" involved in the killing of poultry, rabbits and other small animals and birds, often by

elaborate washing of the meat before cooking is a continuation of the ritual specifically designed to ensure that every particle of blood is separated from the flesh.

[1] See also Leviticus vi. 26-7; xvii. 14.
[2] Quoted in *Slaughter-House Reform in the United States and the Opposing Forces*, by Francis H. Rowley, The Massachusetts Society for the Prevention of Cruelty to Animals, Boston, U.S.A., p. 13.
[3] *Ibid.*, pp. 12-13.

persons who either are not experienced "killers," or who secure a sadistic pleasure from the sight or the infliction of suffering. In a quarter of a century's close connexion with animals and birds, I have seen fowls bled to death slowly; I have seen them "hanged" by degrees; I have seen them plucked while still living; I have seen their heads battered against a wall by those who knew no other way of killing.

Often, too, the manner in which animals and birds are reared and housed makes of their lives one continual torture. There are dogs which are kept chained up, in cramped quarters, for hours and hours at a stretch; there are rabbits and cavies which never see sunlight; there are fowls kept in dirty, insanitary and incredibly small enclosures month after month and year after year. And there are chickens fattened by cramming, a method reminiscent of the "water torture" of the Inquisition; there are others confined until the day of their death in cages, the wire bottoms of which make movement difficult.

There are the methods adopted to catch wild animals, methods which, often enough, result in wholesale mutilations. The steel traps used for catching rabbits break or crush their legs and keep them imprisoned by their mutilated limbs for hours and often for days; the "running noose" often means a lingering and painful death.

Finally and importantly, there are the performing animals which give pleasure and amusement to thousands of patrons of the music-halls, *et al.* These animals are trained, in the majority of instances, by cruel methods. I know this statement has been persistently denied, but I say, without the slightest shadow of doubt, that in *most* cases the tricks that delight audiences are the result of consistent cruelty and often of torture. It was Jack London who wrote:

"What turns my head and makes my gorge rise, is the cold-blooded, conscious, deliberate cruelty and torment that is manifest behind ninety-nine of every hundred trained animal turns. Cruelty, as a fine art, has attained its perfect flower in the trained-animal world." And again: "It was a body of cruelty so horrible that I am confident no normal person exists who, once aware of it, could ever enjoy looking on at any trained-animal turn."[1]

It was the knowledge of what went on behind the performances that spoiled this form of entertainment for Jack London. It is this same knowledge that spoils it for me.

Major F. Yeats-Brown has revealed the way in which, on the Continent, dancing bears are trained. " I am told," he says, that the animal is put " into a deep copper, under which a fire is lighted." Naturally the bear tries to climb out. It is clubbed or whipped on the snout, causing it to dance with pain. All the time this is going on, a drum is beaten, " so that eventually whenever he hears that rhythm he begins to dance."[2] And there is a revealing account in the autobiography of " Lord " George Sanger, the showman, of how " kicking, rearing or buck-jumping horses " are made to order with the help of a sharp pin![3]

[1] Jack London, *Michael, Brother of Jerry*, Mills & Boon, 1917.
[2] *The Spectator*, October 4, 1930.
[3] " Lord " George Sanger, *Seventy Years a Showman*, Dent, 1926, p. 231.

PART FOUR

THE CASE AGAINST TORTURE

CHAPTER XXVIII

THE FUTILITY OF TORTURE IN THE FIGHT AGAINST CRIMINALITY

The Aims of Punishment

ONE might reasonably expect that the objects of punishment would be clearly recognized and rigidly defined. The fact that responsible law-makers and penologists are by no means in agreement on this important matter suggests one of the main shortcomings of the modern method of dealing with crime, as it has similarly suggested the failings of all methods which have been practised in the past.

It has been stated, and it is agreed upon in many quarters, that the aims of punishment are concerned with the prevention of crime and the reformation of the criminal. This statement, in view of the methods actually in force and approved by implication, is contradictory. As regards certain crimes the penalty imposed debars any possibility of the criminal being reformed; and in relation to various other crimes the nature of the punishment is calculated, whether consciously or unconsciously is beside the point, to extend or develop the anti-social attitude of the criminal. Thus the death penalty[1] in every case, and life imprisonment in most cases, absolutely prevent the reformation of the criminal;

---

[1] In England the death penalty can be imposed for four classes of crime, although in two of them it is doubtful if such a sentence would be given or, if given, would be carried out. These crimes are (1) murder; (2) high treason; (3) piracy with violence; and (4) setting fire to dockyards, arsenals, etc. As recently as 1917 there was an execution for high treason.

while long prison sentences, corporal punishment, and the stigma which inevitably attaches itself to imprisonment, in the case of most offenders, are the reverse of reformatory in their effects.

Any deterrent effect of punishment upon the incidence of crime is to some extent bound up with the reformation of the criminal. Its power as a deterrent, however, goes very much farther than this. It deters criminals who have not been apprehended, as well as a considerable number of other individuals who, while they may not actually have embarked upon a career of crime, may be contemplating such a career and therefore rank as latent or incipient criminals.

The basis of any such deterrent effect is fear of the punishment prescribed for the offence and the inevitability of its infliction. The idea that individuals remain moral and law-abiding owing to the dread inspired by the penalties which follow any departures from a fixed code of behaviour is fundamentally true and sound. This formed part of the notion behind the primary concept of vengeance, and was, in turn, responsible for the formulation of the first penal code. Here no idea of reformation entered into the matter. Society was concerned solely with the prevention of the criminal repeating his offence, and the deterring of others from offending in the same manner. To this end punishments were necessarily severe, brutal and spectacular. They were devised to fit the crime, in accordance with the ancient notion of an eye for an eye and a tooth for a tooth. Any divergence from this elemental concept of vengeance concerned itself with exaggerating the punishment rather than showing any sign of leniency.

The Bible confirms and expounds the savage's concept of vengeance. "Whoso sheddeth man's blood, by man shall his blood be shed." And "Vengeance belongeth to me, I will recompense, saith the Lord." And again: "I will execute vengeance in anger and fury upon the heathen, such as they have not heard." And yet again: "I will punish you seven times more for your sins. . . . And if ye walk contrary unto me, and will not hearken unto me; I will bring seven times more plagues upon you, according to your sins. I will also send wild beasts among you, which shall rob you of your children, and destroy your cattle, and make you few in number." Yahveh was a revengeful, cruel, merciless god, who forced his subjects to follow the paths of virtue by fear, and by fear alone.

The fact that the *force* of modern punishment, not only because of its lessened severity, but also owing to the circumstances in which it is inflicted, does not carry with it the fear that applied to punitive measures of the past, largely undermines the effect of the punishment and at the same time does much to destroy any justification for it. Actually the position to-day is that we are continuing to practise a method of dealing with crime which, because of the changed psychological outlook upon penology and its problems, is obsolete. In other words, we continue to use a method which, however effective and suitable it might have been at the time when it was originated, is much less suitable and largely ineffective in the sociological conditions prevailing to-day.

Behind the brutality of the ancients was the sound reasoning that the sight of the criminal undergoing the prescribed punishment for the offence he had committed, was an excellent mode of deterring others as well as preventing a repetition of the crime by the person undergoing the punishment. If there is any justification for brutality or torture, by whatever name it is described, in this lay its sole justification. It did do something to *prevent* crime, and therefore to protect society from the depredations of its criminal element by the enforcement of its laws. This represents the main reason for the existence of any punitive system.

There is, and there can be, no other justification for punishment, because it has not, in any circumstances, any true reformative action. To this extent then the ancient law-makers were on far sounder ground than are those modern penologists who prescribe punishment as an essential feature of any penal system.

With the abolition of the administration of executions and other forms of retribution exacted *in public*, the power of any such punishment to act as a deterring factor was very greatly curtailed. The only person upon whom it could act as a deterrent was the one actually undergoing the punishment. As regards others, knowledge of a penalty that will be imposed in secrecy is not the same as witnessing the culprit writhing under the torture. Thus, by abolishing one of the evils connected with torture, one destroys much of its efficacy in another field.

The Limitations of Fear as a Deterrent

Admitting that punishment imposed in public and in sufficient degrees of severity or brutality, by the fear it induces, has some deterrent effect as regards certain offences, there is no doubt that this effect was exaggerated in the past, and that to-day it is credited with a degree of efficacy far beyond reality. In regard to the more serious crimes, notably murder and rape, it is, in the majority of cases, ineffective.

Here again, our forefathers, in applying their brutal punishments to practically all kinds of offences against law and order, unconsciously no doubt but nonetheless surely, were applying the principle of punishment as a deterring factor upon a far more efficient scale than is the case to-day. The very elasticity and width of their punitive system ensured this, upon the old blundering hit or miss principle. But nowadays, the rigid restriction of torture or severe punishment, by narrowing so tremendously the field of influence, has largely undermined, destroyed or nullified its efficacy.

The reason why an exaggerated value has been and is vested in punishment is because, in the past, the psychology of crime received little attention, and even to-day, the causes of crime are insufficiently understood. The old ideas that the criminal is a member of a specific class of society, and that he has inherited a diseased form of mentality from criminal parents, still persist.

There is no criminal class *per se*. Every member of society is a *potential* criminal. The criminal environment, about which so much has been written and so much nonsense circulated, constitutes the whole of existent society. The old theory, immortalized by Charles Dickens, that every thief or pickpocket carries the marks of his trade upon his countenance, in the manner of Bill Sikes, bears no relation to the truth. The criminal, in appearance, is no different from any respectable member of society. Moreover, the respectable citizen of to-day may be the criminal of to-morrow; and, not inconceivably, the criminal of to-day, if *given the opportunity*, might become the respectable man of to-morrow. This general concept, which postulates the incidence of criminality being due more to accident than to anything else, is applicable increasingly as the life of the citizen gets more complicated and less and less rigidly restricted from birth to death to one specific social environment.

Especially is this applicable to the most serious of all crimes—murder. In ninety-nine out of a hundred cases the murderer, before the crime occurs, has not any intention of committing murder. The crime is committed in the heat of passion, under an emotional storm which reaches such a degree of crescendic violence that no restraining forces or arguments are or can be considered. In such circumstances, the *fear of punishment* cannot enter into the matter. It can have no deterrent effect. The murderer is in a state of mind when anger or hate dominates the scene and excludes from his mind every other possible concept. Were this not so the bulk of murders would never be committed.

The Nullity of Punishment in a Reformatory Sense

The law, in its punishment of murder, harks back to the cry for vengeance so steadfastly reiterated in the social code prescribed by Yahveh for his subjects. Whatever may be the case as regards other crimes, the State, in this twentieth century of Christianity, exacts the same form of vengeance for murder as it did four thousand years ago. By implication, if not by direct statement, it subscribes to the doctrine that the murderer cannot be reformed, it makes the gratuitous assumption that if he is let loose upon society he will proceed to commit more murders. And yet, of all the crimes on the statute book, it is highly probable that murder would be less likely to be repeated than any other. There are relatively few *professional* murderers; and there is little difficulty in deciding which murders are the work of such professionals. It can, of course, be argued that the paucity of such professionals is indicated by the fact of the detected criminal having to face the death penalty. This argument, whatever its value as a means of scoring a rococo debating point, is of little actual significance. Murder, being essentially a crime of passion, the forces which cause an ordinary respectable member of society to commit such an outrage are not likely to be repeated in relation to that same individual. Nor does success in the first instance, as is the case with so many offences, necessarily lead the criminal to repeat his crime. Because of these facts, while it is unlikely that any form of punishment, however severe, which falls short of the death penalty, would prevent a murderer from repeating his crime if such circumstances arose as called for its repetition, it is just as unlikely that any form of punishment would deter a potential murderer (which means every member of society) from becoming an actual murderer; and it is just as unlikely (though society might justifiably think the risk was far too big a one to take) that the released murderer would be encouraged to commit a second murder because he had got away with his initial crime. It is the uncaught murderer, in an effort to escape retribution, who is tempted to commit a second murder.

Turning to crimes which do not incur a capital sentence, the uselessness of punishment as a means of reforming the prisoner has been well established. Indeed, it may be taken as axiomatic that the more severe the punishment the more pronounced is its failure in any true reformatory sense. Severe punishment has a most brutalizing effect upon most prisoners; it induces despair, it makes the culprit feel that he is virtually at war with or outlawed from society. The more likely is the prisoner to profit by his lapse, the more likely is severe punishment to transform him into a *habitual prisoner*. On the other hand it cannot, in any circumstances, have any reformative effect upon the *professional* criminal.

Punishment affects different individuals in different ways. In this lies one of the major evils of a penological system which prescribes the extent, nature and duration of the punishment in accordance with the nature and extent of the crime, neglecting to take into consideration the physical, mental and sociological constitution of the individual offender. Upon these individual psychological factors depend far more the reaction of the prisoner to punishment than the actual extent or mode of punishment.   Thus what to one individual might seem a form of persecution so mild as to constitute the merest bagatelle, to another might represent the most extreme form of torture.   This psychological element of the present day penological system is, in my opinion, of the most profound importance and significance.   I have already indicated the existence of such a thing as psychological torture (cf. page 4).   It is a matter which cannot be ignored in any future consideration of the treatment of crime and the reclaiming of the criminal.

The loss of freedom which imprisonment entails has a most profound effect upon the prisoner.   This effect varies considerably in respect to the individual, for whereas in some cases a long term of imprisonment seems to have no enduring or severe psychological results, in other cases the shortest possible term, so long as it continues, ranks as a form of torture, and leaves scars that are never properly healed.   The effects of deprivation of freedom depend, of course, upon the extent to which the individual had already achieved freedom outside prison.   In this connexion, it is impossible to ignore the fact that the growing tendency towards the restriction by the State of the freedom of the individual in normal life is having a tendency, in conjunction with the greatly improved living and social conditions now available in prison, to make of the complete deprivation of freedom a lesser degree of punishment than would be the case in the ideal State, where the normal member of society enjoyed intellectual and economic emancipation in any real or complete sense.   The growing bureaucracy, which is so sinister a feature of the modern State, is an evil the significance and extent of which society has not even yet begun to have any conception.

In one sense every prisoner who is not senile or impotent, and who is serving a sentence of any considerable length, is severely punished.   I refer to the lack of opportunities for the securing of normal sexual relief.   The persistency with which this aspect of prison life is ignored in most considerations of the problem, in no way reduces its significance, its effects and its complexity.   It represents the greatest suffering, in many cases, that a young and virile man has to face.[1]

Experience Confounds the Arguments of the Floggers

The present-day controversy concerning the merits of the " cat," induced by the proposed abolition of flogging for all except grave prison offences, has caused many judges, magistrates and others to reaffirm the old contention that the " cat " is the only form of punishment which acts as a deterrent in certain crimes, and that its abolition would be followed by a huge increase in the incidence of crimes of violence, assaults on women and children, white-slave trafficking, *et al.* Those conversant with the history of crime and punishment are familiar with this type of argument: an argument which has been brought forward against the abolition of practically every form of torture and cruelty since the days of ancient Rome.

Two hundred and fifty years ago we find Sir R. Wiseman apologizing for and countenancing the use of the rack and other tortures on the ground that they were necessary for the welfare of society, thus:

" Neither does it derogate from the clemency of the Civil Law, that it seems to deal so sharply with those (against whom there are grounds enough to suspect them of some enormous crimes whereof they are accused, but not evidence full enough to condemn them) as to allow such persons to be ' set upon the rack,' thereby to manifest their innocence by an obstinate denial, or to discover their guilt by a plain confession. For the only ground of this austere proceeding was a great tenderness not to take away the lives of any, but upon most manifest and undeniable proof, and yet with a care notwithstanding, that for

---

[1] Joseph F. Fishman, former Inspector of Federal Prisons, in his interesting and valuable book, *Sex in Prison* (New York, 1934), says that " in the minds of many the greatest punishment the prisoner must undergo is the deprivation of normal sex gratification "; and Ernst Toller, in his introductory essay, appearing in the English edition of Fishman's work (John Lane, 1935) says " the sexual imagination of prisoners is stronger than that of people enjoying their ordinary liberty."

want of such full and clear proof (which offenders through their secret workings would always labour to prevent) offences should not go unpunished, to the endangering of the public peace and welfare of other men."[1]

A little over a century ago we find Lord Ellenborough, the Lord Chief Justice of England, in the course of a debate in the House of Lords on the "Privately Stealing Bill," opposing the abolition of the death penalty for thefts, up to the value of five shillings, from shops. He

"trusted their lordships would pause before they assented to the repeal of a law which had so long been held *necessary for the security of public interest*, and which he was not conscious had in any instance produced any injury to the community. . . . In this metropolis, where the retail trade had become so great and so *beneficial to the ends of commerce, and from whence such a considerable proportion of the taxes are raised*, it was the duty of the legislature to protect such property from being plundered. Indeed, were the *terror of death*, which now, as the law stood, threatened the depredator, *to be removed*, it was his opinion the consequence would be that *shops would be liable to unavoidable losses from depredations*, and, in many instances, bankruptcy and ruin must be the lot of honest and laborious tradesmen."[2] (The italics are mine.—G.R.S.)

Coming to the present time, we find that the Home Secretary's proposal to abolish flogging for all except certain serious prison offences, is meeting with much opposition. Mr. Justice Oliver, at Birmingham Assizes, observed, says the *News of the World* (January 8, 1939):

"I have yet to meet anyone with judicial experience of crime who does not feel that the best weapon against this type of offence (robbery with violence) is that of flogging."

---

[1] *The Law of Laws: or the Excellency of the Civil Laws*, 1686.
[2] *Hansard*, London, 1812, Vol. XVII, pp. 196*, 197*.

And says the *Daily Mail* (January 3, 1939), Sir Reginald Coventry, at Worcester Quarter Sessions, stated that if the change in the law occurred

> "the professional garrotters of Liverpool and Cardiff could look forward to being able to ply their occupation without the slightest fear of being punished in the only way which really appealed to them—the cat-o'-nine-tails."

The views so often and so persistently reiterated that the Garrotters Act of 1863, which provided the penalty of corporal punishment with the "cat" for the offence of strangling, and the severe flogging sentences imposed in 1887 by Mr. Justice Day for robbery with violence, were responsible for the stamping out of the "crime waves" in both cases, are founded upon very doubtful evidence. In the *Report of the Departmental Committee on Corporal Punishment* we read that, according to the evidence collected by the Committee, in neither of these specifically cited cases was flogging, directly or indirectly, responsible for the passing of the outbursts of crime. Respecting the Garrotters Act, it is stated that "by the time the Bill was in the House of Commons, the outbreak with which it was designed to deal had already subsided." And two years *after* the Act came into force the number of offences which it was specifically intended to stamp out exceeded those which occurred before the Act was introduced. In reference to the activities of the Liverpool "High-Rip Gang" the Report, after analysing the number of cases of robbery with violence in the period from 1887 to 1894, states:

> "These figures show that Mr. Justice Day made considerable use of the power to order corporal punishment, but they do not substantiate the statement that these methods stamped out robbery with violence. In the first three years of the period the total number of offenders was 176, and in the last three years—after a prolonged trial of flogging—the total number was 198."[1]

---

[1] *Report of the Departmental Committee on Corporal Punishment,* H.M.S.O., 1938, p. 84.

Just as the abolition of hanging for minor crimes did not lead to an increase in the number of such crimes; so it will, I venture to assert, be found that when flogging is abolished there will be no increase in the prevalence of those particular crimes for which it is at present considered to be a deterrent. *The passing of the Whipping of Female Offenders Abolition Act, in 1820, was not followed by any increase in the incidence of crime among women and girls.* This, in itself, is a point worthy of receiving the most serious consideration by all those who still hold that the retention of corporal punishment as a means of preventing crime is either necessary or justifiable. I commend it to their attention.

CHAPTER XXIX

THE EVILS OF TORTURE AS A FORM OF PUNISHMENT

Dangers Incidental to Excessive Pain

THE moment punishment becomes excessive it leads to an extension of crime rather than to its suppression. It does this in two ways. In the first place the *fear* of a dreadful form of punishment often leads to the commission of the crime that was clearly unpremeditated or to the commission of a series of crimes in order to escape the consequences of one crime. For instance, this danger inevitably crops up in connexion with any crime for which the penalty is capital punishment. The old saying " as well be hung for a sheep as a lamb " is a true one. Many a murderer has committed a second and even a third murder in order to silence someone who accidentally witnessed the initial crime or who had discovered the identity of the criminal. In cases of rape and other sexual offences, the culprit, realizing the dreadful nature of the punishment with which he is threatened, commits murder in order to silence the only witness of his crime.

In the second place the severity of punishment inflicted upon the offender is a frequent cause of recidivism. The evidence that a considerable number of prisoners " come back " is consistent throughout Europe and America. They " come back " because the severity of the punishment inflicted induces a feeling of despair, of revenge against society; and because the difficulties which are placed in the way of their return to respectability are often wellnigh insuperable. Even where there is no undue severity in a physical sense; psychologically, punishment, to anyone other than a confirmed or professional criminal, is inevitably severe. For whatever may be the reformative aims in principle, the practical effects of punishment are at war with the theoretical aims. The reaction of society to the criminal continues long after the penalty has been paid, and, in theory, the account squared. Society, in negation of its expressed attitude towards crime, does not apparently consider that the account has *ever* been squared. The very fact of once having suffered imprisonment, like the fact of having engaged in prostitution, or being the mother of an illegitimate child, constitutes an invisible brand which, to those who are aware of its existence, is every whit as effective as were the marks burnt into the faces of social offenders in the Middle Ages. Hence the only opportunity for the ex-prisoner is to move to some district where he is unknown, and by pseudonymity, or other disguise, attempt to conceal the past.

The Brutalizing Effect of Punishment

One of the worst features of severe punishment is the brutalizing effect it has upon *all* concerned. Anyone who is associated with cruelty in any form must either rebel against it or accept it. There is no middle course. Callousness to suffering is an inevitable aftermath of long connexion with the infliction or witnessing of cruelty. The slaughterer of animals, if he continues to perform the task, must become devoid of sympathy for the victims or revulsion for the practice.

It is unfamiliarity with a form of cruelty or torture that arouses resentment or revulsion, just as familiarity leads to toleration. It is unfamiliarity with bull-fighting which leads to its condemnation by Englishmen and Americans. It is familiarity with the sentencing of canaries, parrots, and various other foreign and British birds, to life imprisonment in tiny cages, that causes the majority of Englishmen and Englishwomen to view the practice with equanimity if not approval.

It was because of the comparative rarity of the practice that the executioner to whom was entrusted the task of torturing the suffering Damiens on that never-to-be-forgotten day in Paris, at the last moment revolted from his task :

" Charles Henri Sanson saw the chafing-dish trembling in his uncle's hands. By his pallor, which was almost as deathly as the sufferer's, and the shudder which made his limbs shake, he perceived that he could not proceed with the burning with red-hot pincers; and he offered a hundred louis to one of the valets if he would undertake the horrible task. The man, whose name was André Legris, accepted."[1]

The gradual *growth* of indifference to punishment is indicated particularly in the case of flogging. The tendency, even as regards school floggings, is for the first feeling of revulsion to give place to indifference, and, in time, for the exhibition to change in its character from one of cruelty to one of entertainment. Mr. Brinsley Richards says: " The eyes and nerves soon get accustomed to cruel sights. I gradually came to witness the executions in the Lower School not only with indifference but with amusement."[2]

The Suppression of Humanity

The rights of the individual on the social and humanistic side may easily be endangered by the growth of the State penological machine. The idea that the rights of the individual and the rights of the State are mutual and interchangeable is an illusion diligently fostered by the State itself in furtherance of dictatorial and oligarchistic ideals. The main underlying idea which is behind the penological system, is the importance of preserving the property rights of the State in particular. Offences against property are invariably more severely punished than are offences against humanity. The stealing of a loaf of bread is a more serious offence than is the torturing of an animal.

A significant factor in connexion with flogging with the " cat " is that, in the majority of cases, it is prescribed for *robbery* with violence.[3] Writing on this very point a year ago I said:

" Violence against another individual is not, *in itself*, punishable by flogging; to be so punishable it must con-

---

[1] *Memoirs of the Sansons*, Vol. I, p. 113.
[2] *Seven Years at Eton*.
[3] In 1933, out of a total of 49 offences for which flogging was inflicted, 42 were for robbery with violence or assaults with intent to rob.

stitute an assault with intent to steal. This is *one* point which does much to demonstrate the lack of sanity, justice and logicality in the application of the most degrading, humiliating and psychologically lasting form of punishment approved and sanctioned by English law."[1]

In this we have an instance of how the State has cunningly secured public support for a form of barbaric persecution ostensibly directed against *assault*, but in reality against *robbery* or attempted robbery. A man who has a personal grudge against another individual may batter, kick and maltreat his enemy to his heart's content and he cannot be flogged for the offence, whereas one guilty of a far milder form of assault combined with robbery or attempted robbery can be sentenced to flogging with the " cat."

Some years ago, in the *New Age* (July 14, 1932) attention was drawn to a case of flogging, in which the driver of a car containing four men concerned in a robbery, was sentenced to 20 months' imprisonment with hard labour and 15 strokes of the " cat." The sentence was for taking part in " robbery with violence "; the act of violence consisted of placing a treacle-plaster over the robbed man's face. An appeal against this sentence, on the ground that the prisoner " had not been previously violent," failed. In an editorial in the *New Age* (August 11, 1932) it was further pointed out that " what is interpreted as ' crimes of violence against property ' becomes, in the last analysis, simply thefts of, or damage to, *insured property*," and that " flogging costs less money to the State than imprisonment."

[1] George Ryley Scott, *The History of Corporal Punishment*, second edition, Werner Laurie, 1938, p. xxiv.

CHAPTER XXX

THE PSYCHOPATHOLOGICAL ELEMENT IN TORTURE, AND ITS TREATMENT

The Limitations of Punishment

THE shortcomings and deficiencies of the penological system are never more thoroughly demonstrated than in relation to the treatment of those guilty of sexual perversions. For centuries the State has adopted and it still adopts methods which are not only calculated to prevent all possibility of reformation, but which are also, in many instances, likely to develop the existent anomaly. Thus the homosexual is confined under conditions where there is danger of homosexual vice developing in heterosexual individuals even without the excitatory influence of a homosexual presence; and the masochist is placed in an environment which is almost sure to lead to an extension of his particular aberration.

The punishing effects of pain, persecution, humiliation and degradation, so far as they can apply in any civilized penal system, are to this type of pervert, with rare exceptions, inexistent. On the contrary, the masochist glories in his martyrdom. Even his lack of freedom may be interpreted as a form of persecution inflicted by society, and may prepare the way for an extended form of submission to domination when liberty is regained. The failure of the State to realize the psychological motivation behind masochism, and the futility of any ordinary form of punishment as applicable to the masochistic type of individual, have far-reaching consequences. The masochist is seldom in prison because of his perversion. The anomaly, in itself, is not punishable, and, unlike sadism, it rarely is directly connected with any punishable offence. The masochist is usually in prison for some ordinary misdemeanour or crime, and the fact that his anomalous sexual condition will completely alter his reaction to the punishment implied in a prison sentence is not even considered by either the court in passing sentence or the prison authorities in carrying out that sentence.   If sadism is coexistent with masochism, as it very often is, the position is further complicated, and the danger of punishment developing an existent anomaly is a very great one.

Now the sadist, unlike the masochist, is very often convicted and imprisoned or executed as a direct result of his anomaly. The lust murderer figures occasionally in the English courts. So does the "pricker," the mutilator and, less commonly, the pyromaniac. They all receive prison sentences of various lengths. Other sadists, whose activities take the form of maiming, wounding or otherwise ill-treating animals and birds, are usually punished with fines or let off with a caution. In other words, they are not punished at all, if by punishment we are to accept the usual implications of the term.

It is here, in particular, that the law-makers of the State, and those who are supposed to be qualified to interpret these laws, make a gigantic muddle. In dealing with cases of cruelty to animals, they fail to realize the distinction existing between those with a sadistic basis and those which are initiated as a result of plain unvarnished cruelty. Because the case is concerned with animals only, it is considered to be of little importance. The State and the public are not interested. Actually, however, the distinction to which I have referred is of supreme importance. The sadist, almost without exception, *in the beginning*, confines any practical expression of his perversion to animals. Kürten, the lust murderer, admitted that, as a boy, he tortured animals, and this, he said, was the commencement of the sadism which developed to such an abnormal degree in later life.[1] Flavius Domitianus, the Roman tyrant, in his childhood, amused himself with torturing animals, birds and insects. It is a bitter reflection upon our sense of justice, and a terrible commentary upon the inhumanity of mankind, that the sadist, provided he restricts his operations to animals and birds, may indulge in his aberration continuously and with comparative immunity. What is so remarkably strange is that

---

[1] Karl Berg, *The Sadist*, 1938.

the courts rarely consider that the maiming of animals *is* an expression of sadism; they wait until the pervert transfers his activities to human beings before they class him as a sadist.

Treatment of Sadism and Masochism

The contention that algolagnia, in either of its forms, is hereditary, is founded upon the most dubious premises. The sadist and the masochist carry no physical stigmata, the presence of which might imply some inheritable or congenital factor; and it is extremely doubtful whether, to any degree, mental qualities or predispositions *are* hereditary.

Most children are cruel, it is true, but, as Stekel has sagaciously pointed out, " the child is not actually cruel from the start, because he has not the consciousness of cruelty."[1] It is merely an expression, incipient and perhaps unconscious, of the will to power. It is not, of course, sadism, but it may, in certain circumstances, be converted into sadism; just as the experiencing of cruelty at the hands of another child, or more likely an adult, may be converted into masochism. It was to the floggings with which Mme. Lambercier corrected the juvenile Rousseau that he traced the beginnings of the masochism which was to form so potent an element in his adult life. Similarly, there seems ground for the belief that the sexual perversion of Swinburne was a result of the floggings he received at Eton; a point which is noted by Georges Lafourcade.[2]

It is probable that sadism and masochism, once they are *thoroughly developed to the point of overt expression*, cannot be cured. No form of punishment can prove of any avail. Perpetual imprisonment, under suitable supervision, may be completely repressive, but this constitutes neither cure nor reform. It ranks as a protective measure only. Any method of dealing with these anomalies must concern itself with prophylactic or preventive treatment. That is to say the perversion must be prevented from showing itself, or it must be aborted long before it reaches any form of active expression.

Precisely here we lay bare a primary and powerful argu-

[1] Wilhelm Stekel, *Sadism and Masochism*, The Bodley Head, 1935.
[2] Georges Lafourcade, *Swinburne: A Literary Biography*, Bell, 1932.

ment against any form of cruelty or torture as a judicial punishment in relation to adult or juvenile crime; or as a corrective in the education of children. The use of corporal punishment, either in the case of juveniles or adults, represents, for this reason, a most dangerous procedure. Whatever safeguards one adopts there is inevitably a possibility of developing existent sadism or masochism, or awakening potential algolagnistic trends in either the whipper or the whipped. It is a risk that cannot be disregarded; and the fact that, in nearly every discussion of the case for or against flogging, this aspect is studiously ignored does not in any way detract from its major importance and significance.

The man who wields the " cat " may be a sadist who enjoys performing his brutal task. If he is not a sadist then he is in danger of developing into a sadist. Such development is not inevitable; he may, in cases of *force majeure*, perform his task most unwillingly, but repetition is sure, even where it does not develop sadistic tendencies, to lead to a form of callousness that may be described as sheer cruelty. There is ample evidence as to the truth of this (cf. page 299).

Upon analysis, the imposition of any form of physical torture constitutes a crime on the part of the State. Either the State becomes an accomplice in the commission of cruelty and sadism, or it attempts to create a condition of cruelty or sadism. In either case it is guilty. Prophylactic treatment and prevention must concern themselves with abstention from corporal punishment by the State, and the rigid confinement of those proved to be confirmed sadists.

CHAPTER XXXI

THE ABOLITION OF TORTURE

Preventing the Torture of Children and Animals

IN civilized Europe and America to-day torture, on the part of private individuals, is practically confined in its expression to children and animals, these being the only forms of life which are not in a position to resist or escape persecution. And, incidentally, it may be mentioned that this alone is the reason why cruelty is not more generalized in present-day society.

The incidence of cruelty to children is nothing less than appalling. The total number of cases dealt with, during 1938, under the category of ill-treatment, by the National Society for the Prevention of Cruelty to Children, was 5,269, involving 11,323 children. It is a staggering total. And it must be remembered that these figures represent only such cases as, in one way or another, came to the notice of the Society. There remains that other and probably bigger total of cases, which for one reason or another, are never brought to the attention of the Society or of the police.

The prevention of cruelty to children is indicated in the reporting of every known or suspected case to the local inspector of the Society which has done, and is doing, such good work in the way of ameliorating the lot of so many infants that have been born into a world of sorrow and have known nothing but suffering and neglect.

Cruelty to animals is far more widespread than cruelty to children, and in many more instances does it go beyond the limits of cruelty and become torture. It is more widespread because the cruel individual has more opportunities to indulge in his propensity in relations to animals and birds than in regard to children, and in addition there is no risk involved of his victim causing trouble or being a witness against him.

Unfortunately the means taken by the State to prevent

cruelty to animals are unsatisfactory and negligible. In many ways the State aids and abets the infliction of cruelty. A fine is useless as a deterrent, particularly as, in most cases, it is so small as to represent a very minor inconvenience to the convicted person. Moreover, no adequate measures are taken to ensure that the person guilty of cruelty will not repeat his offence: in a large number of cases all that a fine does is to make him take greater care to ensure that any future cruel acts do not come to light.

The measures that should be taken by the State include the infliction of more severe sentences. In minor cases, the fines should be increased; in major cases the punishment should be imprisonment. And in all cases where there are no extenuating circumstances, the culprit should be *prohibited, under severe penalties, from ever keeping live stock again.*

The Jewish and Mohammedan methods of killing, and the slaughtering of sheep with the knife alone, should all be prohibited. These are steps which the State should take towards the decrease in the torture of animals which is going on all over England every week. The public should *demand* that these steps be taken at once.

The prohibition of *all* blood sports is another step that is long overdue. Stag-hunting, deer-stalking, otter-hunting, badger-hunting, and fox-hunting are a disgrace to the twentieth century and should be abolished, just as a hundred years ago bull- and bear-baiting were abolished. Vivisection calls for more stringent regulation. The conditions under which thousands of small birds, foreign and domestic, are kept in this country amount to cruelty and often to torture. The manner of fattening poultry for marketing purposes is a disgrace to civilization.

The need for the prohibition of animals taking part in performances on the stage has been repeatedly urged. But these performances still go on.[1] Their boycott by the public, on the lines indicated by Jack London, would soon bring this evil to an end.

[1] While the Performing Animals (Regulation) Act 1925, and the Protection of Animals Act 1934, provide certain regulations and restrictions in relation to the training and exhibition of animals for public performances, they do not, in the opinion of many humanists, go far enough. The only way in which cruelty can be prevented in any complete sense is by the prohibition of such performances altogether.

Difficulties in the Way of Abolition

The motives which have led to the retention of the principle of torture, not only in the penal systems of civilization, but also in the private and domestic life of the individual, are the main causes of the difficulties in the way of its abolition. The fundamental reason behind punishment, as we have seen, is the desire for vengeance on the part of the individual in the first instance, and, as civilization evolved, on the part of society as a whole or of some particular section of it. The State has acknowledged this fundamental urge by adopting a system of punishment based upon the concept of vengeance as a form of justice, and has to some extent been dragooned into the acceptance and perpetuation of this concept in the face of humanitarianism and the modern scientific treatment of crime.

The desire of society for the punishment or prevention of crime always outrides any humanitarian feelings; in other words, the call for vengeance is invariably louder than the appeal to mercy. Self-preservation, in both its individual and racial aspects, inevitably overrides humanitarianism. The State, by a careful excitation of the community to the danger they stand in at the hands of certain classes of criminals, can secure support and even a demand for the most ruthless and barbaric forms of torture in the guise of punishment. More, the State, by cunning suggestive methods, can ultimately justify its infliction of torture and persecution by stating, with perfect truth, that it is acting at the request and with the full authorization of the public. In precisely this way, has State after State justified wholesale persecutions of individuals and of races.

It is inevitable that as regards equity or justice, the individual is at a disadvantage in any conflict with the State concerned with the breaking of social or ethical regulations. In the Middle Ages the persecutors acted upon the principle that they were justified in burning a dozen innocent persons to ensure the destruction of one guilty individual.[1] In modern times, society subscribes to

---

[1] In connexion with the Chinese communist atrocities, we read in *The Times* (February 13, 1928) that the motto of the Reds was: " Better 10,000 innocent victims than that one anti-communist escape."

a principle in which it is contended that, in order to deter the commission of crimes against the social order, and to satisfy the cry for vengeance, it were better to sacrifice an innocent subject than not to immolate any victim at all. The cult of deterrence, of which one of the primary principles is the suggestion of the *inevitability* of punishment, indicates the necessity for sacrificing an innocent victim in the interests of society as a whole.

It is due to these facts that the members of society allow themselves to run the risk of playing the role of martyrs in an inquisition of their own making. Rules of self-preservation, made under the stress of blinding emotionalism, lead to the putting of themselves always in a position of potential danger. Thus the persistence, in America, of "third-degree" methods which are admitted and tolerated; and the persistence in England of "third-degree" methods which are not admitted by the authorities and are denied by the public. Thus the persistence of an atmosphere in which the mere fact of being charged with an offence has a prejudicial effect and goes a long way towards conviction. "Even an innocent man stands at a disadvantage before a jury when testifying alone against police officers."[1]

There is a danger that the mob element in society, if it is convinced that the State is not satisfying the primeval concept of vengeance, may be tempted to take the law into its own hands; witness the lynchings in the southern American States and the congregation of mobs of outraged citizens in England and other countries at moments when emotional responses have been aroused.

The danger of sporadic outbursts of mob emotion fructifying in demands for vengeance is always with us, and is likely to be with us as long as human beings, whether as individuals or in the mass, have forfeited the respect of their kind. This danger is greater, and its recurrence more inevitable, owing to the fact that nothing is more likely to reduce all component members of society to the level of a common denominator than the appeal to those basic ideas of vengeance and brutality that are so apparent when

[1] *Harvard Law Review*, February 1920, p. 623. This statement applies as strongly in Great Britain as it does in the United States of America.

a mob is actuated by the primitive desire for vengeance, the call for self-preservation and the stress of panic. It is in such circumstances that all forms of class distinction are *temporarily* overwhelmed, just as in panic fear caused by the unknown and the mysterious the tiger, the lion and the deer may commune in a common gregariousness. When the gladiators were being literally thrown to the wild beasts in the amphitheatres of ancient Rome, emperors and commoners fraternized in a spirit of democratic idealism; and when the crowds followed the blood-dripping Titus Oates through the London streets, all classes hobnobbed together and cheered lustily; and when Damiens was tortured and torn limb from limb in Paris the aristocrats found themselves exchanging pleasantries with the peasants. The bull-fights of Spain, and, to a lesser degree, the boxing matches of Britain and America, show something of the same democratic feeling.

"Not infrequently," writes Dr. Raper, "more unanimity can be had on a lynching than on any other subject. Lynchings tend to minimize social and class distinctions between white plantation owners and white tenants, mill owners and textile workers, Methodists and Baptists, and so on."[1]

Reinhardt, in relation to the whippings that were such features of the nineteenth-century bridewells in Germany, made much the same observation. It is an ironic commentary upon democracy with its ideals of equality and fraternity, that it functions most thoroughly in circumstances where the most brutal and despicable traits of humanity are given an opportunity for manifestation.

The iconoclast is always in some danger of mob persecution. There is a distinct degree of affinity between the mental persecution which is meted out to the intellectual heretic and the persecution which was the lot of the religious heretic of the Middle Ages, and which conceivably might be the lot of the sociological and political heretic of to-day, were the occasion to arise. In any time of stress or panic, the heretic, irrespective of the precise nature of his heresy,

[1] Arthur F. Raper, *The Tragedy of Lynching*, 1933, p. 47.

is in danger of persecution, and might well become a victim of mob violence. To the mob, held together, mentally congested, and fructifying as nearly on the level of animal mentality and psychology as is possible, the voicer of anything beyond the comprehension of the lowest common denominator of collective intelligence is a heretic and an enemy. He is as much an enemy of the mob, whether he be of the same nationality or not, as is a foreign subject at the moment when war is declared upon his country. He stands in much the same potential danger, and the question of whether that potential peril may be transformed into actual physical danger depends upon circumstances which are nearly always trivial and illogical.

The Real Solution

The foregoing analysis of the difficulties in the way of the abolition of torture suggests the means that must be taken to accomplish such abolition. Abolition is neither a fantastic theory nor an impossible dream. Admittedly there are many and great obstacles in the way. Society as a whole has a long road to travel before the goal is anywhere within reach of achievement.

The despair of the humanitarian has always been largely the result of those sporadic bursts of torture and persecution with which the history of the world is so liberally punctuated. Just at the moment when one is congratulating oneself on the progress made, and upon the vastly increased humanity observable on every side and in every country, there is an outbreak of torture which, in its details and in its extent, equal anything that occurred in the worst days of the Spanish Inquisition. And every time one of these sporadic epidemics occurs one feels, with much justification, that the clock has been put back a hundred years in as many minutes. One sighs for the future of humanity. One is inclined to subscribe wholeheartedly to a gospel of futility.

The solution lies mainly in the cultivation of humanitarianism, not humanitarianism in any parochial sense or circumscribed *bravura*, but universally. This implies a penal system in which there is no brutalizing form of punishment providing State encouragement for private cruelty. One of the greatest objections to corporal punishment, as I have stated elsewhere,

"is the danger inseparable from the practice by the State of cruelty in any form. Man does not need the stimulating and fortifying influence of either precept or example. It is an essential feature of any State campaign against cruelty that torture shall form no feature of its own armamentarium."[1]

It implies, too, sociological changes, of which the most profound is an extension of freedom. No greater obstacle to the development of humanitarianism exists than the denial of intellectual freedom to the individual, a denial to which society assents by its policy of penalizing free thought in any adequate sense. Only in this way is it possible to develop, on any extensive scale, a frame of mind which will be sufficient to invalidate the primeval tendency of the mob to exact vengeance upon the expression of any heresy. The State by its policy of propaganda, patriotism, pluto-democratic or dictatorial and intransigent domination, defends and tolerates where it does not encourage mob persecution.

A very great deal could be effected by a reform in the educational system. Children must be taught humanitarian ideals. The liking for cruelty which manifests itself in the torture of all kinds of domestic animals and birds, must be strictly repressed. The parent, by encouraging his child to keep pets may think he is exerting his influence along right lines, but only too often this same parent fails to ensure that the child is kind to the animals or birds which are put in its charge. Nothing is better calculated to develop a love for animals and the formation of humanitarian ideals than the keeping of pets, provided care is taken to ensure that kindness is manifested. Nothing is better calculated to develop cruelty than to allow that child to persecute and torture the pets he is allowed to keep.

[1] George Ryley Scott, *The History of Corporal Punishment*, second edition, 1938, p. xxii.

In the cruel and thoughtless treatment of animals that is so marked throughout all civilized countries, it seems to me lies much of the blame for the cruelty and inhumanity of mankind towards one another. The child is allowed to be cruel to animals, and grows up to look upon cruelty as an everyday affair. It becomes callous as regards the sufferings of animals, and there is, in consequence, all the elements present for the development of callousness towards its own kind. Or the adult is observed by the child to be cruel to the domestic cat or dog. What more natural, what more inevitable, than that the child, reared in such circumstances, should equal, if not excel, in cruelty, its parent. Where is the blame to be apportioned : to the parent, or to the child, or to the both of them? It is a vicious circle, the effects of which can only be broken by wholesale reforms along the lines I have endeavoured to indicate.

Much of the education of society along humanitarian lines must of necessity be bound up with a wholesale reform in the methods of treating crime. These methods, as at present conducted, after hundreds of years of experiment, largely fail. They fail because they are still motivated by the old feeling of vengeance. They are concerned far too little with the reformation of the criminal.

Because there is nothing in the world more likely to manufacture a habitual criminal than the present gaol system, and because the *bulk* of first offenders are victims of environment, bad luck, accident, *et al.*, we may say that this system is mainly concerned with the manufacture of recidivists.

The system of sentencing offenders to terms of imprisonment fixed either in accordance with the crime or the whims of the judges, and which treats certain crimes involving property and morality in a harsher manner than other crimes which are of a far more serious nature, is neither fair to the criminal nor to society. Moreover, such a system of dealing with crime suggests that the criminal, after paying the price, is free to repeat his offence provided he is willing, if caught, to again pay this price; a suggestion which, in itself, does much to rob the penal system of any reformative value. The prisoner, in a huge number of cases, is prepared to repeat his offence the minute he secures his liberty, and the police, well aware of this, and, in point of fact, implying by their conduct that he is almost certain to repeat his crime, are always ready to haul him back again.

The lack of consideration for the psychology of the individual criminal is a major factor for evil in the methods at present adopted in dealing with crime. The punishment decreed and the treatment given are based upon the crime and not upon the individual. Until this method is to some extent reversed, any reformative action will be prevented or aborted.

More and more does it appear that only a small proportion of the erring (habitual criminals, confirmed sadists, *et al*.) are altogether irreclaimable, resistant to every form of educative or therapeutic treatment. These would constitute the permanent inmates of the prisons or their analogues. The others, after a course of reconciliatory, propitiatory or prophylactic treatment, based, as regards duration, upon results rather than upon actual time, should re-enter society and contribute to the utility and formulativeness of the State.

BIBLIOGRAPHY

W. Alexander, *The History of Women*, London, 1779.

Gregor Alexinsky, *Modern Russia*, translated by Bernard Miall, London, 1913.

J. Arago, *Narrative of a Voyage Round the World*, London, 1823.

Aristophanes, *Lysistrata*.

Corinne Bacon (compiled by), *Prison Reform*, New York, 1917.

John Barrow, *Travels in China*, London, 1804.

F. W. N. Bayley, *Four Years' Residence in the West Indies*, London, 1830.

Cesare Bonesana Beccaria, *An Essay on Crimes and Punishments*, London, 1764.

Charles T. Beke, *The British Captives in Abyssinia*, London, 1867.

Karl Berg, *The Sadist*, authorized translation by Olga Illner and George Godwin, London, 1938.

Theodore Besterman (edited by), *The Travels and Sufferings of Father Jean de Brébeuf*, London, 1938.

George Bishop, *New England Judged by the Spirit of the Lord*, London, 1703.

Abbé Boileau, *History of the Flagellants, Otherwise of Religious Flagellation among Different Nations*, etc., London, 1783. This is an English translation of Boileau's *Historia flagellantium*, 1700.

John Brand, *Observations on Popular Antiquities*, London, 1813.

W. H. Brett, *The Indian Tribes of Guiana*, London, 1868.

G. W. Bridges, *The Annals of Jamaica*, London, 1828.

Bishop Burnet, *History of His Own Time with the Suppressed Passages*, Oxford, 1823.

Bishop Burnet, *The History of the Reformation*, Oxford, 1829.

Francis Caron and Joost Schorten, *A True Description of the Mighty Kingdoms of Japan and Siam*, translated from the Dutch by Roger Manley, London, 1671.

Geo. Catlin, *Letters and Notes on the Manners, Customs and Conditions of the North American Indians*, London, 1841.

Chambers's *Book of Days*, 1863.

Cicero, *Works*.

Samuel Clarke, *A General Martyrologie*, London, 1677.

Thomas Clarkson, *An Essay on the Slavery and Commerce of the Human Species*, London, 1786.

Thomas Clarkson, *The History of the Rise, Progress and Accomplishment of the Abolition of the African Slave Trade*, London, 1808.

Thomas R. R. Cobb, *An Inquiry into the Law of Negro Slavery in the United States of America*, Philadelphia, 1858.

Cobbett's *State Trials*, London, 1742-60.

Wm. M. Cooper (James Glass Bertram), *Flagellation and the Flagellants: A History of the Rod in all Countries from the Earliest Period to the Present Time*, London, 1868.

John Graham Dalyell, *The Darker Superstitions of Scotland*, Edinburgh, 1834.

Josse de Damhouder, *Praxis Rerum Criminalium*, Antwerp, 1562.

John Francis Davis, *The Chinese*, London, 1840.

Johannes Baptista de Cavaberüs, *Ecclesiae Anglicanae trophaeo*, Rome, 1584.

Dellon's *Account of the Inquisition at Goa*, London, 1815.

De Lolme, *The History of the Flagellants or the Advantages of Discipline*, London, 1777.

Hippolytus de Marsiliis, *Practica Criminalis quae Averolda nuncupatur*, Venice, 1532.

T. W. Doane, *Bible Myths*, New York, 1882.

Alice Morse Earle, *Curious Punishments of Bygone Days*, London, 1896.

Bryan Edwards, *The History of the British Colonies in the West Indies*, London, 1793.

Bryan Edwards, *The History of the British West Indies*, London, 1819.

Eusebius, *Ecclesiastical History*.

Eusebius, *History of the Martyrs in Palestine*, 1861.

E. P. Evans, *The Criminal Prosecution and Capital Punishment of Animals*, London, 1906.

Edward G. Fairholme and Wellesley Pain, *A Century of Work for Animals*, London, 1924.

Prosper Farinacius, *Praxis et Theoricæ Criminalis*, Frankfort, 1622.

Ch. Féré, *The Sexual Instinct: Its Evolution and Dissolution*, authorized translation by Henry Blanchamp, London, 1900.

Fereal, *Mysteries De L'Inquisition*, Paris, 1846.

James Forbes, *Oriental Memoirs*, London, 1813.

Richard Ford, *Tauromachia, or the Bull-Fights of Spain*, London, 1852.

John Fox, *Acts and Monuments of Martyrs*, London, 1684.

J. A. Froude, *History of England*, London, 1863.

Father Antonio Gallonio, *De SS. Martyrum Cruciatibus*, Antwerp, 1668.

Father Antonio Gallonio, *Tortures and Torments of the Christian Martyrs*, translated by A. R. Allinson, Paris, 1903. The English translation of *De SS. Martyrum Cruciatibus*.

James Gardner, *The Faiths of the World*, London, 1858.

D. Antonio Gavin, *A Master-Key to Popery*, London, 1725.

E. Gibbon, *History of the Decline and Fall of the Roman Empire*, London, 1776-88.

Horace Greeley, *The American Conflict*, Hartford, 1864.

James Greenwood, *Curiosities of Savage Life*, London, 1863.

Francis Grose, *Military Antiquities*, London, 1788.

George Grote, *History of Greece*, London, 1850.

Henry Hallam, *Constitutional History*, London, 1827.

Henry Hallam, *Middle Ages*, London.

Hampton, *The General History of Polybius*, London, 1772.

Herodotus, *History*.

Holinshed's *Chronicles*, London, 1807.

John Howard, *The State of the Prisons*, London, 1777 and 1784.

George Ives, *A History of Penal Methods*, London, 1914.

David Jardine, *On the Use of Torture in the Criminal Law of England*, London, 1837.

R. Mounteney Jephson and Edward Pennell Elmhirst, *Our Life in Japan*, London, 1869.

Flavius Josephus, *Works*.

Sir John Kelyng, *A Report of Divers Cases*, London, 1708.

R. V. Krafft-Ebing, *Psychopathia Sexualis, with Especial Reference to the Antipathic Sexual Instinct: A Medico-Forensic Study*. Authorized English adaptation of the twelfth German edition, by F. J. Rebman, New York, 1925.

J. Lewis Krapf, *Travels, Researches and Missionary Labours During an Eighteen Years' Residence in Eastern Africa*, London, 1860.

Paul Lacroix, *Manners, Customs and Dress During the Middle Ages*, London, 1874.

Paul Lacroix, *The Eighteenth Century*, London, 1874.

Emanuel H. Lavine, *The Third Degree*, London, 1931.

Henry Charles Lea, *A History of the Inquisition of Spain*, New York, 1906.

Henry Charles Lea, *A History of the Inquisition of the Middle Ages*, New York, 1906.

Henry Charles Lea, *Superstition and Force*, Philadelphia, 1878.

W. E. H. Lecky, *History of European Morals*, London, 1869.

W. E. H. Lecky, *History of the Rise and Influence of the Spirit of Rationalism in Europe*, London, 1865.

Philip a Limborch, *The History of the Inquisition*, translated by Samuel Chandler, London, 1731.

John Lingard, *A History of England*, London, 1823.

William Lithgow, *The Totall Discourse of the Rare Adventures and painefull peregrinations of long nineteene yeares Travailes from Scotland, to the most famous Kingdomes in Europe, Asia and Affrica*, London, 1640.

D. Jean Antoine Llorente, *The History of the Inquisition of Spain*, London, 1826.

Joseph H. Longford, *The Story of Old Japan*, 1910.

Lucian, *Works*.

Macaulay, *History of England*, London, 1848.

B. Vicuna Mackenna, *Francisco Moyen: or the Inquisition as it was in South America*, translated by James W. Duffy, London, 1869.

John Marchant, *A Review of the Bloody Tribunal or The Horrid Cruelties of the Inquisition*, Perth, 1770.

Cotton Mather, *Magnalia Christi Americana*, 1702.

Henry Mayhew and John Bunny, *The Criminal Prisons of London*, London, 1862.

Johannes Heinricus Meibomius, *Tractatus de usu flagrorum in re medica et venerea*, 1643.

Johannes Heinricus Meibomius, *A Treatise on the Use of Flogging in Medicine and Venery*, Paris, n.d. An English translation of the above work.

Sergey Petrovich Melgounov, *The Red Terror in Russia*, London, 1925.

J. G. Millingen, *Curiosities of Medical Experience*, London, 1837.

John Milton, *The History of Britain*, London, 1777.

Montaigne's *Essays* (Charles Cotton's translation), London, 1711.

Henry Moore, *The History of the Persecutions of the Church of Rome and Complete Protestant Martyrology*, London, 1809.

Samuel Morland, *The History of the Evangelical Churches of the Valleys of Piedmont*, London, 1658.

James Murdoch, *A History of Japan*, revised and edited by Joseph H. Longford, London, 1926.

Major-General Charles J. Napier, *Remarks on Military Law and the Punishment of Flogging*, London, 1837.

Henry Norman, *The People and Politics of the Far East*, London, 1895.

L. A. Parry, *The History of Torture in England*, London, 1933.

Rueben and Sholto Percy, *The Percy Anecdotes*, London, 1820-3.

B. Picart, *Religious Ceremonies*, London, 1737.

Luke Owen Pike, *A History of Crime in England*, London, 1873.

George Pinckard, *Notes on the West Indies*, London, 1806.

Robert Pitcairn, *Ancient Criminal Trials in Scotland, Compiled from the original Records and MSS.*, Edinburgh, 1833.

Pliny, *Epistles*.

Robert Plot, *The Natural History of Staffordshire*, London, 1686.

Plutarch, *Lives*.

William H. Prescott, *History of the Conquest of Mexico*, London, 1843.

D. Antonio Puigblanch, *The Inquisition Revealed*, London, 1816.

Arthur F. Raper, *The Tragedy of Lynching*, Chapel Hill, North Carolina, 1933.

Antony Real (Fernand Michel), *The Story of the Stick in all Ages, Lands*, New York, 1891.

R. A. Reiss, *Report Upon the Atrocities Committed by the Austro-Hungarian Army During the First Invasion of Serbia*. English translation by F. S. Copeland, London, 1916.

Jean Jacques Rousseau, *Confessions*.

Francis H. Rowley, *Slaughter-House Reform in the United States and the Opposing Forces*, Boston, n.d.

St. Augustine, *De Civitate Dei*.

Henry S. Salt, *The Flogging Craze*, London, 1916.

Harry Sanson (edited by), *Memoirs of the Sansons*, London, 1876.

George Ryley Scott, *The History of Corporal Punishment: A Survey of Flagellation in its Historical, Anthropological and Sociological Aspects*, London, 1938.

F. Alvarez Semedo, *History of China*, London, 1655.

John Shipp, *Flogging and its Substitute*, London, 1831.

Frederic Shoberl, *Persecutions of Popery*, London, 1844.

Lieut.-Col. W. H. Sleeman, *Rambles and Recollections of an Indian Official*, London, 1844.

W. Smith, *Dictionary of Greek and Roman Antiquities*, London, 1842.

Alexander Somerville, *The Autobiography of a Working Man*, London, 1848.

Lord Sommers, *Tracts*, London, 1795.

Sir George Thomas Staunton, *Penal Code of China*, London, 1810.

J. G. Stedman, *Narrative of a Five Years' Expedition Against the Revolted Negroes of Surinam in Guinea on the Coast of South America from the year 1772-1777*, London, 1796.

Jesse F. Steiner and Roy M. Brown, *The North Carolina Chain Gang, A Study of County Convict Road Work*, Chapel Hill, 1927.

Wilhelm Stekel, *Sadism and Masochism*, London, 1935.

James Stephen, *The Slavery of the British West India Colonies Delineated*, London, 1830.

John Stow, *A Survey of London*, London, 1720.

Harriet Beecher Stowe, *A Key to Uncle Tom's Cabin*, London, 1853.

Joseph Strutt, *Manners and Customs of the Inhabitants of England*, London, 1775.

Joseph Strutt, *The Chronicles of England*, London, 1779.

W. G. Sumner, *Folkways*, Boston, 1907.

John Swain, *Brutes and Beasts*, London, 1933.

John Swain, *The Pleasures of the Torture Chamber*, London, 1931.

Tacitus, *Annals*.

Ulric Tengler, *Layenspiegel*, Strasburg, 1511.

R. Therry, *Reminiscences of Thirty Years' Residence in New South Wales and Victoria*, London, 1863.

John Timbs, *Curiosities of London*, London, 1855.

H. J. Timperley (Compiled and edited by), *What War Means: The Japanese Terror in China*, London, 1938.

Thomas Timpson, *The Inquisition Revealed*, London, 1841.

C. Suetonius Tranquillus, *The Lives of the XII Cæsars*, 1717.

Philip Vincent, *The Lamentations of Germany*, London, 1638.

Voltaire, *Philosophical Dictionary*.

Sir Cecil Walsh, *Crime in India*, London, 1930.

John West, *The History of Tasmania*, Launceston, 1852.

Jacob D. Wheeler, *A Practical Treatise on the Law of Slavery*, New York, 1837.

John White, *Journal of a Voyage to New South Wales*, London, 1790.

John Whiting, *Truth and Innocency Defended Against Falsehood and Envy*, London, 1702.

W. J. Wilkins, *Modern Hinduism*, London, 1887.

G. T. Wilkinson, *The Newgate Calendar*, London, 1820.

Mark Wilks, *History of the Persecutions Endured by the Protestants of the South of France, 1814-1816*, London, 1821.

Daniel Wilson, *Prehistoric Annals of Scotland*, London, 1863.

R. Wiseman, *The Law of Laws: or the Excellency of the Civil Laws*, London, 1686.

Robert Wodrow, *History of the Sufferings of the Church of Scotland*, Glasgow, 1828.

Thomas Wright, *A History of the Domestic Manners and Sentiments of England*, London, 1862.

Thomas Wright, *The Archæological Album*, London, 1845.

Dr. Jacobus X, *Discipline in School and Cloister*, Paris, 1901.

A Collection of the Most Remarkable Trials, London, 1734.

A Collection of Reports on Bolshevism in Russia, London, 1919.

Anti-Slavery Monthly Reporter, London, 1829.

Archæologia, London, 1838.

A Relation of the Bloody Massacre in Ireland, London, 1689.

A True Relation of the Most Cruell and Barbarous Proceedings Against the English at Amboyna, London, 1624.

Catholic Encyclopædia.

Encyclopædia Britannica (ninth edition).

History of Flagellation Among Different Nations. A narrative of the Strange Customs and Cruelties of the Romans, Greeks, Egyptians, etc., with an account of its practice among the early Christians as a religious stimulant and corrector of morals, New York, 1903.

Report of the Committee Appointed to Inquire into the Conditions of Treatment of the Prisoners Confined in Birmingham Borough Prison, London, 1854.

Report of the Departmental Committee on Corporal Punishment, London, 1938.

Report on the Natives of South-West Africa and their Treatment by Germany, London, 1918.

The History of the Trial of Warren Hastings, London, 1796.

Theatrum Crudelitatum Haercticorum, Antwerp, 1592.

The Memoirs of a Protestant Condemned to the Galleys of France for his Religion, Written by Himself, translated by James Willington, Dublin, 1765.

The Treatment of Armenians in the Ottoman Empire 1915-16. Documents Presented to Viscount Grey of Fallodon by Viscount Bryce. Presented to both Houses of Parliament by Command of His Majesty, October 1916, London, 1916.

INDEX

ABYSSINIA, torture in, 267
Adamites, 256n.
Aesopus, 186
Africa, South-West, torture in, 267, 268
Albigenses, torture of the, 145
Alexander, W., 209
Algolagnia, forms of, 21
Amboyna, torture of English prisoners at, 177 et seq.
American Humane Education Society, 140
American Indians, initiatory rites of, 38 et seq.
American Indians, tortures of, 42, 43
Animals, cruelty to, 138 et seq., 278 et seq.
Animals, cruelty to, in modern times, 282 et seq.
Animals, cruelty to, difficulties in abolishing, 308 et seq.
Animals, cruelty to, incidence of, 306
Animals, cruelty to, prevention of, 307
Animals, performing, cruelty in connexion with training of, 284, 285
Animals, persecution of, 11, 13
Antiochus, 164, 166
Antiphon, 44
Anundal, 113
Apostolicals, torture of the, 146
Apphianus, torture of, 157
Arago, J., 41
Aristophanes, 44
Aristotle, 46
Artaxerxes, 222
Astor, Lady, vii
Athenaeus, 180
Australian Blacks, mutilations practised by, 37
Auto da fé, description of, 70 et seq.

BASTINADO, 104, 188, 200
Bath, torture of the, 242
Bayley, F. W. N., 13
Bear-baiting, 280, 281
Bears, dancing, how trained, 285
Beccaria, Cesare Bonesana, 63, 97, 135, 136
Bentham, 138
Berg, Dr. Karl, 16
Bilboes, 236

Bill of Rights, 134
Birmingham prison, 251
Bishop, George, 61
Black Death, 257
Black Hole of Calcutta, 221
Boats, torture of the, 222
Boiling to death, 164, 165
Boiling to death in England, 166
Boot, torture of the, 90, 183
Branding as a punishment in ancient Rome, 49
Branding in France, 164
Branding in Great Britain, 91, 163
Branding slaves, 125
Brand, John, 99
Brazen Bull, torture of the, 166, 167
Brett, W. H., 37
Bridewells, ducking-stool used in, 240
Bridewells, flogging in, 207
Brodequins, 185
Brownrigg, Elizabeth, notorious sadist, 205
Bull-baiting, 280
Bull-fight, Spanish, 281
Bull's-hide torture, 118
Burckhardt, 228
Burdett, Sir Francis, 136, 199n.
Burke, Edmund, 148
Burnet, Bishop, 183, 236
Burning at the stake, 72, 73, 92, 147, 157 et seq.
Burt, Captain, 101
Burying alive, torture of, 217
Butler, 138
Bzovius, 145

CALIGULA, 142
Canning, George, 138
Capital punishment and torture, 63
Cart's tail, flogging at, 200, 201
Casanova, 17n.
Castration in ancient Rome, 49
Castration, torture by, 208
Catlin, George, 38, 39
Cat-o'-nine-tails, flogging with, 197 et seq.
Cat-o'-nine-tails, flogging with, a cause of death, 198
Cat-o'-nine-tails, flogging with, futility of, 296
Ceylon, torture in, 112

Children, incidence of cruelty to, 306
Children, prevention of cruelty to, 307
China, capital punishment in, 105, 106
China, Communist atrocities in, 268, 269
China, forms of torture used in, 104, 105, 216
China, judicial torture in, 102, 103
China, punishment of fornication in, 103
China Year Book, The, 269
Choctaws, methods of torture practised by, 42
Christianity and torture, 53 *et seq.*
Cicero, 48, 134
Clarke, John, torture of, 177 *et seq.*
Clarkson, Thomas, 127
Code of Gentoo Laws, 117
Columbus, Christopher, 119
Constantine, 45, 49, 158
Coustos, John, torture of, 170
Coventry, Sir Reginald, 296
Cromwell, Oliver, 182
Crozier, General, 273
Crucifixion, antiquity of, 153
Crucifixion in ancient Rome, 49, 154
Crucifixion of Jesus, 153
Crucifixion, technique of, 154
Cruelty in relation to self-preservation, 9
Cruelty in relation to torture, 2, 3
Cruelty of Scythian women, 49
Cucking-stool, 239
Czekanowski, 37

Daily Mail, 296
Dalyell, J. G., 237
Damiens, Robert François, torture of, 17*n.*, 213, 299
D'Archenholz, 90
Dartmoor prison, mutiny in, 253
Dav, Mr. Justice, 296
" Death by the Thousand Cuts " in modern China, 269, 270
" Death by the Thousand Cuts," torture of, 105
De Brébeuf, Father Jean, torture of, 43
Decapitation, 216
Decius, 144
De Coceicao, Maria, torture of, 69
Defoe, Daniel, in the pillory, 235
Delicieux, Bernard, 31
Dellon, 75
De Lolme, 259, 261
De Marsillis, Hippolyte, 246
De Rais, Gilles, 68, 146, 158
De Sade, Marquis, 15
" Dice," torture of the, 154
Dickens, Charles, 290
Diocletianus, 143

Discovery of Witches, The, 98
Dogs, torture of, 139
Domitianus, 303
Drawing and quartering, torture of, 212 *et seq.*
Drowning, 222
Dublin Review, 259
Ducking-stool, punishment of the, 239

EARLE, ALICE MORSE, 244
Edwards, Bryan, 181
Egan, killed on the pillory, 235
Elizabeth, Queen, 88, 89
Ellenborough, Lord, 295
Encyclopædia Britannica, 230
Encyclopædia of Religion and Ethics, 230
Encyclopædia of Rural Sports, 280
Endicott, Governor, 60
England, judicial torture in, 86 *et seq.*
English Protestants, torture of, 93, 94
Epickaris, 143
Epiphanes, Antiochus, 141
Erskine, Lord, 139
Essay on Crimes and Punishments, 97, 135
Estrapade, torture of the, 187
Eusebius, 144, 157

FARINACIUS, 63
Farquhar, Sir Robert, 128
Fasani, Raniero, doctrines of, 256
Fear as a deterring force, 290
Féré, Ch., 19
Fire, torture by, 162, 163
Firmillianus, Governor, 144
Fishman, Joseph F., 294*n.*
Flagellants, the, methods adopted by, 257, 258
Flagellants, the, origin of, 256
Flagellation among Pueblo Indians, 259
Flagellation as a form of punishment in ancient Rome, 46, 48, 49, 144
Flagellation, erotic, 22
Flagellation, implements used in, 188, 189
Flagellation in Australia, 202, 203
Flagellation in China, 104, 105
Flagellation in England, 86, 89, 136, 197*n.*
Flagellation in Japan, 200
Flagellation in Mauritius, 194, 195
Flagellation in Russia, 200
Flagellation in the army and navy, 199
Flagellation in the United States, 203, 204
Flagellation, methods of, employed in Middle Ages, 188 *et seq.*
Flagellation of galley slaves, 190, 191

Flagellation of witches, 96
Flagellation of women, 193, 196
Flagellation, penal, 137, 200 *et seq.*
Flagellation, penal, injuries connected with, 300, 301
Flagellation practised as a religious rite, 37
Flagellation, sadistic, 205, 206, 207
Flagellation, voluntary, 260, 261
Flagellation with the Jamaica cart-whip, 192, 193
Flagellum, 48, 144
Flaying alive, 216
Flogging. *See* Flagellation
Forbes, James, 111, 114, 229
Ford, Richard, 281
Fox, George, 59, 158
France, torture in, 63
Frederick the Great, 135
Frying to death, 164, 165

GALLEY-SLAVES, torture of, 190, 191
Gallonio, 180
Gallus, 144
Gardner, James, 257
Garrotters Act, 34, 296
Gastaldo, Andrew, 56
Gavin, D. Antonio, 189, 278
Gibbon, 44
Girard, Father, 22
Gladiators of ancient Rome, 50, 51
Glove, torture of the, 238
Goncourt, 17
Graefe, Johann, 135
Greece, torture in ancient, 44 *et seq.*
Greenwood, James, 40, 42
Grimm, 180, 227
Grose, Francis, 244

HADRIEN, CORNELIUS, 22
Hale, John P., 133
Hallam, 89
Hammond, W., 22
Hanging alive in chains in England, 219
Hanging alive in chains in West Indies, 218 *et seq.*
Hari-kari, 110
Hastings, Warren, 148
Hate, psychology of, 9
Heineccius, 32
Heiss, Dr., 283
Henry II, 260
Heresy, burning alive as punishment for, 158
Heresy punished by various tortures, 54, 55
Herod the First, 141
Herodotus, 182, 211
History of Circumcision, 208n.
History of the Inquisition, The, 168

Hodge, Hon. Arthur William, 150, 151
Hogarth, 138
Holinshed, 215
Hooper, Bishop, burnt at the stake, 158 *et seq.*
Hopkins, Matthew, 98, 232
Horace, 48
Horse-baiting, 281
Howard, John, 237, 240, 249, 250
Humanity, suppression of, 300, 301
Hutchinson, Lord, 136, 199n.

IGNATIUS, 143
Imprisonment, psychological effects of, 293
Incest, punished by burning alive, 158
India, children tortured in, 117
India, methods of torture employed in, 111 *et seq.*, 148
Infibulation, 38
Inge, Very Rev. W. R., vi
Innocent III, 145
Innocent VIII, 95
Inquisition, activities of, 74
Inquisition, examination of prisoners by, 66
Inquisition, formation and development of, 64 *et seq.*
Inquisition, influence of, 73 *et seq.*
Inquisition, torture chamber of, 66
Inquisition, tortures employed by, 67, 82, 168 *et seq.*, 190
Inquisition, victims of the, 81 *et seq.*
Ireland, judicial torture in, 90
Ireland, terrorism in modern, 272
"Iron Gauntlets," torture of the, 237, 238
Italy, torture in, 62
Ivan the Terrible, 147

JAMAICA cart-whip. *See* Flagellation
James I, 97
James II, 147
Japan, forms of torture employed in, 107
Japan, judicial torture in, 106, 107
Japan, methods of punishment in, 110
Japan, torture of Christians in, 108, 109
Jardine, David, 88
Jeffreys, Judge, 147
Jennings, Al, 203
Joan of Arc, 158
Josephus, 164, 165, 180
Jougs, 241
Justinian, 45

Kian hao. See Pillory, Chinese
Kittee, 112, 113
Knaresborough prison, 249

Kraemer, Henrich, 95
Krafft-Ebing, 19, 22
Kürten, Peter, 16, 19, 303

LACROIX, PAUL, 185, 212, 247
Lafourcade, Georges, 304
Las Casas, B., 119, 162
Lavine, E. H., 277
Lawrence, John, 138
Lea, H. C., 62, 67, 243, 246
Lecky, W. E. H., 53
Leeds Mercury, 236
Letters from the North of Scotland, 101
Libel, punishment for, 210
Lilburn, John, in pillory, 234
Limborch, Philip a, 67
Lisle, Lady Alice, burned at the stake, 147
Lithgow, William, torture of, 172 *et seq.*
" Little Ease," torture of, 89, 246, 247
Llorente, 81
Locke, 138
London, Jack, 284, 285, 307*n.*
Long, Rev. J., 117
Lucian, 166, 180
Lynching, effects on public opinion of, 310
Lynching, torture of, 273, 274

MACAULAY, 201
Maccabees, tortures of the, 164 *et seq.*
Maconochie, Governor, 251, 252, 253
Magna Charta, 134
Malleus Malificarum, 96, 99
Martial, 51
Martin, Isaac, flogging of, 83, 84
Martin, Richard, 139
Masochism and martyrdom, 22, 23
Masochism, extension of psychological, 23
Masochism, futility of punishment in cases of, 302
Masochism, pleasure principle in, 21 *et seq.*
Masochism, treatment of, 304, 305
Master Key to Popery, A, 75
Mauritius, torture of slaves in, 129 *et seq.*
Maximinus, 143
Maximus, 45
Mayer, Dr., 224, 225
Melgounov, S. P., 266
Memoirs of the Sansons, 210
Michelet, 222
Mika operation, 38
Millingen, J. G., 207
Mithridates, 222
Montaigne, 25, 49, 135

Morning Chronicle, 123
Moyen, Francisco, torture of, 84
Murdoch, James, 107
Mutilation, torture by, 91, 208 *et seq.*
Mutiny Act of 1869, 197

NABIS, 144
Napier, Major-General C. J., 136, 198, 199*n.*
National Society for the Prevention of Cruelty to Children, 306
Nero, 51, 143
New Age, 301
News from Scotland, 99
News of the World, 295
Norman, Sir Henry, 105, 106
Notes and Queries, 219*n.*, 220

OATES, TITUS, flogged at cart's tail, 201
Oliver, Mr. Justice, 295
Once a Week, 218, 219
Onondaga County Penitentiary, treatment of prisoners in, 254
Ordeal of boiling water, 229
Ordeal of cold water, 231 *et seq.*
Ordeal of the hatchet, 228
Ordeal of the " venomous gloves," 40
Ordeal, red-hot iron, 227, 228
Ordeal, trial by, in England, 228, 232, 233
Ordeal, trial by, in India, 229, 230
Orobio, Isaac, torture of, 178 *et seq.*
Osborne, Ruth, trial by ordeal of, 232
Outlook, The, 254
Ovid, 16, 167

" PADDLE," use of the, 132
Pearsall, R. L., 224, 226
Peine forte et dure, 87, 89, 90, 91, 155, 156
Peine forte et dure in America, 156
Peine forte et dure in Ireland, 156
Penal Code of China, 103
Pendulum, torture of the, 242
Percy Anecdotes, The, 116, 166
Performing Animals (Regulations) Act, 307*n.*
Perilaus, 166, 167, 186
Persecution by the State, 28
Persecution, modern aspects of, 27
Persecution, physiology of, 26, 27
Phalaris, 166, 186
Picart, B., 36, 103
Picketing, 244
Picton, Sir Thomas, convicted for torture, 149
Piedmont, torture of Protestants in, 182
Picture of England, 90
Pike, Luke Owen, 155
Pillory, Chinese, 104

Pillory, Egan killed on the, 235
Pillory, John Waller pelted to death on the, 235
Pillory, torture of the, in England, 210, 234 *et seq.*
Pinckard, George, 126
Pit and the Pendulum, The, 242
Plato, 46, 278
Pliny, 143
Plot, Robert, 240
Plutarch, 217, 222
Poe, Edgar Allan, 242
Polybius, 44
Polycarpus, 143
Praxis et Theoricæ Criminalis, 63
Prescott, William H., 25
Pressing to death. *See Peine forte et dure*
Prison forte et dure, 222
Prisons, conditions in English, 247 *et seq.*
Prisons, conditions in foreign, 247, 250
Prisons, floating, 247
Prostitution, burning alive a punishment for, 158
Protection of Animals Act, 307n.
Pueblo Indians, flagellation rites of, 259
Pulley, torture of the. *See* Squassation
Pulteney, Sir W., 138
Punishment, aims of, 286 *et seq.*
Punishment, brutalizing effects of, 299 *et seq.*
Punishment, fear of, and its effects, 291
Punishment for reformative purpose, nullity of, 291 *et seq.*
Punishment, lessened force of modern forms of, 289
Punishment, limitations of, 302 *et seq.*
Punishment, relation of torture to, 40, 91 *et seq.*
Putuanius, 186

Quakers, persecutions of the, 59 *et seq.*

Rack, Chinese, 102
Rack, Isaac Orobio tortured on the, 178 *et seq.*
Rack, John Coustos tortured on the, 170 *et seq.*
Rack, William Lithgow tortured on the, 172 *et seq.*
Rack, technique of torture of the, 69
Rack, technique of torture of the, as employed by the Inquisition, 169 *et seq.*
Rack, technique of torture of the, in England, 87, 88
Raper, Arthur F., 274, 310

Remondino, 208n.
Report of the Departmental Committee on Corporal Punishment, 296
Richards, Brinsley, 300
Rome, torture in ancient, 44 *et seq.*
Romilly, Sir Samuel, 136, 198
Rope, torture of the, 118
Rousseau, 304
Rowley, Dr. Francis H., 283
Royal Society for the Prevention of Cruelty to Animals, 140
Russia, Bolshevist atrocities in, 265, 266
Russia, torture in, 264

Sacrifice and torture, 24 *et seq.*, 35
Sacrifice, human, 25
Sadism and flagellation, 205
Sadism and gladiatorial exhibitions, 50
Sadism and modern surgery, 20
Sadism and the Inquisition, 75
Sadism, danger in wrong treatment of, 303
Sadism, encouragement of, 18
Sadism in relation to torture, 14 *et seq.*
Sadism, private, 18
Sadism, treatment of, 304, 305
St. Augustine, 56, 134
St. Domingo, torture in, 128
St. Liguori, 260
Sanger, "Lord" George, 285
Saunders, W. D., 203, 254
Scalping, methods of, 212
Scalping, torture of, 211
Scavenger's Daughter, 89
Scavenger's Daughter, torture of, 185
Scold's Bridle, 240, 241
Scotland, judicial torture in, 89, 90
Scotland, methods of torture used in, 183, 184, 185
Scottish Historical Review, 220
Select Committee on Slavery, 193
Self-torture of saints and penitents, 260, 261
Semedo, F. A., 102, 103, 104
Seneca, 134
Serbia, torture in, 271
Severus, 45, 143, 144
Sex in Prison, 294n.
Shaw, Bernard, 207
Sheridan, 138
Shipp, John, 197
Short Account of Scotland, A, 185
Shortest Way with Dissenters, The, 235
Simson, Cuthbert, torture of, 171
Slaughter-House Reform, 283
Slaughtering animals, Jewish methods of, 282, 283
Slavery and torture, 119 *et seq.*
Slaughter of Animals Act, 139, 282

Slaves, bizarre forms of punishing, 127
Slaves, branding of, 125
Slaves, flogging, 122, 123, 124, 125
Slaves, horrors in connexion with transport of, 121
Slaves, methods of torturing, 122 et seq., 150, 151
Slaves, mutilations of, 126
Slaves, torture of, in ancient Greece and Rome, 46 et seq.
Slaves, whipping of, in West Indies, 193
Slaves, whipping of, in Mauritius, 194, 195
Slaves, whipping of, in United States, 196
Slave-trade, extent of, 120
" Slicing process," torture by. See " Death by the Thousand Cuts "
Smith, W., 246
Solon, 46
Sophocles, 227
" Spanish Boot," torture of the, 184
Spectator, 118, 254
Sprenger, Johann, 95
Spreull, John, torture of, 183
Squassation, 168
Squire, Dr. Amos, 4
Star Chamber, 59, 87, 234, 237, 275
Staunton, Sir George, 103
Stedman, J. G., 126, 181
Stekel, Wilhelm, 20, 304
Stephen, James, 218
Stocks, punishment of the, 236
Stoning to death, 182
Stow, John, 155, 200, 214
Strutt, Joseph, 160, 235
Suetonius, 142
Sumner, W. G., 10
Survey, 202, 254
Survey of London, 155
" Suttee," rites of Indian, 261, 262, 263
Swinburne, 304
Symmachus, 50

Tait's Edinburgh Magazine, 198
Templars, torture of the, 87
Tertullian, 134
Therry, R., 202
" Third Degree," methods employed, 276, 277
" Third Degree," torture of, 275
" Third Degree," torture of, in England, 277
" Third Degree," torture of, in India, 277
Thoodasavary, 114
Thumbkins. See Torture of the thumbscrews
Thumb-tying, 87

Tiberius, 141, 142
Times, The, 233, 270, 272
Timperley, H. J., 272
Toller, Ernst, 294n.
Torquemada, 69
Torture, abolition of, 306 et seq.
Torture among savage and primitive races, 35 et seq.
Torture and the Holy Inquisition, 66 et seq., 168 et seq.
Torture and the will to power, 7
Torture as a means of developing sadism, 16
Torture as a means of discovering witches, 99
Torture as a means of enacting vengeance, 6 et seq.
Torture as a religious rite, 35
Torture, attitude of church towards, 52 et seq.
Torture, bizarre forms of, 117 et seq., 245, 246
Torture, causes of wholesale or mass, 24 et seq.
Torture, decline of, 136, 137
Torture, definition of, 1, 2
Torture, development of, 12
Torture, effects of, 29 et seq.
Torture, effects of mental, 4, 29 et seq.
Torture, evils of, 298 et seq.
Torture, futility of, 30 et seq., 286 et seq.
Torture in ancient Greece and Rome, 44 et seq.
Torture in Great Britain and Ireland, 86 et seq.
Torture in initiatory rites, 37 et seq.
Torture in modern warfare, 270 et seq.
Torture, judicial, 61 et seq., 86 et seq.
Torture, justification of, vii, 10
Torture, legal meaning of, 2, 3
Torture, masochistic aspects of, 20 et seq.
Torture, modern forms of, 264 et seq.
Torture, modern forms of, in Abyssinia, 267
Torture, modern forms of, in America, 273 et seq.
Torture, modern forms of, in China, 268, 269
Torture, modern forms of, in Russia, 264, 265
Torture, modern forms of, in South-West Africa, 267, 268
Torture of animals, 11, 13, 138 et seq., 278 et seq.
Torture of boiling to death, 164, 165
Torture of branding, 163, 210
Torture of burning alive, 157 et seq.
Torture of burying alive, 217

Torture of castration, 208
Torture of crucifixion, 153, 154
Torture of decapitation, 216
Torture of drawing and quartering, 212 et seq.
Torture of drowning, 222
Torture of flagellation, 188 et seq.
Torture of flaying alive, 216
Torture of hanging alive, 218 et seq.
Torture of hurling from a tower, 186
Torture of " Little Ease," 246
Torture of lynching, 273, 274
Torture of mutilation, 208, 209, 210
Torture of peine forte et dure, 155, 156
Torture of scalping, 211
Torture of school children in India, 117
Torture of slaves in America, 130 et seq.
Torture of slaves in Mauritius, 129
Torture of slaves in West Indies, 119 et seq.
Torture of squassation, 168
Torture of starvation, 222
Torture of stoning to death, 182
Torture of the bath, 243
Torture of the boats, 222, 223
Torture of the boot, 183
Torture of the brazen bull, 166, 167
Torture of the Brodequins, 185
Torture of the " dice," 154
Torture of the ducking-stool, 239
Torture of the estrapade, 187
Torture of the frying-pan, 164, 166
Torture of the glove, 238
Torture of the " Iron Gauntlets," 237
Torture of the ordeal, 227 et seq.
Torture of the pendulum, 242
Torture of the pillory, 210, 234 et seq.
Torture of the rack, 169 et seq.
Torture of the rats, 247
Torture of the Scavenger's Daughter, 185
Torture of the " Scold's Bridle," 240, 241
Torture of the " Spanish Boot," 184
Torture of the stocks, 236
Torture of the " Third Degree," 275, 276, 277
Torture of the thumbscrews, 236
Torture of the " Virgin Mary," 223 et seq.
Torture of the wheel, 180 et seq.
Torture of water, 171 et seq., 243
Torture, principle of, 6 et seq.
Torture, prohibition of, 5
Torture, psychological effects of, 3 et seq., 33, 302 et seq.
Torture, reintroduction into Europe, vi

Torture, relation of punishment to, 1, 2, 40 et seq., 91 et seq.
Torture, sacrifice in relation to, 24
Torture, self-inflicted, methods of, 256 et seq.
Torture, surreptitious, 5
Torture, technique and methods of, 153 et seq.
Torture, toleration of, 9
Torture, war upon, 134 et seq.
Torturers, notorious, 141 et seq.
Torturers of the Middle Ages, 145 et seq.
Tortures, military, 243, 244
Tortures, prison, 248 et seq.
Tower of London, tortures used in, 171, 174n., 185, 237, 246, 247
Tragedy of Lynching, The, 274
Trajanus, 143
Treadmill, 251
Treason Act, 34
Trinidad, torture of slaves in, 126
Turkish prisons, conditions in, 255

ULPIAN, 134
Urbanus, 144

VALERIANUS, 144
Van Halen, Don Juan, torture of, 238
Vengeance in relation to torture, 6 et seq.
" Virgin Mary," mechanism of the, 226
" Virgin Mary," torture of the, 223 et seq.
Vives, Juan Luis, 135
Vivisection, 307
Voltaire, 135, 136, 230

WALDENSES, persecution of the, 56 et seq.
Waller, John, pelted to death on pillory, 235
Walsh, Sir Cecil, 277
Warfare, torture in modern, 270 et seq.
Water, torture of, 171, 243
Water, torture of, modern methods, 277
Wesley, 138
Wheel, breaking on the, 180 et seq.
Wheel, breaking on the, as practised in Surinam, 181
Whipping. See Flagellation
Whipping of Female Offenders Abolition Act, 297
Whirlgig, 244
Wilberforce, 138
Wildman, J. B., 193
Wilkins, W. J., 263
Wilson, Daniel, 241
Windham, William, 138

Wiseman, Sir R., 294
Witches, persecution and torture of, 95 *et seq*.
Witches, pricking test for discovering, 97, 98, 99
Witches, torture of, in Great Britain, 99, 100
Witches, trial of, by ordeal, 232, 233

Witch's Bridle. *See* Scold's Bridle
Wood, Stuart, 253
" Wooden Horse," torture of the, 243, 244

YEATS-BROWN, MAJOR F., 285

ZENO, EMPEROR, 186